Discounts, Deals & Steals

For Those over 50 Who Don't Want to Pay to Play

TAKE ADVANTAGE OF ALL YOUR BENEFITS

Discounts, Deals & Steal$

For Those over 50 Who Don't Want to Pay to Play

Reader's
Digest

The Reader's Digest Association, Inc.
New York

Project Staff

Executive Editor
Elissa Altman

Writers
Sharon Bowers, Susan Randol,
Karen Kelly

Designers
Michele Laseau, Erick Swindell

Copy Editor/Proofreader
Marcia Mangum Cronin

Indexer
Cohen Carruth Indexes

Illustrations
Chuck Rekow

Reader's Digest Home & Health Books

**President, Home & Garden
and Health & Wellness**
Alyce Alston

Editor in Chief
Neil Wertheimer

Creative Director
Michele Laseau

Executive Managing Editor
Donna Ruvituso

Associate Director, North America Prepress
Douglas A. Croll

Manufacturing Manager
John L. Cassidy

Marketing Director
Dawn Nelson

The Reader's Digest Association, Inc.

President and Chief Executive Officer
Mary Berner

President, Global Consumer Marketing
Dawn Zier

A READER'S DIGEST BOOK

Library of Congress Cataloging-in-Publication Data

Discounts, deals and steals : for those over 50 who don't want to pay to play / from the editors at Reader's Digest.

   p. cm.

Includes index.

ISBN 978-1-60652-133-5

1. Discounts for older people. 2. Older people--Recreation--United States. 3. Older people--Travel--United States. 4. Shopping--United States. I. Reader's Digest Association.

HQ1064.U5D57 2010

332.0240084'60973--dc22

          2010035620

We are committed to both the quality of our products and the service we provide to our customers. We value your comments, so please feel free to contact us.

The Reader's Digest Association, Inc.
Adult Trade Publishing
44 South Broadway
White Plains, NY 10601

For more Reader's Digest products and information, visit our website: **www.rd.com** (in the United States)

Printed in The United States of America

  3 5 7 9 10 8 6 4 2

Note to Readers

The information in this book has been carefully researched, and all efforts have been made to ensure its accuracy and safety. Reader's Digest Association, Inc., does not assume any responsibility for any injuries suffered or damages or losses incurred as a result of following the instructions in this book. At the time of printing, all information herein was checked for accuracy; information pertaining to personal finance, government, or health may change by the time of publication. Before taking any action based on information in this book, study the information carefully and make sure that you understand it fully. The mention of any brands, products, retail businesses, or Web sites in this book does not constitute an endorsement by the writers or by The Reader's Digest Association, Inc. All prices and product names mentioned are subject to change and should be considered general examples rather than specific recommendations.

All character illustrations ©Chuck Rekow.

The Early Bird Mantra

I will strive to unearth every discount I deserve, in every part of my life.

I will proudly ask for senior discounts, in the knowledge that those who offer them want and need my patronage today and in the future.

I will be a savvy consumer not only because having extra money is useful, but also because I believe in the values of simple, frugal, clever living.

I will enjoy the spectacular rewards of being over 50 and share my Early Bird wisdom with others.

I will understand that part of being an Early Bird is being lighthearted and joyful about everyday life, and that the pursuit of savings is a game I will always win!

Contents

Wake Up, Early Bird! It's a Whole New Day!

Imagine this: You arise one sparkling and lovely morning. The skies are blue, the birds are chirping happily, the sun is shining. You proceed with your day as you always do: have a nice breakfast, maybe do a little bit of exercise, and take your pooch for a walk. You accomplish that long list of busy errands—paying a few bills, taking the car to be serviced, making arrangements to visit the grandkids, calling the oil company to have your furnace cleaned, visiting the doctor for a checkup. Perhaps you have a cafe lunch with one of your friends before hitting up the library for the newest bestseller you've been waiting for. You come home, have a nice dinner, watch some television, send a few chatty e-mails, and hit the sack.

What's different about this particular day?

Dear reader, *this* day is an Early Bird Day!

As an invigorated member of the Early Birds, you will take advantage of absolutely everything that the world now offers you, in every part of your life. You will reap the extensive rewards that you deserve, now that you are on the right side of 50, whether you're filling up your car with gasoline, buying airline or train tickets, or doing grocery shopping of any proportion. Discounts will appear as if by magic when you go to the movies or go golfing. You will absolutely expect "senior" discounts (little do they know how youthful you are!) to be handed to you as often as possible; be they small or great. They will make a terrific, joyful, thrifty impact on virtually every aspect of your life, and turn the clever art of savvy savings into a game that you win each day, every day. What could be more rewarding?

The Sunny Side of 50

Gone are the days, Early Bird, when you might have felt just a little bit funny asking for senior discounts, or even assuming they existed at all in some places. Never again! And here's why: Businesses want you. *Desperately.* They're not offering "senior" discounts out of respect, pity, or moral obligation. Quite the opposite. We Americans are living longer than ever before; we are living more actively than ever before; and we Early Birders have much more available cash on average than people under 50. Retailers know all this! So if they can win your patronage by offering you special deals, they're banking on you being a regular customer for many years to come. It's the proverbial "win-win" equation that makes our economy so great!

So in the coming pages, our top flight team of Early Bird experts will show you how to live better than ever by knowing exactly what to ask for, how to get it, and making your wisdom, your experience, and your smarts pay off BIG! If you're on the sunny side of 50, the world is your oyster! Here are just a few of the ways in which you can save:

Ka-Ching! Staying at a hotel or a motel? There are hundreds of valuable discounts just yours for the asking.

Ka-Ching! Get your morning coffee for much less—even free—at this national fast food chain.

Ka-Ching! Fill your fridge, your pantry, and your freezer for a song.

Ka-Ching! Take classes at this world-class university for free.

Ka-Ching! Turn your favorite hobby into a cool cash cow.

Ka-Ching! Get totally free checking at your local bank.

Ka-Ching! Get deeply discounted cell phone service.

And so much more—all just for being you!

Discounts, Deals, and Steals is filled with more than 1,900 invaluable tips, techniques, and secrets to great living for far less than you spend now, freeing up time and cash for the things you really want in your life. You'll learn how to get expert medical advice for less; how to look and feel your best for virtually nothing; how to keep in touch with family and friends the world over; how to get the best deals on the right insurance for you, and much, much more. The icing on the Early Bird cake? An A-Z section chock-full of quick, clever, savings ideas for making life not only great, but joyful, fun, *and* thrifty.

So sharpen your pencils and get ready to reap all the benefits that are yours for the taking. The time is now!

Elissa Altman

EXECUTIVE EDITOR,
READER'S DIGEST HOME BOOKS

1

Finding Gold in Your Golden Years

Get Discounts, Strike Bargains, and Give Scammers the Boot

Top Strategies for Getting the Best Bargains

There's no single way to get the best bargain all the time. You have to be ready to go with the flow, to know what to ask for, and then be prepared to ask again, or differently, if you're not getting what you want. Keep your eyes on the prize, stay focused on what you're looking for, and be ready to change tactics, change questions, or even call back later and change whom you're talking to!

Ask for a discount whether it's marked or not. The price on the tag is rarely the price. We've all been deeply conditioned to believe that the number on the tag is the number we have to pay, with tax added on top. But how did that number get on the tag? It's the amount the retailer paid to make or acquire the item wholesale plus a prorated amount that he has to spend to pay his staff and keep the lights on and advertise to get you to come to his store, plus however much more he thinks you, Mr. and Mrs. Public, are willing to pay on top of that (that is, the profit).

Be a savvy senior shopper. Unless you're dealing with a big commercial operation like Wal-Mart or Costco, most retailers and service providers are a lot more interested in moving goods out the door and closing the deal for the service than in making you pay a set price. We are prepared to negotiate when it comes to buying a house or a new car, where we wouldn't dream of paying the asking price, but when it comes to retail shopping, we think that the price on the tag is the final price, and we wouldn't consider negotiating over the price of a coat or skirt. Think again. Depending on where you are and who you're dealing with, you can probably get an additional 10 percent off just for the asking. And if you don't ask, you'll never know.

Tap into your Inner Bargainer. If you've never asked for a discount in your life, that first request can be hard. But guess what? People who do commercial transactions get asked all the time. They're not going to think twice about you and your request. It's all in a day's work to them. You may feel like it's a bigger deal, until you ask for the first time, get your discount, and realize it's nothing but money back in your pocket. So open your mouth and take a stand: "Can you do any better on that rate?" "Is there a lower-priced option?" "Would you be willing to cut your commission?"

Be nice about it. Even though the person you're asking doesn't mind at all if you ask, you've got a better chance at success—and a better chance for a deeper discount—if you ask politely. Even though nobody *minds* giving you a discount, they don't *have* to give you one, either, so if you make the transaction pleasant, you might find the person taking your credit card will do a better deal for you if they've enjoyed dealing with you.

Don't forget about cold, hard cash. Cash is almost always good for a percentage off, and many people find it easier to ask for a discount when using it. There are no residual credit card fees for the merchant, and they can do what they like with cash in hand. If you're new to bargaining, you may find a good place to start is with this classic line: "Can I have a better price if I pay cash?"

Early Bird Secret

Take 10 Off the Top!

Ten percent is the standard amount that any employee will have the ability to take off of a bill without getting additional authorization, so don't expect to go too much higher on a normal transaction. If you're somewhere that the employee is just minding the store and running the cash register, such as a chain restaurant or a mini-mart, for example, then those employees have probably never even been asked for a discount and will think they do not have the authority to give you one. But if you're somewhere where you're dealing with the owner or manager—a small clothing store, a café, or a garage, say—you can likely have 10 percent off just for asking, whether or not you're a senior!

Don't bargain for stuff you don't need. When you start asking for discounts and find that you're racking up savings right and left, you may also find that the practice is addictive. "I got 5 percent off here, 10 percent off there, and a whopping 25 percent off over there!" It's like discovering a secret that was hiding in plain sight but one that hardly anyone else can see. However, you have to curb your impulse if it's simply making you shop more to exercise your newfound negotiating powers. There are no savings in that. Like a comic-book superhero, be sure to use your powers for good—which means scoring discounts only on the stuff you truly want and need.

Always take your due. In addition to asking for special discounts, never overlook anything that was already yours to begin with. There are dozens more subgroups of Americans in addition to senior citizens who are entitled to special consideration. Money off for being a veteran? I was, indeed, in the armed services. Special discounts for firefighters, clergy, police, schoolteachers, nonprofit workers, or municipal employees? Here's my ID.

Free entry for those with disabilities? Yes, thank you. If you're a member, either active or retired, of a special group that America seeks to reward or honor through special offers or discounts, proudly claim the rights that are your due and that are offered with open hearts and hands. You can find out about special offers through professional organizations and special-interest groups that support your profession or status.

Did You Know?

It Pays to Be Carded! You might think you'll be offended if someone offers you a senior discount when you totally don't look like a senior. But you'll likely be far more frustrated and annoyed if you go to the trouble of asking for a senior discount and can't get it because the person doesn't believe you! Be sure to travel with the ID required to take full advantage of any discounts you can get. Whether it's your driving license, your AARP membership card, your AAA card, or any other senior program that you've signed up for, don't get caught out without your little piece of paper that may be your key to senior savings.

Stay one step ahead. Even when the economy feels stable, things change all the time, and in a period of rising inflation or economic downturn, they change even faster. You can stay informed about the big stuff—tax breaks, write-offs, federal benefits—by reading the papers, listening to the news, talking to tax professionals, or inquiring about federal programs directly through the government. Nobody can stay on top of everything all the time, but you owe it to yourself to figure out what you care about and pursue it. Does your tax bill feel out of whack? Read about getting free assistance through the AARP on page 246. Are you tired of paying full-price for ball game tickets, but you love Major League Baseball? Find out how to search for Senior Discount Days hosted by your favorite team on page 138. Are you distressed by your skyrocketing energy bills and want to know what all the fuss is about with new energy-saving lightbulbs? Check out terrific sources of info on federally mandated power saving tips on page 74. The help you need and savings you probably never considered are just waiting for you.

Use your noggin. A little common sense can go a long way toward cutting your spending and saving you money, with or without a special senior discount. Clipping coupons, for example, is a big waste of time and money if you're saving 50 cents on a major national brand when you could have bought the store brand for $2.50 less in the first place. And ordering the three-course lunch special that comes with a free drink is a waste if all you really wanted for lunch that day was a sandwich and a glass of water. Learn to see through the hype to find what the special offer really is and what's in it for you. Don't be swayed by promises of saving a certain amount on an item when you didn't necessarily want that item anyway.

Take a chance. Be willing to take a chance on a big payoff when it makes sense. For example, why pay for all the coverage offered on a rental car if one of your credit cards offers that extra coverage automatically, as so many cards do? If you've had a lifetime of safe driving and you don't do much driving besides the grocery store and church on Sunday, you're probably a safe bet to take a higher deductible on your car insurance. Similarly, if your basement has never flooded and you don't have any ominous trees leaning over your eaves, you're a good candidate to take a higher deductible on your homeowner's insurance, with the payoff of big annual savings in exchange for assuming more of the risk.

Get creative. Don't just take what's offered, and don't just ask for a discount and wait to see what you get. Come up with an idea that helps the service provider help you. Your doctor, for example, may be able to open her sample cabinet and supply you with two weeks' worth of the high-priced antibiotic she's just prescribed—if you ask. Finding the price of beef too high for comfort? See if an area farmer can provide you with a butchered cow to share with a handful of friends who have big freezers. You'll get good local meat for a fraction of the supermarket price. Is the price of gas too high for you to make your monthly trip to the doctor without worry? Ask the receptionist at the doctor's office to help you put together a carpool with patients who live near you, so that two or three of you could make appointments for the same morning and all drive together. It saves money for everyone, it's sociable, and, if you need any more convincing, it decreases your carbon footprint and is good for the planet!

Get thee to the Internet! If you haven't done so already, it's time to face up to the fact: we're living in an Internet world, and if you're not online, you're simply not getting the best deals possible. Many airlines, for example, offer Internet-only fares that are significantly cheaper than anything you can get by booking through a human being on their toll-free reservations lines. In fact, generally, most airlines will tell you that they can't offer you that price over the phone, even if you call and say you saw or heard about it at their Web site.

Let people help you. Always take advantage of an offer of help or a freebie. If your doctor says, "Don't fill that prescription—I have a handful of samples for you," or if your neighbor says, "I'm driving to the grocery store—want to come along, or is there anything I can pick up for you?" then all you have to do is say, "Yes, thank you." If the checkout girl at the grocery store says, "Hey, did you know that we have a senior discount?" she's not trying to offend you (or say that it's time you touched up your grays). Take all offers in the spirit in which they're made, and don't assume anything other than kindness or good nature.

Use both old and new classifieds. You can read the classified ads in newspapers, both in hard copy and online, so there's nothing to limit your search for the best possible price, whether you're in the market for airline tickets or a new car. And if you're not part of the phenomenon that is Craigslist, you should be. Once a tiny site of free ad listings based in California, it's now the go-to site worldwide for classified listings with sites for every major city in the United States and around the world. Looking for an apartment to rent when you go to a wedding in Seattle? Want to find a babysitter for your grandkids at the same time? Need a roofer to fix that leaky spot in the eaves? You can find everything at the listing for your city at www.craigslist.org.

Comparison shop. Even if it seems like the deal of the century, it's always worth doing a little comparison shopping before you buy. It's up to you to use the Internet or the phone, but check to find out what price the competition is offering before you buy anything big, whether it's a lawn mower or a life insurance policy.

Keep your eyes peeled for deals. Special offers are all around, as retailers and service providers seek to draw in new customers. Whether it's a discount aimed at seniors or not, there's no reason you shouldn't take full advantage! Ben & Jerry's ice cream shops, for example, hold a free cone day every year, when you can enjoy a luscious scoop on the house. Starbucks recently took out ads in local papers that included a card that entitled the bearer to a free iced coffee every Wednesday for six weeks. Read the papers, listen to the news, and enjoy everything that's offered!

Let Uncle Sam extend a helping hand. Your tax money goes toward countless free services that are available to all citizens simply for the asking, from tax help to tips on cutting your energy costs. There are countless services available to specific groups, from seniors to veterans to the disabled, and you've already paid for your share through your annual income

Ka-Ching!

Easy Ways to Get Started on the Internet

Don't have a computer? Worried about getting started? Here are some ways to go online for less.

Ask for a hand-me-down. Your son or daughter or one of your grandchildren has probably recently upgraded one of their computers, and you should be first in line to get the old computer. As prices have come down on new computers and laptops and as the technology changes so quickly, people have begun to upgrade more frequently. That castoff might be the perfect thing for you to surf the Internet and send e-mail.

Get an inexpensive laptop. Nowadays, you can buy a new laptop for several hundred dollars, complete with software installed, which will likely include a step-by-step online tutorial on how to use it. There's no excuse!

Use the library. Nearly all public libraries in the United States now have public computers. At busy branches, you may have to register for a time slot, but you can spend your hour online surfing for good deals for that upcoming trip to Mexico or finding the lowest price prescription drugs.

Get connected with a high-speed package. If you've got cable TV, you're just clicks away from having a high-speed Internet connection. "Dial-up," the kind of connection that goes through your phone line, is so slow to download information that many Web sites won't even work through dial-up anymore. Ask your cable provider if it has any special offers to bundle high-speed service along with your regular cable service—and then ask if it has a senior discount as well!

Take a tutorial. Get moving fast with one of the excellent free Web sites that focus on teaching seniors how to use computers and the Internet as quickly and easily as possible, without assuming that you already understand some aspects, the way your teenage grandson might! Here's a list of terrific sites, many written by seniors for seniors:

www.seniorsguide tocomputers.com

www.computers forretirees.com

www.seniornet.org (Click on "E-Learning" and "Online Courses.")

tax. Be sure to get your benefits, too. A good place to start is at the main Web portal for the U.S. government, www.usa.gov, which links you to every single Web page administered by the federal government.

Early Bird Secret

Get Online for Less

Your cable company's high-speed access is fast and simple to set up, but even with a special introductory offer, you'll still pay anywhere from $20 to $30 a month, possibly more with taxes and fees. Instead, consider a free or discount high-speed provider. Few of these services are completely free, but some still offer free connection for a limited number of hours, typically 10 hours a month. That may be great for you to get started, but once you figure out how to use the Web to your advantage, you may want to upgrade. These services are still very inexpensive by comparison, generally no more than $20 a month, for unlimited Internet access as well as full technical support. Check out these reliable providers and get online the cheap way!

www.juno.com   www.mfire.com   www.arcZip.com

Go local. Although there are tons of national discounts just waiting to help you save money as a senior, from national clothing stores, restaurants, and more, the real savings might be hiding in your region. Local and state-wide senior discounts can be a real seam of gold to mine, from towns that focus on making themselves amenable to seniors to states, such as Ohio, that pay more than lip-service to the idea of aid and respect for their senior citizens. While it's comforting and easy to know, for example, that Perkins will always have the same (or similar) Senior Menu from restaurant to restaurant, wherever you go, you can find better and deeper discounts if you push outside the box a bit and ask about senior benefits at your local mom-and-pop stores and restaurants. They may even cook up a senior discount on the spot just for you!

Skirting Scams and Dubious Deals

While you're out there looking for your senior discounts, other, much more insidious operators, are out there looking for you—to separate you from as much of your money as possible. One study says that the average amount a senior loses in a telemarketing scam is as much as $7,000! You'd have to save a lot of money at the grocery store to make up for that kind of loss out of your nest egg. It's crucial throughout life to avoid scams and scurrilous offers, to dodge fakes and protect yourself from tricksters and con artists, but it's a particular problem that plagues seniors. Anyone can get taken in—and a lot of people do. But the fact is that a lot of scam artists tend to target seniors for a variety of reasons, not least being that we're more likely to politely hear them out. You need to keep your head on your shoulders and pay attention when you're the person writing the check or handing over the credit card or bank account info.

Protect yourself with a little bit of care and a modicum of suspicion. Check out these tips for avoiding cons and scams, and take them to heart when navigating the sometimes deep waters of commercial transactions.

10 Secrets to Shielding Yourself (and Your Money) from Con Artists

Although it may seem there are pitfalls around every corner, in fact you can protect yourself pretty easily by taking some standard precautions and sticking to them.

1. Ignore junk mail. Just throw it in the trash. The likelihood is practically nil that there is some kind of offer in unsolicited mail that will benefit you instead of the mailer.

2. Buy a shredder. Shred and tear up all documents containing personal or banking information before you dispose of them. It's not very likely that someone will go through your trash—but if they do, why hand them your identity?

3. Create a trustee or assign a power of attorney. Although this person can be a trusted family friend or family member, you can also have it be a financial adviser or attorney—in other words, a disinterested party. The benefit is that, as you get older, you won't find yourself writing a check for $50,000 from your life savings to some scurrilous operator when you need that money for your medical bills! Your trustee will be able to step in and help prevent it. You may feel that you're giving up a certain measure of control, but in fact it's about protecting yourself and your assets to the best of your abilities.

4. Don't have checks mailed to your home. If you get regular payments, be it Social Security, dividends, royalties, or whatever, have them deposited directly into your bank account whenever possible.

5. Get a Medicare-approved list of drug discounters. You should not buy a drug discount card from a telemarketer, and when you buy the card, you should not need to provide your personal financial information—Medicare already has access to it! If you're asked for personal financials, run the other way, or call Medicare to check on the company's record, at 1-800-MEDICARE (800-633-4227).

6. For home repairs, get referrals. If you need work done on your house, ask friends for referrals to a reputable contractor. Do not hire the guy who knocks on your front door and asks whether you need a new roof or a new driveway surface. If you *do* need these things, you should go looking for the worker, not the other way around. You can ask someone who knocks on your door for a business card and tell that person you want to think about it first. If you do want to use that person's services, contact your local Better Business Bureau first. And never pay more than half of the fee up front—if you do lose money, you won't lose the entire amount.

7. The government does *not* call to drum up business. If someone calls you offering a government grant for repairs on your house, for example, and then asks for a processing fee to give you the grant money, do *not* give them your bank account number. This is a particularly tricky scam because it all sounds very official and correct, right up to the moment you give the caller your personal info. There are indeed government grants for home repair for seniors, but you need to go looking for them by calling your local housing authority and asking for further information. The U.S. government has a lot of programs out there to help you, but they do not have the resources to call and offer you the help—and if they do, it will never come with a fee. You can contact www.grants.gov, the federal clearinghouse for government grants, or call them at 1-800-518-4726 to check the authenticity of the offer.

Did You Know?

Reporting Fraud and Scams There are a number of authorities who want to hear if you've been scammed or approached by a con artist. If someone has come to your home and physically threatened or frightened you, always start by calling the local police or dialing 911. For less urgent matters where your life or health is not endangered, try these:

Federal Trade Commission, www.ftc.gov

National Consumers League's Fraud Center, www.fraud.org

U.S. Department of Justice, www.usdoj.gov/criminal/fraud

8. Have scam, will travel. Be wary of travel clubs that promise you special rates and discounts in exchange for steep annual fees. Why pay an organization thousands of dollars a year to get room rates that you can probably find for less on the Internet? When you agree to accept something, such as a night at a resort, in exchange for listening to a sales pitch, the person doing the pitching is going to be *extremely* persuasive, and will press on your feeling of obligation, thanks to whatever you got: free dinner, hotel, or show tickets, for example. Accepting anything in exchange for listening to a sales pitch does *not* obligate you to buy whatever service is offered. Refuse to sign a contract then and there.

9. Be sure your bills are real. Suppose you receive a notice that your subscription to *Gourmet* is nearly up. You reach for your checkbook, but then think, "Wait, didn't I just pay that?" Check the return address on the bill, which is probably something like, "National Magazine Renewal Service." These scammers make money by collecting from a huge range of victims, who don't balk at writing small amounts for magazines that will never arrive. Many of us are so careless in our bookkeeping that we never even notice and might pay our actual *Gourmet* bill again when the real thing arrives nine or 10 months later. If you want to renew a magazine, check your subscription label or call customer service and find out when it's actually due—and then write your check *only* to the magazine, not to anyone else.

10. Stop and think before you act. The world might seem to be moving quickly, but there's *always* time to stop and think. Ask that the request be put in writing or tell the caller you can't write a check or give out

info without the okay of your trustee (even if you don't have one!)—that will generally be enough to end a solicitation. If you do want to pursue the offer, check with the Better Business Bureau or the National Consumer League's Fraud Center. And you can always check the Web at www.snopes.com, a wonderful site that debunks myths, scams, and urban legends right and left, with frequent updates and authoritative research.

Keep Your Privacy Private

The Privacy Rights Clearinghouse is a nonprofit organization that provides a huge range of information on protecting your privacy, from avoiding identity theft to dealing with cell phone abuse. Here's the place to find out exactly what rights you have to privacy when it comes to your medical records or background checks in the workplace. You can also find out how junk mailers get your name and address and how to get off their lists—including how to stop getting junk mail in the name of a deceased loved one. Visit its Web site at www.privacyrights.org.

Simple Ways to Dump Those Pesky Telemarketers

It is estimated that more than half of the victims of telemarketing fraud are over 50. The sad truth is that dishonest telemarketers target seniors for a variety of reasons, not least being that basic courtesy for many seniors makes it hard for them to hang up and impossible for them to accept that the helpful-sounding person at the other end of the line might wish them harm. As your own parents may have said long ago, "There's no free lunch." There are great discounts and bargains, but hardly anything that's just being handed to you for free, especially when it sounds too good to be true. But there are a number of ways to tell whether the call is a scam and the caller is a con artist, and, more important, ways to avoid these calls altogether.

Free things don't cost money. If a caller tells you that you've won a free gift and that all you have to do is pay taxes or shipping or a "claim fee," it's a scam. Never send money to claim a prize or pay a tax or any other reason. Most telemarketing fraud is in the field of prize winning and investments, with "contests" and "sweepstakes" making up a major part of it. Remember that it is illegal in the United States to charge people a fee to enter a contest or claim a prize.

If you have to make a decision *now*, say "No." When a caller rushes you and says that you have to accept the offer right away or it will be rescinded, that's your cue to let it go. There simply are no deals that have to be done in that time frame. If they called you, not the other way around, what's the rush? The only person who's in a hurry is the caller. Even legitimate merchants like to sew up deals quickly, but it's fraudulent telemarketers who insist upon it.

Tell the caller to put it in the mail. A list of terms and conditions reeled off at speed is no way to close a contract. Whatever the rush, whatever the terms, tell them to send the offer to you in the mail if you have any actual interest in it—but keep in mind all the other warnings here when it comes! Nice-looking letterhead is easy to fake, so that's no indication of legitimacy.

Let Your Fingers Do the Walking

There's one foolproof way to know whether the person on the other end of the line is making you a legitimate offer for a service or product that you actually want and need. *Did you look them up in the phone book and dial the call?* If not, all other calls can fall by the wayside. If you really needed or wanted the product or service, you would have gone looking for it yourself and made the call to a reliable purveyor. Anybody calling you is just trying to sell you something that you probably don't need, even if the call is "real."

Don't share. Ever. Never give out personal information to someone who calls you, including your Social Security number or your credit card or bank account numbers.

Have a standard refusal, say it, and hang up. Use whatever phrase you like, but repeat it to all callers, and include the request that they not call again—otherwise you get people saying things like, "I'll call again later." Here's a very useful phrase that's polite and effective: "I'm sorry, this house does not accept solicitation phone calls. Please take my name off your list and do not call this number again." The last sentence is the most important part, and you can say simply that, "Please take my name off your list and do not call back." Practice saying it, keep it on a piece of paper on the wall by the phone to read it aloud if necessary, and then *hang up.*

They're not just making a living. Don't assume that the caller is just someone working a tough job and trying to make a living by selling something on the phone—even if that's what the person tells you! Anyone who cajoles, threatens, pleads, or offers to work out a special price or deal "just for you" (and tries to get your bank account or credit card number) is not just making a living. Is this how you earned your money, or how your parents earned a living before you? Probably not. Protect yourself and your money and hang up.

Put yourself on the Do Not Call Registry. You won't even need most of these defensive measures if you put all your phone numbers, including your cell, on the National Do Not Call Registry. Call 1-888-382-1222 from your home phone to register it automatically, or register your home and cell phone numbers at www.donotcall.gov. After about a month, you should notice a significant reduction in the number of calls you receive, although you may still receive calls from legitimate charities, political organizations, telephone surveyors, and companies with which you have an existing relationship. The rules still apply, though! If you want to donate, ask for the request in writing, or offer your stock rejection phrase.

Delicious Food Savings for Seniors

Big Savings on Dining Out, Cooking In, and Eating Great!

Super Savings at Supermarkets

To be clear, you don't have to be over 50 to want (or get) a great deal on basic necessities—but the fact is that some of the best deals at supermarkets are *only* available to seniors. Many national and regional supermarket chains offer discounts on certain days of the week, and all you have to do is be sure to shop that day rather than another. Since you have the freedom to shop when you like, be the first in line to rack up the savings!

Note: The sample list below was accurate at time of printing, but age requirements, percentage of discount, and other restrictions can vary from store to store, even within the same chain of supermarkets, so be sure to get the specifics from the store where you shop.

A&P Supermarket If you have an A&P Club Card and you're 60 or above, upgrade to a Live Better Wellness Club Card and get a 15 percent discount on fruits and vegetables, a 25 percent discount on healthcare products, plus a 10 percent Senior Citizen Prescription and Family Pet Prescription discount. Details at www.apsupermarket.com.

Bi-Lo Once you register for a Bi-Lo Bonus Card, if you're 60 or older, every Wednesday you can get the Senior Bonus program, which means an additional 5 percent savings. Visit www.bi-lo.com.

Earth Fare This chain of grocery stores in North Carolina, South Carolina, Georgia, and Tennessee offers 5 percent off to seniors 60 and older everday. To find locations, visit www.earthfare.com.

Foodland Some Foodland stores offer a senior discount of 5 percent one day a week. The day of the discount, discount amount, and age requirement varies for each store. Call your local branch for specifics. Find locations and phone numbers at www.foodlandstores.com.

Fry's If you register for Fry's VIP savings card (registration is free) and you're 55 or older, you can save 10 percent on your food bill (less VIP savings, taxes, and coupons) the first Wednesday of every month. Register by visiting www.frysfood.com.

Kroger The first Wednesday of each month, seniors 60 and older receive a 10 percent discount off total purchases, but you have to go to Customer Service to get it rather than having the discount rung up when you pay. You must have a KrogerPlus shopping card and ID. Get details at www.kroger.com.

Ralphs You can get a Ralph's rewards card that lets you save 20 percent on some store brands. You can also save an extra $1 after accumulating $10 in spending on Ralphs private label products. Get details at www.ralphs.com.

Shop 'n Save The day of the week varies according to location, but most offer a 10 percent discount to seniors once a week. Visit www.shopnsave.com.

ShopRite If you're 55 or older, you can get a discount off your purchases at your local ShopRite. The amount of the discount and day of the week it applies varies with each individual store, so be sure to check in advance. You can find your nearest ShopRite by visiting www.shoprite.com.

Wegmans Wegmans wins when it comes to the biggest effort to accommodate seniors among grocery chains: They send Medical Motors buses with wheelchair access to 70 senior-subsidized housing complexes, and they take the residents for free to a Wegmans store to shop. Note: This offer is only open to seniors who live in government-subsidized housing. Find out more at www.wegmans.com.

25 Grocery Items Never to Buy Again

Let's face it: We'll probably never stop shopping in a grocery store for many reasons, nor should we. We just have to be smarter and savvier about it, and vow to never, ever buy certain prepackaged items again because, simply, we don't have to. Why spend when we don't have to? So shelve those mixes and say good-bye to canned broth, once and for all!

1. Gravy Mixes

Got flour? Some butter? Canned or homemade broth? We thought so. If you have these three pantry ingredients, you've got the makings for gravy that will take you from Thanksgiving to July Fourth and every day in between. Here's an easy version that you can modify to your heart's content (try a handful of mushrooms or a splash of wine).

 The Gravy Train Gravy

Makes about 2 cups

> **4 tablespoons unsalted butter**
> **1/4 cup all-purpose flour**
> **2 cups turkey, chicken, or beef broth (low-sodium if using packaged)**
> **1/4 teaspoon salt (or to taste)**

1 In a medium saucepan, melt the butter over medium heat and add the flour, whisking until a smooth paste is formed.

2 Continue cooking until the mixture browns to a light toasty color, about 3–5 minutes. Reduce the heat to low and slowly add broth, whisking constantly. Once the liquid is incorporated (about 2 minutes), turn the heat back to medium, and bring to a slow boil until thickened.

3 Taste and adjust for seasoning if necessary. Refrigerate leftovers for 3–4 days or freeze gravy within 24 hours of making it for up to one month.

Modifications: Replace 1/4 of the liquid with dry white wine; add sautéed mushrooms; add oregano, basil, rosemary or sage; adding a tablespoon of sherry at the end gives a sweet, sophisticated punch; likewise, a bit of cream—just a tablespoon—adds decadence and makes this truly "special sauce."

2. Canned, Bottled, or Boxed Soup Stocks

Sure, the canned or boxed stuff is easy, and who doesn't like easy? But if you've bought a chicken for $6, you can make a virtual vat of homemade stock from the leftover carcass (and those veggies and herbs that might be lurking in your crisper) and save yourself a lot of dough in the long run. Once made (usually from stuff that you'd just throw away), stocks freeze well, so make them when you have the ingredients and the time, and you'll never run out. Here's our favorite chicken stock recipe (which can also be made with a turkey carcass, but then it would be turkey stock):

 Move-Over-Martha Chicken Stock

Makes about 5 quarts

Carcass, bones, and any attached meat from one 4-pound chicken
1 onion, peeled and quartered
1 large carrot, peeled and cut into 2-inch chunks
1 celery stalk, cut into 1-inch chunks
1 bay leaf
1 parsley sprig
1 thyme sprig

8 whole black peppercorns

1/2 teaspoon salt

1 In a large soup pot over medium-high heat, combine chicken carcass, onion, carrot, and celery. Add 7 cups of cool water, and bring to a boil. Skim off foam and discard.

2 Add bay leaf, parsley, thyme, peppercorns, and salt. Reduce heat, cover, and simmer for 2 hours.

3 Strain stock through a fine mesh sieve into a heatproof bowl. Let cool completely, then refrigerate until cold, and remove fat from surface. Use within 3 days or freeze and use within 3 months.

Freeze this stock in 1-cup containers or ice cube trays for a quick hit of flavor in everything from soups to stews.

3. Packaged Bread Crumbs and Stuffing Mixes

How many "heels" of old bread do you toss out or give to the birds? If you saved them and grated them in a food processor or blender, you would never run out of fresh bread crumbs; if you cubed, tossed them with dried herbs, and toasted them, you'd never run out of stuffing. Freeze crumbs, cubes, and slices in storage bags for up to 6 months.

Early Bird Secret

Stale Bread Reborn

Like croutons on your salad? If you like bread, you'll never have to buy them again. Bread of any kind can be sliced and toasted for croutons or as a surface for any kind of dip or topping.

4. Commercial Tomato-Based Pasta Sauces

Forget about premade pasta sauces, even if they are supposedly made by Butch Cassidy. They can be very expensive because you're paying extra for the bottle. Make your own sauces from inexpensive canned crushed tomatoes or, in late summer, fresh tomatoes, when they're plentiful and CHEAP!

Even better: *you* control the amount of salt, pepper, herbs, and other seasonings that go inside. Here's a quick, simple, and frugal version:

 Totally Terrific Tomato Sauce

Makes about 2–3 quarts

2 tablespoons extra-virgin olive oil
2 cloves garlic, peeled and minced
1 medium onion, peeled and diced
2 celery stalks, diced
2 carrots, peeled and diced
2 cans (28 ounces each) crushed tomatoes
Salt and pepper, to taste
Optional: red pepper flakes, dried basil, dried oregano

1   Heat the olive oil in a large soup pot set over medium-high heat. Add the garlic, onion, celery, and carrots, and cook until soft, about 8 minutes, stirring frequently to keep them from sticking to the pan.

2   Add the tomatoes and stir to blend well. Bring to a boil, and immediately lower heat to slow simmer. Cover and continue to cook for 30 minutes, stirring frequently, seasoning to taste with salt and pepper. Add red pepper flakes, basil, and/or oregano as desired. Use within 5 days, or freeze in individual 1-cup containers.

5. Meat and Pasta Helpers

These convenient boxes filled with dried pasta and some flavorings are basically a very expensive way to buy macaroni, whether it's a blend to add to hamburger or tuna, or good old boxed mac and cheese. Bottom line: You're paying between $1.79 and $2.79 for a few ounces of pasta and fake cheese or freeze-dried herbs and spices. On the other hand, 16 ounces of pasta costs about 99 cents. You can mix up your own ground beef, herbs, pasta, and tomato sauce just as easily—and it will taste better, too!

6. Bottled Salad Dressing

The cheap stuff tastes like motor oil so that's no bargain. And the expensive stuff—at $5 and up—can be matched by your own (very frugal) culinary magic at home. Here's how:

Fabulous and Frugal Italian Dressing

Makes about 1/2 a cup

1/2 teaspoon Dijon mustard

2 tablespoons vinegar (red or white wine)

1/3 cup olive oil

Pinch of sugar, to taste

Optional: snipped chives, fresh or dried parsley, fresh or dried tarragon

1 Place the mustard in a medium-size bowl and add the vinegar. Whisk well.

2 Drizzle in the olive oil in a steady stream, whisking to incorporate.

3 Add sugar, to taste, and optional herbs. Pour into a glass jar, seal, and refrigerate for up to 4 days. Shake well to reincorporate ingredients.

 Fabulous and Frugal Ranch Dressing

Makes about 1 1/2 cups

1/2 cup mayonnaise

1/2 cup sour cream

2 tablespoons lemon juice

2 tablespoons each chopped fresh parsley and scallion

1 clove garlic, minced

1/2 teaspoon black pepper

Combine all ingredients in a small bowl. Pour into a small glass jar and store for up to 4 days. Shake well before serving.

7. Boxed Rice Entrée or Side Dish Mixes

These consist of two inexpensive ingredients—rice and salt—yet they're priced way beyond either ingredient sold individually. Sure, there are a few flavorings included, but they're probably ones you have in your pantry already.

Buy a bag of rice, measure out what you need, add your own herbs and other seasonings, and cook the rice according to package directions.

The Manager's Special

In addition to the sales advertised in the weekly flyer, supermarkets very often have unadvertised "Manager's Specials"—sales that often occur when the supermarket has an overstock of perishable items such as produce, dairy, bakery, meat, poultry, or seafood. Savings can range from 50 percent to 80 percent off, depending on the item. Inquire at your store's service desk to see if there are any "Manager's Specials" that day or week. These items will be clearly marked on the shelves and, in the case of meat, poultry, and fresh seafood, tagged on the item itself. You may get lucky and find half a turkey breast for $2 (for the entire thing, not "per pound"), and a 3-pound pork roast for $3.

8. *Premade Frozen Noodle Side Dishes*

No matter how you carefully you prepare these "according to package directions," the noodles and veggies will still come out mushy, because pasta wasn't meant to be cooked in its sauce, and precooked veggies just get softer with every reheating. Again, you have all the items in your pantry to make a perfectly delicious side dish of, say, Pasta Alfredo (okay, you may have to buy fresh Parmesan cheese), or chicken with pasta in cream sauce.

9. *Granola Bars*

These expensive, calorie-and-sugar laden bars are stacked at the checkout counter because they depend on impulse buyers who grab them thinking they are more wholesome than a candy bar. (They're not.) If you need a quick boost, enjoy a piece of fruit, a hard-boiled egg, a cup of yogurt, or a small handful of nuts.

10. *Flavored Water*

Why pay a premium price for tap water or spring water with a shot of lemon or orange juice—and food coloring—when you can concoct your own flavors at home? Simply add a tablespoon of cranberry, orange, lemon, or lime juice to seven ounces of cold water, and you've got yourself a refreshing, low-cal thirst-quencher.

11. Powdered Iced Tea Mixes or Prepared Flavored Iced Tea

Do the math: If you buy a bottle of packaged iced tea twice a day, every day, at $2 a bottle, you've spent $28 a week (or $112 a month, or $1,344 a year!) on what you can make at home for just pennies. Here's how:

 Summertime Anytime Iced Tea

Makes 32 ounces, or 8 to 10 large glasses of tea

About 32 ounces of *fresh cold* **water**

8 bags of black tea or 10 bags of herbal, green, or white tea, or a combination of 10 black and herbals bags

Ice cubes

Optional: Granulated sugar or other sweetener such as fruit juice, and lemon, orange, or lime slices

1 Place tea bags in a *heatproof* glass or ceramic pitcher large enough to hold 32 ounces of water. Bring water to a rapid boil, and pour over the bags in the pitcher. Allow the tea to steep for about 20 minutes, then remove bags with a slotted spoon.

2 Cover and chill for at least an hour and a half or overnight. To serve, pour in an ice-filled glass. Stir in a teaspoon of sugar (or to taste) if you like your tea sweet. Add citrus slices for another layer of flavor. (Note: If you include fruit juice, you will likely not have to use additional sugar or other sweetener.)

12. "Gourmet" Frozen Vegetables in Sauce

Sure, you can buy an eight-ounce package of peas in "herbed butter sauce." But why do so when you can make your own? Just cook fresh or frozen peas, add a pat of butter and a sprinkle of herbs you already have on hand.

13. Spice Mixes

Spice mixes like grill seasoning and rib rubs might seem like a good buy because they contain a lot of spices that you would otherwise have to buy individually. Right? Wrong! Look in your pantry, and you'll likely find the same ingredients, so why not make your own like we do? Stored in an airtight container in a cool part of the kitchen, these babies will keep for up to 2 months.

 Mama Mia Italian Spice Rub

Makes about 1/2 cup

2 tablespoons dried basil
1 tablespoon dried oregano
1 tablespoon fennel seeds
1 tablespoon garlic powder
1/2 tablespoon salt

Mix all ingredients together in a small bowl, and spoon into an airtight container or jar. Label, and store in a cool, dark cupboard for up to 6 months.

 Ooh-La-La French Spice Rub

Makes about 1/2 cup

2 tablespoons dried parsley
1 tablespoon dried lavender
1 tablespoon fennel seeds
1 tablespoon thyme
1/2 tablespoon salt

Mix all ingredients together in a small bowl, and spoon into an airtight container or jar. Label, and store in a cool, dark cupboard for up to 6 months.

5 Things

Not to Buy in a **Supermarket**

We love grocery stores. Their stock and trade is food—fresh, frozen, canned or prepared—and kitchen staples like paper towels and laundry detergent. But there are a whole host of other items that cost a premium in grocery stores because of the "convenience" factor. You can get them cheaper at a discount department or hardware store, dollar store, or drug store so leave the following items off your shopping list:

1. **COOKWARE AND KITCHEN UTENSILS**

   It may be convenient to pick up a frying pan while you're buying your bacon, but you'll be paying much more than you ought to for it.

2. **COSMETICS, TOILETRIES, AND PERSONAL CARE ITEMS**

   Keep rolling! It might save time to buy your lip-gloss, moisturizer, toothpaste, razor blades, and deodorant at the same time and place you're getting your food, but you'll be paying a premium price.

3. **SMALL APPLIANCES**

   Why buy a toaster for $40 when you can buy the same toaster for $20 dollars at a discount house? The same theory applies to coffee makers, electric teakettles, and hot plates.

4. **PARTY SUPPLIES**

   Okay, you can get your balloons, funny hats, place cards, candles, and name tags in the grocery store. But you could pay a whole lot less getting them in bulk at a party supply store.

5. **BATTERIES, LIGHTBULBS, EXTENSION CORDS**

   Again, these are pricey specialty items at the grocery store, but cheap impulse buys at a discount hardware, department, or dollar store!

All-American Barbecue Dry Rub

Makes about 1/2 cup

1 tablespoon coarse salt
2 tablespoons dark brown sugar
1 tablespoon paprika
1/2 teaspoon cayenne pepper
1/2 tablespoon garlic powder

Mix all ingredients together in a small bowl, and spoon into an airtight container or jar. Label, and store in a cool, dark cupboard for up to 6 months.

14. Premium Frozen Fruit Bars

At more than $2 per bar, frozen "all fruit" or "fruit and juice" bars may not be rich in calories, but they are certainly rich in price. Make your own at home—and get the flavors you want. The only equipment you need is a blender, clean yogurt cups, and pop sticks or wooden skewers.

 Save-ery Fruit Pops

Makes 4 pops

2 cups cut-up fruit (strawberries, pitted peaches, nectarines, melon, pitted cherries, pitted plums, pitted apricots)
1 tablespoon sugar or the equivalent amount of your favorite replacement sweetener (optional, depending on sweetness of fruit)
1 teaspoon fresh lemon or lime juice
Water

1 Place the fruit, sweetener if using, and lemon or lime juice in a blender. Cover and blend until smooth. Add 1–2 tablespoons water, if necessary, to create a thick "slush."

2 Pour evenly into 4 yogurt cups or a Popsicle mold. Insert sticks. Freeze until solid.

15. Cocktail Mixes

Premade bottled cocktail mixes (Just add gin! Just add vodka! Just add rum!) are another waste of money because you end up paying for a lot of *water* (!), sugar, and artificial ingredients. It's just as easy and cheaper to make your own drinks "from scratch" with your own fresh fruit juice, sugar, and water.

16. Buttermilk

It's tangy, it's low-fat, and a little bit of it will give zip to all sorts of baked dishes. Why buy an extra grocery item when you can make it yourself? It's simple!

 Better than Bought Buttermilk

Makes about 1 cup

1 tablespoon white vinegar or lemon juice
1 cup milk (preferably whole)

Combine vinegar with milk and let stand for 5 minutes before using it (which you should do immediately).

17. Brown Sugar

The more people we asked, the more our suspicions were confirmed: How many of you have an ancient box of brown sugar from a long-ago presidential administration (Kennedy? Carter?) kicking around your pantry, and it's rock hard. Don't chisel away at it; make your own instead with two basic pantry ingredients, and never buy it again. Ever. (Meanwhile, you can still use that rock-hard block if you microwave it in the bag for 1–2 minutes on high, squeezing and checking it frequently until it's soft enough to use.)

Even Better Brown Sugar

Makes about 1 cup

1 cup white granulated sugar

2 tablespoons molasses

Using a fork, combine the sugar and molasses until blended completely. For dark brown sugar, use blackstrap molasses; for light brown sugar, use lighter molasses. Store in an airtight resealable bag in a cool, dark location.

18. Canned Cake Frosting

Ick. The cheap brands taste like petrochemicals, and the premium products are super-expensive. Frostings from scratch are simple and easy to make. Here's our favorite simple one:

Old-Fashioned Chocolate Frosting

Makes about 2 cups (enough to frost a 1-layer cake or a dozen cupcakes)

2 cups confectioners' sugar

1/2 cup unsweetened cocoa

1 stick unsalted butter, softened to room temperature

7-8 tablespoons whole milk

1 teaspoon vanilla extract

1 tablespoon brewed coffee (instant is fine)

Combine all ingredients in a medium bowl, and beat with an electric mixer or by hand until combined and spreadable. Use immediately or store in an airtight container in the refrigerator for up to 3 days.

2 Ways to Avoid Slippage

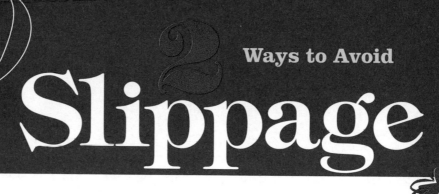

"Hey, wasn't that cottage cheese?"
"Wasn't this once a green pepper?"
"We ate chili two nights running,
    so let's just throw the rest away."

Sound familiar?

It's so common to throw out food that we rarely stop to consider that it's like standing on the front porch feeding dollar bills into the wind. "Slippage" is an economic term for the difference between the estimated costs of a transaction and what you actually pay. When it comes to food, "slippage" is when you buy bananas, eat three, and throw away two. Stop now and save big.

FIGURE OUT WHAT YOU USE FREQUENTLY AND BUY IT—AND ONLY IT—IN BULK.

Everyone knows their staples: cereal, coffee, toilet paper—anything your family always has on hand or might make a special trip to buy. These are the only things you should ever buy in bulk at wholesale stores or discount clubs.

MAKE A MEAL PLAN AND A GROCERY LIST—AND STICK TO THEM.

Your list can be definite while your meal plan is hazy. Say you know you're going out Friday and have something already for Monday but still need to cook Tuesday, Wednesday, and Thursday. Choosing the actual meat or vegetable or pasta can depend on what might be on special at the store, but you're still sticking to your list in terms of basic items to acquire.

19. Flavored Yogurt

Instead of spending money on pricey flavored yogurt, flavor your own plain yogurt with already-in-your-kitchen pantry items: fruit spread or jam, honey, maple syrup, a drop or two of vanilla extract, mashed bananas, walnuts... the possibilities are endless!

Did You Know?

You can save big by blending your own inexpensive, customized specialty sauces and dips, and you'll never look back. Here's how to get started:

1. Trick out a cup of plain yogurt with lemon juice, salt, pepper, and curry powder for an elegant dip for raw veggies.

2. Make honey mustard by mixing half honey, half mustard (either Dijon or spicy brown), and a dash of cider vinegar.

3. Homemade onion dip is fresh, easy, and preservative-free if you mix half sour cream, half mayo with some caramelized onions, chopped fresh parsley, Worcestershire, ground black pepper, and a dash of hot sauce.

20. Trail Mix

Our experts did a national price check and found that, on average, those little bags of candy-coated chocolate nuts and raisins cost about $10 a pound! Make your own for much, much less with a one-pound can of dry-roasted peanuts, a cup of raisins, a handful of almonds, another of candy-coated chocolate, and perhaps some other kind of dried fruit. Keep it in a plastic or glass container with a tight lid for up to three weeks.

21. Granola

Gourmet granola breakfast, especially organic brands, can also run in the $7 to $10 per pound range. If you love granola for breakfast (or as a snack to munch on during the day) make your own with good old-fashioned rolled oats.

Simply Grand Granola

Makes about 6 cups

1/2 cup vegetable, sunflower, or canola oil
1/3 cup honey or maple syrup
1/4 teaspoon salt
3/4 teaspoon cinnamon
1/3 cup skim milk
3/4 cup brown sugar
5 cups whole oats
Nonstick cooking spray
1/2 cup each of any of the following:
Unsalted slivered almonds
Unsalted chopped walnuts
Unsalted chopped cashews
Raisins
Shredded unsweetened coconut
Dried cranberries
Dried apricots, chopped

1 Preheat over to 375°F. Combine the first 6 ingredients in a large saucepan over medium heat until the sugar melts and the mixture is well blended. Remove from heat and add oats, and continue to mix well with a wooden spoon.

2 Spray 2 cookie sheets with nonstick cooking spray, and spread the granola mixture evenly on the sheets. Bake for about 15–20 minutes, checking every few minutes and stirring a few times for even browning and to prevent burning. Remove from the oven, and cool on sheets.

3 When the mixture has cooled completely, transfer it to a large bowl and add the nuts and dried fruits. Store in an airtight container for 3–4 weeks.

22. Canned Soup

Sure, they are convenient, but they are also expensive, not all that tasty, and often contain unhealthy amounts of salt. Make your own healthier, tastier soup in minutes with your homemade stock Add in some fresh veggies, beans, leftover chicken or beef, and freeze what you can't eat right away in portion-sized containers.

Early Bird Secret

We Can Get It for You Tomorrow

Supermarkets sell baked goods and produce that are just approaching or have slightly passed their sell-by dates at 50 percent off (or more) of the regular price. Don't buy baked goods that are rock-hard (unless you want stale bread to make stuffing, for instance) or fruit or vegetables that are badly blemished, and never buy badly dented cans or packages that have been opened—they could harbor bacteria. But with a little care, you can find some excellent buys, such a ripe cantaloupe for a third of the price of its younger cousin in the regular produce department.

23. Salad Kits

Washed and bagged greens can be a time-saver, but they're three and four times more expensive than a head of lettuce. Even more expensive, however, are "salad kits," where you get some greens, a small bag of dressing, and a small bag of croutons. Skip these—you already have the ingredients for croutons (toasted or fried bread) and salad dressing (mayonnaise, vinegar, oil, and mustard, plus whatever herbs you like) at home.

24. Preformed Meat Patties

Frozen burgers—beef or otherwise—are more expensive than buying the ground meat in bulk and making patties yourself. (We timed it—it takes less than 10 seconds to form a flat circle and throw it on the grill!) Also, there's some evidence that preformed meat patties might contain more *E. coli* than regular ground meat. In fact, all the recent beef recalls have involved premade frozen beef patties. Fresh is definitely better!

25. Cooking Spray

Don't pay big bucks for compressed air. A small oil-misting bottle will pay for itself when you fill it with your own olive oil or canola oil (the two healthiest).

Off-the-Beaten-Path Food Savings

In addition to getting discounts at your favorite grocery store, there are plenty of other ways for us seniors to get the jump on savings. Shopping for everything in the same place, like your local supermarket, may be convenient but it will never save you the biggest bundle. To do that, you need to shop around a bit more to be sure you're hitting the right places for the right items. So where are your best bets? Here's a rundown of your basic grocery shopping options and of which places tend to have better prices on what.

Visit Your Local Farmers' Market in Season

Stock up on whatever is in season, which will usually make it easier on the wallet. A fringe benefit is that produce might be grown locally, and if it is, it'll likely be cheaper. A dozen eggs fresh from a free-range hen will usually cost the same or less than that mass-farmed refrigerated dozen at the grocery store, and they'll always taste much better. The farmers who sell their goods are not big, commercial, high-volume producers, and the prices they set for their produce may *seem* higher than they are at the supermarket. Guess again.

The farmer is your friend. Make friends with the owners, and let them share their passion for what they do (they may even give you a free sample or at least a taste). Once they recognize you and your tastes, they may save their very best tomatoes or apples for you. Once again, the best of the best is almost always a bargain, since you'll be more likely to eat all of it rather than throw some of it out at the end of the week.

Did You Know?

Farmers' markets are among the best places to pick up free recipes straight from the food source. Farmers are often fabulous cooks and are very willing to share advice on how to prepare the vegetables and herbs that they grow. Don't be shy. Take a pad and a pencil, and promise that you'll always give them credit when your family swoons and says, "Where did you get this recipe?"

It's okay to negotiate the price. Farmers are entrepreneurs and are more than willing to do a bit of haggling, especially if you are willing to buy in bulk those items that can be stored or frozen, like winter squash, apples, potatoes, and green beans.

Time it right for savings. If you want to eat fresh food cheap, hit the market an hour to a half hour before closing and scoop up fruits and veggies, even baked goods and flowers, at a discount, sometimes as much as 50 percent to 75 percent off. Growers always want to unload as much as they can at the end of day, rather than haul it home. Just be sure your afternoon foraging begins with an open mind and palate and empty shopping bags (they often run out of bags at the end of the day). Some sellers are even willing to give away items. If you've never tried Chinese cabbage or fresh fava beans, this may be your chance. If you don't fall in love with the flavor, there's always the compost bin.

Enjoy a berry nice price. Love blueberries and cherries but cringe at the checkout when you buy them in the dead of winter? Shop for them in season, and if you know you love them, buy as many as you can. Place them on a large, lipped baking sheet, pop them into the freezer, and four hours later, you'll have individually frozen, fresh-as-a-daisy berries. Store them in heavy-duty freezer bags for up to six months, and you'll never have to shell out hard-earned dough again to make a succulent, fresh blueberry pie or cherry tart in the middle of January.

Other Food-Buying Choices

Find an ethnic market. One man's butt is another man's tender-loin—*pork butt*, that is! One of our researchers discovered an entire pork butt (which is really shoulder) for 99 cents a pound in her local ethnic market and the same cut—from the same producer—at $4.99 per pound in the case at a neighboring gourmet shop. Ethnic markets will cater directly to clientele who have to stretch their dollars as far as they can go. If you live near an Italian, Spanish, Asian, or African market, take advantage of everything you'll find there. And if something looks unfamiliar to you, ask the people around you for help. You'll be thrilled you did!

Don't forget the dollar store! Paper products, cleaning supplies, and even plenty of canned or dry foods can be bought at the dollar store for...you guessed it: a dollar! Many of these stores sell "odd lots" of brand-name products, generally from overstock. There's no stigma in paying a tiny fraction of the original price for perfectly good products.

Ka-Ching!

The Ethnic Market Versus the Supermarket

We shopped for the same 15 items, below, in a small, East Coast ethnic market and a major chain supermarket in the same neighborhood. Here's what we discovered:

	Ethnic Market	Supermarket
Soy sauce (1 quart):	$2.99	$4.99
Pork butt (6 pounds):	$5.99	$10.98
Corn tortillas (pack of 24):	$1.59	$3.99
Organic eggs (1 dozen):	$2.19	$3.99
Sheep's milk cheese (1 pound):	$3.99	$15.99
Canned garbanzo beans (16 ounces):	$.89	$2.99
Chili sauce (1 quart):	$2.99	$4.99
Broccoli (2 heads):	$2.99	$4.50
Imported Italian pasta (1 pound):	$2.19	$4.99
Imported basmati rice (10 pounds):	$8.99	$19.99
Organic milk (1/2 gallon):	$1.19	$3.29
Imported coffee (1 pound):	$3.69	$9.00
Imported tea (150 bags):	$6.50	$12.00
Chicken sausage (1 pound):	$5.75	$8.00
Canned tomatoes (28 ounces):	$1.99	$4.99
TOTALS	$53.92	$114.68

Split the goods, share the discounts. A dozen rolls of toilet paper won't go stale sitting in your closet, but unless it's wrapped well and your freezer is huge, 12 pounds of beef just may! What to do? Split a discount club membership fee between a few friends, and then divvy up the goods at the end of your shopping trip. You'll reap the benefits of the lower price, without needlessly throwing out food that's gone bad before you've had a chance to use it.

If you're an avid cook, buy spices in bulk. The markup on spices from major brand names in the grocery-store spice aisle is hair-raising. If you can find a store that sells spices and dried herbs from large bins, you may be pleasantly surprised to discover that the little jar of spices you paid $5 for at the supermarket is 89 cents for about three-quarters of a cupful, weighed out in a little paper bag—when bought in bulk.

Meaty Discounts

If you love meats of all kinds but think they'll cost you a fortune, you're in the right place. With a little ingenuity, you can regularly fill your freezer with the tastiest cuts, and dine like royalty. What's the secret? Read on!

Good-bye, prime time. While it's true that prime meat—the highest quality, dry-aged stuff that the top restaurants peddle for mortgage-payment amounts—is the cream of the crop, it's the less-expensive, more frugal cuts that offer both flavor *and* value. Look for hanger steaks, skillet steaks, London broils, chuck steaks, and bottom rounds, and keep your wallet full!

Do the braise craze. If you've got a few hours to kill on a rainy afternoon, you've got time to make a flavor-packed stew that will yield leftovers for days and weeks (if you freeze them). Brown a chuck roast on all sides in a heavy oven-proof casserole (cast iron is best), throw in a handful of chopped onions, carrots, and celery, pour in a cup or two of inexpensive red wine and a cup of beef broth, cover it, and place it in the oven at 300°F. Voila! Three hours later, and dinner is served.

Give it an airing for more flavor. For maximum taste at minimal cost, unwrap your beef when you get it home, put it on a plate, sprinkle it with a tiny bit of salt, and let it stand, unwrapped, in your refrigerator for up to four hours before you cook it. (Let it come to room temperature before preparing your recipe.) Air-curing is the natural way to age meat and to give it an incomparable flavor boost for practically nothing. Note: Only do this if you're going to be preparing the meat the day you bring it home.

Grind your own and save big!

Sure, we know it's easy, but those immense packages of ground beef are nothing more than an overpriced convenience. What to do? Grind your own! Buy what's on sale (if it's on the bone, slice the bone away and discard it), cube it, and pulse it in your food processor. Store in heavy-duty, resealable bags, and use as you would ground beef—for much less.

Buy in bulk and freeze.

Meat, when wrapped well, can keep for up to six months. Remove your purchase from its grocery store wrapping, double-wrap it in your own plastic wrap, and place it in a dated, labeled, heavy-duty freezer bag.

Go hog wild!

If you're a fan of pork, you're in luck. Some yummy parts of pig can be had in bulk for surprisingly little money. "Country-style" pork ribs—meatier, more flavorful than their baby back cousins, and far more frugal—are generally sold in large "family size" packages. If it's just two of you, break up the big package into smaller ones and freeze; if you're having a crowd, haul out the slow cooker, layer them on top of sliced onions, add a few garlic cloves and your favorite barbecue sauce, cook it on high for a few hours, and call it summer!

Be a ham. Again and again.

Don't bypass that big ham on sale at the grocery store, even if there are only two or three of you at the table each night. It's simple to prepare, and leftovers can be cubed and tossed into pea soup, noodle dishes, burritos, and more. Even the bone can be added to cooking soup for incomparable flavor. Anything left over? Freeze it for up to four months.

Buy the whole bird.

Grocery stores count on us to skip the whole bird in favor of cut-up parts, like breasts, thighs, and legs. What do they give us in return? Unnecessary expense. If you learn to cut a chicken into parts, you can save up to $2.99 *a pound* on your next chicken-shopping excursion. (Our researchers found whole chickens on sale on the West Coast for as little as 69 cents per pound!) Here's how to do it, simply and easily:

1. Using a clean, strong pair of poultry shears or kitchen scissors, snip up the backbone and flatten the bird.
2. Turn the bird over, and snip right up the breast bone.

3. Snip one half in half again.
4. Snip the other half in half again.

Removing legs and wings is up to you (keep snipping); if you want boneless breasts, simply pull the bone away from the meat. And feel free to pull off the skin while you're at it. What do you have? Expensive chicken parts, for the frugal price of a whole bird.

Caviar Tastes on an Early Bird's Budget

Living the life of a discerning over 50 gourmet is by no means at odds with big savings. Food is something we have to eat every day, and buying good food doesn't have to be expensive. You, too, can be a gourmet while still taking advantage of big discounts!

Be a cheese wiz! Real Italian Parmigiano-Reggiano (not the stuff in the green cardboard can) is a classic addition to everything from pastas to salads and soups, but it can cost a big bundle. Forgo the fake stuff in the green can, and opt for a clever, more frugal substitute for the real thing: Look for easy-to-find Asiago or Grana Padano—very similar cheeses that cost a fraction of Parmigiano-Reggiano and still deliver a punch of flavor.

Early Bird Secret

Keep olive oil cool.

Olive oil should be stored in a cool, dry place, such as a pantry or on a bottom shelf of a lower cabinet. Kept this way, it will stay fresh for a year or more. Never refrigerate it, and never expose it to heat, or it will turn rancid.

You say expensive imported tomato, I say *not!* Fancy Italian canned tomatoes, called San Marzanos, are delicious, sweet, available all year round, and incredibly expensive. Our secret way around the price? Buy other canned tomatoes on sale, and drizzle them with rice vinegar. The result will be so sweet and succulent you'll wonder why you haven't done this before!

Shelve imported pastas where they belong (on the shelf). Fancy imported pastas are rarely worth their price, and sometimes little more than costly packaging wrapped around an inexpensive product. What to do when faced with a choice? Buy the less expensive brand and

Ka-Ching!

Holy cow!

We don't mean to be disrespectful to Elsie, but that iconic cow is responsible for cuts of beef that can run the gamut from very, very expensive to downright cheap. The best-tasting cut is not always the most expensive; the key is knowing what you're buying, what you can save, and how you can use it to make the most succulent, money-savvy meals around.

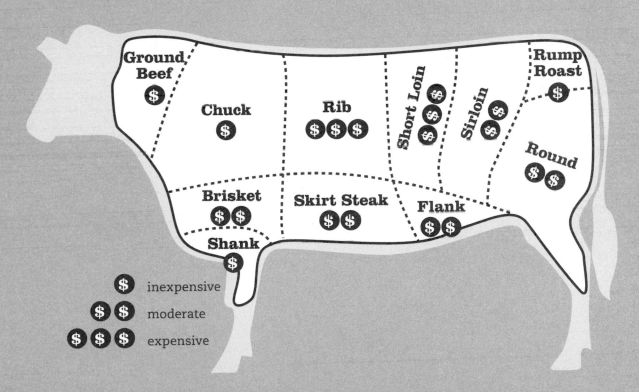

TIP Although ground beef traditionally comes from the neck of the animal, every cut can be bought whole, cubed at home, and ground by pulsing it gently in a food processor. If a particular cut, like chuck or round, is on sale, it may be less expensive to grind it yourself than to purchase it preground.

cook it one or two minutes less than the box suggests; toss it with already hot sauce of your choice, and serve it al dente—to the tooth, in Italian—for a qualitative, delicious boost at a lower cost.

Dressed to the 99s. Sure, you can find everyday items at your local 99-cent store. But if you look a bit more closely, you'll find loads of tempting gourmet goodies: we found fancy, imported chocolates; wild smoked salmon; smoky Spanish almonds; and sweet roasted peppers. Who knew? (Now, you!)

Grow your own herbs; don't buy them. Why spend $2 to $3 for a tiny packet of fresh herbs in a grocery store, when the same amount of money would have bought you a potted plant of the same herb that could live in your windowsill? Rosemary is an amazingly hardy plant, as are thyme and mint, and the only problem with growing chives is to make them *stop*. Cutting chives merely encourages them to grow faster, so if you toss a handful of snipped chives in your scrambled eggs every few days, you'll never lack for them.

Did You Know?

The Whole Truth about Basil. You can freeze fresh basil leaves whole when they're plentiful in summer or, of course, turn them into pesto that will flavor soups and pastas for months afterward. The secret to keeping pesto is to always pour at least half an inch of olive oil over the surface of the jar to block all oxygen from it. Oxygen browns pesto quickly, but a sealing coat of olive oil (which you can spoon right through when you use the pesto) will keep it fresh and fragrant for weeks in your refrigerator. Better yet? Freeze a batch and enjoy a taste of summer during the winter.

Stock up when the price is right. Buying a gallon of extra-virgin olive oil and decanting it into a smaller bottle as needed adds up to big savings. A gallon will run about $25, depending on the brand and country of origin, but even the most inexpensive oils usually run about $8 a quart—or $64 a gallon!

Want lox around the clock? No problem. You can treat your brunch guests to bagels and smoked salmon without spending a fortune. Just find ways to spread it further: mince up a small package (3 to 4 ounces) of high-quality smoked salmon, and blend it gently with one 8-ounce package of softened cream cheese. Refrigerate it overnight in an airtight container, and it'll be perfect by the time your guests arrive.

Get online instead of standing in line. Looking for the best price on a spiral-cut honey ham? Want that special cheese that your mother used to buy? Get thee to the Internet! Online specialty purveyors can offer a much wider range of goods and often at better prices than brick-and-mortar retailers, even with shipping costs added in. Shop around and compare online prices to get the specialty food you want at the lowest cost.

Be a gourmet saler. Even fancy, high-end gourmet shops will generally price expensive products lower than regular grocery stores, especially during sale times. For example, a busy gourmet market will often have lower prices on better-quality coffee than your supermarket, as well as big sales on items like cheeses and sausages, condiments and jams. The super-sharp Cheddar for which you're paying $6.99 a pound at the supermarket may well be selling for $2.99 a pound at a fancy cheese shop, where it may have come from a small cheese maker and not from a major food conglomerate.

Dining-Out Secrets from the Bird That Knows

For many of us, eating out is fun, and it's also entertainment. We don't go to restaurants simply to get food. We go to enjoy new taste sensations and find interesting flavors, to expand our horizons, and enjoy conversations in a relaxed setting. And if we're heading out to an old favorite, we usually do it because it makes us feel good. And that's a wonderful thing!

But too much dining out is a budget-buster—unless you're getting your full due of discounts. Tuck in a napkin and see.

The Early Bird gets the…discounted meal. Yep, the term came from restaurants, and we'd be remiss not to remind you. Have an early lunch so you can enjoy an early dinner at your favorite restaurant during those hours that seem to be specially set aside to please seniors! Restaurants began Early Bird Specials to fill their dining rooms during the quiet early evening hours when they still had the lights on and the stove hot, but the staff was standing around. They're thrilled to have you there and thrilled to offer you a lower price, so take full advantage of it. Best of all, you'll be home and rested and digested while the later diners are just staggering out to their cars with stuffed stomachs!

Split an entrée. Restaurant portions are so big these days that even if you could eat the whole thing, you probably shouldn't. If you're ordering appetizers and drinks, most restaurants are fine with two diners splitting a main course—some of them will even plate it for you separately in the kitchen and add an extra portion of vegetables!

Early Bird Secret

Get a doggy bag. You paid for it, it's yours, and throwing it away is wasteful and not good for the planet or your wallet. It's hard to find a restaurant that's not delighted to pack up your extras for you. Some fancy restaurants will bring you a chit rather than your food in a bag: You exchange the chit at the coat check for your packaged meal, which is waiting in a small fridge on your way out.

Make a meal out of appetizers. Two appetizers, one after the other, likely offer a more normal portion size and can often be more interesting to eat than a big main dish. For two people, you might order four small appetizers and share everything, and still wind up paying less than ordering entrées.

"Do" lunch. Eat exactly the same food that's on the dinner menu, at nearly half the price—lunch can be even cheaper than the Early Bird Special at dinner! The practice may have begun to lure diners into quiet lunchtime restaurants, but now it's a given, and even busy places are still significantly cheaper than they are at dinner. Some high-end restaurants also offer a three-course lunchtime special that's less than the price of a single entrée ordered off the dinner menu.

Go ethnic. Mexican, Cuban, Middle Eastern, Greek, anything Asian—whether it's Chinese, Thai, Vietnamese, or Indian—can be a bargain. Better yet, you'll probably get food cooked with care and love by people who want you to love their native cuisines, so don't be shy about trying out all your local ethnic restaurants. And don't forget they'll be even cheaper at lunch!

Feed kids free. Whether it's kids-eat-free or buffet night or just the Early Bird Special, be sure to compare prices with the senior discount—the special that week may end up being a better deal! That's especially true when it comes to the grandchildren. Feeding two or three (or more) grandchildren for free, even if you're paying full price for your own meal, will probably end up saving you a lot more than bringing them all for the Early Bird.

Go out for breakfast. The first meal of the day is usually cheaper than any other in a restaurant, whether you're having eggs, bacon, potatoes, and toast for $3 or $4 in a diner or croissants and coffee in a high-end hotel restaurant. It can start your day off right whether it's a Sunday brunch or a weekday vacation. Better still: find a place that serves breakfast all day, and have it for dinner.

Order a whole bottle of wine instead of by the glass.
Wine by the glass can add up very quickly, so if there's any chance you or your companion will want a second glass, you're better off ordering a whole bottle. Even if you have wine left over at the end of the meal, you may be able to have the bottle recorked so that you can take it with you. (Laws vary state to state about whether you're able to take leftover alcohol with you, but your waiter will know.)

Fast Food Treats and Tricks

Many fast-food restaurants have unadvertised discounts and special offers for seniors. The reason that they're not widely advertised or visible is mostly because the discount or offer varies from store to store in these franchised restaurants, rather than being a corporate policy across the board. Thus, be sure you check with your local store—one Burger King in town might give you a free cup of coffee while another may not. If it's available, however, the staff is happy to dole out your discount when asked, so don't be shy.

Arby's Company-owned Arby's (more than 1,100 nationwide) offer seniors a value size soft drink or a small coffee for 50 cents. Discounts at franchise-owned restaurants may vary so ask before you order.

Baskin Robbins Got a craving for ice cream or need a special ice-cream cake for your grandchild's birthday party? If you're 55 or older, you can get it at a 10 percent discount.

Early Bird Secret

The Truth about Bottled Water

The moment you sit down, many waiters will ask "Bottle or tap water?" *Never* feel intimidated into ordering bottled water! Tap water is fresh and free, and if you need any better reason, it's also a much "greener" choice because it didn't require a truck to transport it from some spring across the country. Beyond that, bottled water can add untold dollars to your bottom line. One of our experts compared bottled water prices in some of our nation's restaurants, and here is what they found, by city.

Average Restaurant Price of Bottled Water by City

New York $12	Miami $5
Los Angeles $15	New Orleans $6
San Francisco $15	Portland (Maine) $4
Dallas $9	Fargo ($0. You'll never find it.)
Seattle $5	

Burger King Most outlets offer a senior discount on beverages. Some stores also extend a free cup of coffee to senior patrons in the morning until 10 a.m.

Dunkin Donuts American seniors run on Dunkin Donut's standard discount of 10 percent for those who are 55 and older.

Fresh Choice Patrons 60 and above get 15 percent off the price of their entire meal every day at Fresh Choice.

Jack in the Box Senior citizens 55 or older receive 50 cents off on any size soft drink beverage of their choice, combo meals excluded.

KFC The buffet at KFC has special prices for customers 55 and above, and some locations offer a 10 percent discount on the cost of your meal, but the senior benefit varies from store to store.

McDonald's As with other franchises, the owner of each store has the right to set any senior discounts or promotions, and the outcome varies widely between stores. Be sure to ask at your local McDonald's and at any other one you visit when away from home.

Pizza Hut Discounts for seniors vary from store to store but in nearly all branches, the senior prices are for dine-in patrons only, not for take-out.

Souper Salad Sign up for the Souper Fresh Club at soupersalad.com to get printable discounts on food as well as a special discount on your birthday.

Taco Bell Many Taco Bell locations offer discounts for seniors, but the details vary by restaurant. Check with your local Taco Bell to see if they participate in a senior discount program.

Tim Horton's This popular Canadian doughnut chain has infiltrated ever deeper into the American market, and they offer seniors a small coffee for 98 cents.

Wendy's Most Wendy's restaurants offer a discount to seniors, such as a percentage off the customer's order or a free small beverage. Discounts vary with individual restaurants, so customers should inquire about the details when they place their order.

Better Dining Restaurants

A wide range of restaurants beyond fast food offer senior discounts, and some of them are corporate-wide, such as the Applebee's Golden Apple program. Others vary from location to location, so be sure to ask when you're trying a new restaurant to make sure you haven't missed any special deals. Some restaurants will offer you a discount based on your membership in AARP if they have no other program—it never hurts to ask!

Applebee's Sign up for and receive your Golden Apple Card at participating locations if you're 60 and older. You'll get 15 percent off the total of your check at any Applebee's all over the United States.

Bob's Big Boy Patrons 55 and older can sign up for a Senior Discount Card, for a 10 percent discount at participating locations.

Boston Market Chicken-loving patrons who are 60 and above (okay, you don't *have* to love chicken but why else would you be here?) can get a 10 percent discount on their entire order.

Carrows Be sure to order from the special senior menu to get the best prices for Carrows' diners who are 55 and older.

Early Bird Secret

Birthday Discounts

In addition to the senior discount, check around to see if a restaurant you like has any other specials you can profit from as well—and there are few discounts and specials at any restaurant so generous as those they offer for your birthday. Many national chains allow you to register your birthday with them on their Web site or directly at the restaurant, and then they'll send you a coupon or invitation before your birthday to get a variety of freebies and specials that range from a free coffee drink at Caribou Coffee to a free dessert at the Cheesecake Factory to a $30 dinner certificate at Benihana Japanese Steakhouse.

Find out what birthday goodies your own favorite restaurant has to offer, and then sign up your whole family—everyone you love can have birthday treats all year long!

Chili's A senior discount of 10 percent for diners who are 55 and older is available at some Chili's locations, so be sure to ask (and some locations may ask to see your AARP card).

Coco's Bakery Restaurant This western chain has a senior menu called Club 55 for patrons who are—you guessed it—55 and above.

Cracker Barrel Most Cracker Barrel locations have a senior section on the menu offering somewhat smaller portions at a lower price.

Denny's Denny's takes the tastes of their senior patrons very seriously since the company estimates that seniors make up approximately one-third of its customers. It has a senior menu for those who are 55 and above with lower prices for slightly smaller portions.

Elephant Bar Restaurant If you're 60 or older, sign up for the Senior Explorer Card, good for 20 percent off the cost of food at these restaurants.

Friendly's These East Coast establishments with a focus on ice cream have a special senior menu for diners who are 60 and older, which, besides offering lower prices and smaller portions, allows the diner to have a free coffee with breakfast or a small sundae with lunch or dinner.

Golden Corral It varies widely according to location, but most Golden Corral restaurants offer special prices for diners who are 60 and above.

International House of Pancakes IHOP has a senior menu for diners who are 55 and older, but if you want to order off the regular menu, they'll still extend to you a 10 percent discount on your meal.

Old Country/Old Town Buffet/Country Buffet This popular chain of buffets offers a Senior Club Card to patrons 60 and older for $1. The card is good for a year and gives you approximately 10 percent off the cost of your meal when you present it to the cashier at the end of each meal. Using it also enters you in the weekly drawing for a free meal.

Picadilly This Louisiana-based chain of cafeterias, now more than half a century old and popular across the South, offers 10 percent off the cost of the meal for seniors 60 and older from 2 to 5 p.m. every day except Sunday with your Prime Time for Seniors Card. Ask your store manager for one today.

Ponderosa Steakhouse Most locations have special senior menu items at reduced prices for smaller portions. Menu items vary by steakhouse.

Did You Know?

Get a Promotion! Ponderosa Steakhouse occasionally offers some terrific promotions and special offers that you can only get online. Go to www.ponderosasteakhouses.com and sign up for its eClub newsletter to receive news and notices of special promotions. You'll get a special offer on your birthday and other offers throughout the year. While nobody wants to sign up for a lot of junk mail in their e-mail inbox, it's worth it if it's going to bring you savings!

Shoney's If you're 55 and older, be sure to ask your server about their senior discounts.

Silver Diner Diners 55 and older can get 10 percent off the cost of their meals at some locations, while other locations have Early Bird Specials from 4 to 6 p.m. Check with your local restaurant for specifics.

Sizzler If you're 60 and above, you can order from the senior menu, and some locations also have special offers for AARP members when you present your membership card.

Strings Italian Cafe Discounts vary from location to location, but most offer 10 percent to 15 percent off the price of the meal (or sometimes just the entrée) for patrons 62 and above. Sign up for special discounts on your birthday.

Great Life Entertaining

Does having a big crowd of people over and feeding them a lot of delicious food and drinks seem the opposite of saving money? Well, it can be, but guess what? It doesn't have to be. Read on, and you'll see how to save big on food *and* party big with your friends and family.

Cocktails, anyone? Invite people to come from 5 to 7 p.m., which suggests that dinner is not on the menu, even if you end up serving plenty of food, and even if they stay well past 7 (someone *always* does). Serve lots of smaller things—veggies and dips, chips and salsa, hummus and carrots, quiche cut into bite-size pieces—that are inexpensive, tasty, and filling.

Have a sangria bash. You don't have to have a full bar (or anything like one!) just because you're having a party. Sangria is inexpensive, delicious, easy-to-make, and a little goes a long way. Add red wine, carbonated water, sweetener such as honey or orange juice, and a small amount of spirits, such as brandy or triple sec, to a pitcher full of chopped or sliced oranges, apples, or other fruit, and refrigerate for two hours before your guests arrive. Add ice, stir, and your guests will be delighted. For a variation, use white wine, and you have *sangria blanca*.

Have a buffet. Casual buffets lend themselves to clever spending because you can make a large amount of hearty and inexpensive foods, whether it's a giant pot of three-bean chili, a big vat of chicken and dumplings, or a mammoth portion of spaghetti and meatballs.

Don't skimp on starch. There's a reason so many world cuisines center around rice and pasta: they're filling, they're inexpensive, and they can be absolutely delicious. You can serve a smaller amount of an inexpensive meat-based topping, such as beef stew, and an absolutely enormous mountain of buttered egg noodles, and you'll be met with cries of delight rather than whines of hunger.

Early Bird Secret

Serve Caviar Pie

Want to serve something really special but don't want to spend a fortune on it? Make your special ingredient go further. Caviar pie is a great example (domestic caviar can be had for as little as $6 or $7 a jar): Spread a layer of homemade egg salad on a decorative serving dish and smooth over it a layer of softened cream cheese that you've combined with a finely minced red onion. On top, smooth over a small jar of inexpensive caviar, such as "red lumpfish roe." Serve it with crackers—or toast, to make it a little fancier. You just saved yourself $200 on a tin of Beluga!

Go vegetarian. Skip the meat altogether and make a large pot of three-bean chili, a spicy stir-fry with lots of red peppers and broccoli over rice, or a towering bowl of pasta that you can serve with tomato sauce and heaps of cheese. Make a giant pan of cheesy cornbread with chopped jalapenos in it and serve it up with beans. Nobody will even notice there's no meat on the table. (Trust us!)

Start with soup. Most folks love a bowl of homemade soup, which is wonderful because soup is super-inexpensive and supremely delicious—plus, it fills people up before they get to the roast beef! Make a savory leek-and-potato or creamy butternut squash soup. Float some croutons on top of each bowl or—even easier—some bruschetta (toasted slices of hearty country bread brushed with olive oil on both sides and rubbed with a raw garlic clove).

Slow-cook a bigger, cheaper cut. Whether you fancy chicken thighs or boneless country ribs, take advantage and haul out your slow cooker. Sure, you'll have to plan ahead to do this, but the result is a much more deeply flavored dish that you've prepared ahead, which brings down the stress levels on the day of your party, and you'll save lots of money. Your low-priced and plain protein—slow-cooked or in a nice sauce—suddenly becomes dinner-party fancy.

Don't forget the fruit. Fresh fruit in season can turn into inexpensive, show-stopping purées for dessert: try raspberries, blueberries, or peaches (peeled and pitted) in a blender with sugar and lemon juice to taste, and pulse until the sauce is completely smooth (raspberry puree may need to be pushed through a mesh strainer to take out the pesky seeds). The colors of a simple fruit puree are stunning and absolutely delicious when poured over store-bought ice cream. Your guests will swoon!

Take advantage of sales. A batch of "fancy" homemade beef stew can be made ahead and frozen for three months, so if you see something on sale, buy it, make the dish, and freeze it. Why? It may not be on sale when you want to have that big bash, and it'll give you one less thing to worry about come party night.

Decorate seasonally. Don't feel that you need to spend money on flowers or centerpieces when you're having a party. Try using whatever produce looks beautiful just now. If it's spring, place a glass bowl of bright lemons in the center of the table, with a couple of smaller bowls of perfect strawberries to either side. If it's autumn, put a few pomegranates in the center of the table. In the winter, arrange some holly branches and berries. In summer, pick wildflowers or heap up some lovely summer tomatoes. The star of the show should always be the food, so decorations shouldn't be the slightest drain on your party budget.

Turn down the lights and save! When you have votive candles flickering around the room and tapers on the table, surfaces seem to gleam and people's faces glow, making everyone look—and feel—younger, prettier, and happier. If a few cheap votive candles can accomplish that, they're worth every penny. Candles are the easiest, best decorations you can buy, they have the added benefit of hiding dust, and they'll keep your electricity costs down.

Ka-Ching!

The 55-Cent-Per-Person, Slow-Cooked Taco Party

Makes
20
Servings

One of the most delicious ways to entertain a crowd of hungry friends is to slow cook a pork shoulder, pull it off the bone, and have guests assemble their own tacos from the absolutely delicious meat. A recent excursion to our local branch of a national supermarket chain revealed this most frugal, fabulous cut for $1.99 per pound; the biggest one in the case cost a little over $11.00 and served 20 people, making each serving approximately 55 cents. Now *that's* a bargain!

8-pound pork shoulder, on the bone, skin and fat removed
Salt and pepper, to taste
2 tablespoons dried oregano
1 large white onion, peeled and sliced
1/2 cup orange juice

1. Rub pork shoulder all over with salt, pepper, and oregano, and set aside.

2. Place sliced onions in the bottom of a large slow cooker, and place the pork shoulder on top of the onions.

3. Drizzle with orange juice, turn the slow cooker to low, and cook for 6 hours, until the meat is falling off the bone.

4. Let cool and pull meat off bone with a fork. Serve with soft tortillas or hard tacos, and pass around bowls of salsa, shredded lettuce, and grated cheese.

Paper, Plastic, or Ceramic?

Get ready for a *big* surprise: one of our experts was convinced that buying good-quality paper plates and plastic cups for a bash she was having would be *more* expensive than buying the real thing. We didn't believe her, until she went out and did it. The result? We'll never buy paper plates and plastic cups again (they're expensive *and* not good for the environment—a double whammy), and well, neither should you. Here's what we discovered:

Quality Paper and Plastic	99 Cent Store Porcelain and Glass
25 paper dinner plates ($8)	25 porcelain dinner plates (50 cents per plate)
25 paper dessert plates ($6.50)	25 porcelain dessert plates (25 cents per plate)
25 paper soup bowls ($9.95)	25 porcelain soup bowls (25 cents per bowl)
25 plastic soda cups ($6)	50 heatproof glasses (25 cents per glass)
25 plastic hot cups ($6.75)	
Total: **$37.20**	Total: **$37.50**

Make it a potluck. If you're having a big crowd, don't be shy about calling for potluck. It's sociable and cheery, and people love to participate and even show off a little with a special dish. Keep things manageable by providing a main course or two yourself (meatloaf and fried chicken, perhaps), and ask others to bring salads, sides, desserts, and drinks. By having a general idea of who's bringing what, you won't end up with 15 pies and very little else on the table.

Splurge on dessert. You might serve a budget-conscious meal of soup and meatloaf, for example, but then pull out the stops with a flourless chocolate cake made with top-quality chocolate and topped with super-premium vanilla ice cream and fresh raspberries, perhaps. Or brew a pot of fragrant coffee and serve it with wrapped chocolates, homemade caramels, or bakery biscotti. One special item or course is the showpiece and everything else can be more ordinary. Not only will nobody mind, but they'll be very grateful for the good time!

Restaurant-Style Dining at Home

You don't have to eat out to enjoy the experience of fine dining. Make it a special night in, and dramatically cut costs on your restaurant-going by arranging a restaurant-type evening for your family in the comfort of your own home. The plan here is to do something very different from your usual routine so that your family gets the entertainment value of a night out at a fraction of the cost.

Light some candles. Put a lovely tablecloth on the table and some fresh flowers. Don't be afraid to treat yourself well. Get out your nice crystal or your wedding china—it's yours, and who better to enjoy it than you? Put on some background music. And turn off the TV!

Did You Know?

The Real Value of Restaurant Wine. Shocking, but true: most restaurants mark up the wines they sell by the bottle at least 100 percent from the price in a wine shop. In other words, if your favorite wine costs $12.99 in a local wine shop, a restaurant will likely put it on its wine list for $25 or $30 or higher. The way around this? Ask if you can bring a favorite bottle from home. The restaurant will likely charge you a corkage fee if it doesn't have a BYOB policy. Better still? Make dinner at home, and keep the wine bill low.

Start with some nibbles. Signal that this meal is going to be something special with the sorts of appetizing little snacks you get when you sit down at a nice restaurant. Put a dish of flat bread or crackers on the table or warm some rolls or slice some hearty bread from the bakery. Put a pat of butter in a small dish, drizzle it with olive oil, and sprinkle with chopped fresh herbs such as chives or rosemary. Add a dish of nuts or olives, and a cocktail—alcoholic or not—and you're ready to enjoy your evening.

Order in. If concocting an interesting dish is your idea of torture rather than a fun afternoon, order in something you've been wanting to try but never have. Picking up one main dish to go will be cheaper than dining out, and you'll save the cost of starter, sides, marked-up beverages, tax, and tip at a restaurant.

Invite everyone to cook. Whether it's family or a small group of friends, organize a group activity in the kitchen that makes dinnertime fun. Set up an assembly line to let everyone fill and crimp dumplings, decorate their own mini-pizzas, or stuff and fry egg rolls. Alternately, let them assemble their own desserts. Put out the fixings for hot fudge sundaes after dinner.

Discount Cooking Gear

Need to replace some kitchen equipment? You won't get a senior discount at Williams-Sonoma! But you can create your own: Open the phone book and find a restaurant supply store. These places are piled high with plain-looking equipment that is actually more professional than the fancy stuff sold in retail kitchenware stores, and *much* less expensive. Do you really need a $75 electric knife sharpener? A rubber garlic-skin remover? No, we didn't think so. (That's why you'll never find one here!)

Free cookware? You bet. One of the cleverest and most frugal ways to stock up on cookware is to hit your local flea market—at the tail end of the day! Most of the sellers are interested in packing up and generally don't want to repack what they didn't sell. One professional cook we spoke to was handed a heavy-duty flame diffuser because the seller didn't want to have to cart it home; another was asked to relieve the seller of a set of nesting cast-iron frying pans for the same reason. Sometimes, it pays to be late.

Make cookware go the distance. Who says you need a special meat pounder? Or an olive pitter? Save $10 instantly (or $20 or $30) by inventing new ways to use the same objects. For example, if you have an empty wine bottle, you don't need a rolling pin (just flour the sides of the bottle). If you have a heavyweight skillet, you don't need a meat pounder. If you have a good knife, you don't need an olive (or cherry) pitter. (Just smash the olive with the flat side of a heavy knife, and the pit will make a hasty exit.)

Shelve the mixing bowls. Need to marinate something? Pour the contents into a resealable plastic bag, toss in the meat, fish, chicken, pork, or vegetables, zip it up, and stow it in the fridge for its marinating time. Need to mix something? Use an empty plastic container. Need to mix something big? Do it in your biggest soup pot.

The Good-Deal Wine Cellar

New research shows that resveratrol, an organic compound in red wine, may help extend your life! If that's not a good reason to enjoy an occasional glass, nothing is. Best of all, there are plenty of bargains and good deals on wine to be found. It helps to know that "expensive" doesn't always equal "good" in the wine world—the challenge is to seek out inexpensive bottles that suit your tastes. Here's how to do that:

Buy by the case. Many wine stores will offer you a 10 percent case discount if you pay with a credit card, or, even better, a 15 percent discount if you pay with cash or a debit card. Some stores offer smaller discounts on half cases.

Ka-Ching!

Buy Where Restaurants Buy

We took a trip to three restaurant supply houses—one in New York City, another in rural northeastern Pennsylvania, and the last in Texas—and came away with a kitchen full of equipment that would make any four-star chef proud. The same selection, priced at a well-known kitchen shop chain, rang in at nearly $2,000, almost 10 times the supply house cost.

The Basics	Supply Store	Gourmet Store
Wire whisk (10-inch)	$5.00	$10.95
Stainless-steel spatula	$2.00	$22.00
Rubber spatula	$1.50	$22.50
Chef's knife (8-inch, plastic-handle, stainless alloy)	$20.00	$399.00
Instant-read thermometer	$6.00	$20.00
Oven thermometer	$3.00	$18.00
Slotted spoon	$1.25	$22.00
3 wooden spoons	$3.00	$29.95
3 graduated-size, stainless-steel bowls	$9.00	$129.95
Metal tongs (9 1/2-inch)	$2.50	$9.50
Sheet pan (18-by-12-inch)	$8.00	$17.00
Plastic cutting board	$7.00	$20.00
Paring knife	$5.00	$13.95
Manual can opener	$2.00	$10.00
Vegetable peeler	$3.00	$14.00
Box grater	$5.00	$34.95
Stainless-steel colander (8 quart)	$8.00	$59.95
Set of cast-aluminum saucepans	$50.00	$450.00
Nonstick frying pan (10-inch)	$15.00	$160.00
Stock pot (10-quart)	$25.00	$340.00
Universal lid	$6.00	$39.00
TOTALS	$187.50	$1,842.70

Try a different producer. Go looking for smaller or newer producers from lesser-known regions.

Try a different grape. Seek out a less expensive crisp and acidic dry Riesling instead of yet another chardonnay. Ask for a less pricey Argentinian malbec instead of merlot. Go for a Spanish Rioja instead of an expensive pinot noir.

Don't be afraid to ask. People who work in wine stores often do so because they love wine and like to talk about it. When someone says, "May I help you?" tell them you want a terrific, highly drinkable bottle of everyday red for $10, and see what they recommend.

Early Bird Secret

A World of Wine

Who is producing high-value, low-cost wines? Spain remains a good place to look, but don't forget Chile, Argentina, Australia, and even Hungary for lots of good-quality wines at competitive prices. South Africa used to export some bad wines, but the consistency of quality has improved dramatically in recent years while the prices have remained comparatively low.

Go for quantity. The one-and-a-half liter bottles usually cost less than two typical 750-militer bottles, and if you're entertaining, this is the ideal way to go.

Buy the box! The plastic bag-in-a-box style is, oddly enough, an ideal way to store wine. Because the bag is airtight and collapses as you draw off the wine through the box's spigot, air never touches the wine. You can store an opened box for weeks or months without the quality of the wine changing.

Try your luck with Two-Buck Chuck. Trader Joe's famous discount wine sells for less than $4 a bottle. Charles Shaw wines, as they are more formally known, are worth stocking up on. Some wine critics champion them, others scoff at them, but ordinary wine drinkers feel the extremely low price helps the wine slip down easily.

3

Your Castle and Your Car

Easy Ways to Cut Home and Car Costs

DIY Discounts

Not everyone needs a big remodel or renovation (thank goodness!). But do you need a lot of plumbing or lawn work done or tips on where to find the best hardware deals? Check out these senior discounts on everyday items, projects, and special services before you spend another penny.

Ace Hardware Ace is the place where seniors age 60 and above can usually receive 10 percent off their purchases. Both age requirement and discount amount vary by location, and some discounts may be restricted to certain days of the week, so call ahead. You can find your local Ace store at its Web site at www.acehardware.com (click on "My Local Ace").

Roto-Rooter This national chain of plumbers offers 10 percent off labor (but not parts) to customers who are 60 and older. The age and discount can vary according to location and may not be available for holidays or emergencies, so be sure to ask when you call. At its national Web site, where you can find a number for your local branch, you can also sign up to receive special promotions and coupons via e-mail, which may end up saving you more money than the senior discount. Visit www.rotorooter.com.

Early Bird Secret

City Slickers Can Save Big

If you're on a fixed income and you're finding that home costs are getting the better of you, have no fear! Check out the Department of Housing and Urban Development (HUD), where you can find a national list of budget-friendly urban senior apartments. If you have access to the Internet, visit the HUD Web site, where you can search by state to see what the income limits are and what residences are available in your immediate area. Requirements vary region to region.

U.S. Department of Housing and Urban Development
451 7th Street S.W., Washington, DC 20410
(202) 708-1112
www.hud.gov/apps/section8/

ServiceMaster This umbrella company for a family of brands includes many home services, such as Terminix Pest Control, TruGreen lawn care, and ServiceMaster carpet cleaning. Senior discounts vary widely depending on what service you require and what local company performs the service for you, but you can sign up at its main ServiceMaster Web site to receive special offers and promotions that will also help save you money, such as $20 off a carpet cleaning or a free termite inspection and then 10 percent off the first treatment. Visit the Web site at www.servicemaster.com or call the toll-free number: 1-888-WE-SERVE.

Did You Know?

The Poison-Free Way to Get Rid of Pests Alcohol—plain old cheap-as-dirt rubbing alcohol—kills ants, not to mention roaches, better and more safely than dangerous poisons. Place the undiluted alcohol in a spray bottle and squirt when you see a roach. Just a few squirts will do. Clean your counters and areas where you see ants and then spray with the alcohol. Don't rinse it. The ants will become dehydrated when they walk through the alcohol and die. Simply buff away any "clouding" from countertops if necessary.

35 Ways to Accident-Proof Your Property

It's a beautiful day, and you are looking forward to visiting with friends out on the deck or maybe serving a special dinner in front of a roaring fire. But instead, you or one of your friends ends up sitting in the emergency room because you fell, got burned, or got cut. Serious household accidents do happen—more than 7 million times a year. Taking simple precautions and making easy changes around the house can help avoid personal harm and related hospital and aftercare bills.

1. Make sure you have secure, easy-to-grip handrails along all stairs.
2. Ensure loose carpeting and tiles are secured to the floor.
3. Use a contrasting paint color to draw attention to short flights of stairs. Or, place nonskid tape on the edge of each tread.
4. Arrange furniture so it provides ample space for walking, especially if there is someone in your home who uses a cane, walker, or wheelchair.
5. Secure light pieces of furniture so they do not move if someone leans on them.
6. Secure electrical and telephone cords to walls to minimize tripping hazards.

7. Use nonskid safety strips or a nonslip bath mat in the tub and shower.

8. Consider installing a grab rail on the edge of the vanity or shower wall. (Do not use a towel bar. It's not a substitute for a genuine grab rail.)

9. Use automatic night-lights that turn on in the dark and stay off when light.

10. Make sure tile and vinyl floors are dry after cleaning or spills before walking on them.

11. Keep outdoor walkways and paths clear of leaves and other debris.

12. In wintertime, be sure to clear walkways of snow and ice, and place kitty litter, rock salt, or gravel on wet, potentially icy surfaces.

13. Fence in pools and water features, and keep surrounding areas clear of toys, leaves, and other items that someone could trip or slip on.

14. Store outdoor extension cords when not in use.

15. Pick up tools when not in use, and never leave a rake, manual rotary mower, or shovel on the ground.

16. Install smoke alarms on every floor—and make sure they work. About one-third of all smoke detectors don't function because the batteries are dead or missing.

Safety First

Fires kill more than 4,000 Americans and injure an additional 25,000 people. The leading cause of fire deaths: careless smoking. Another great reason to butt out of that bad habit! Other causes of accidents at home include taking medicines or swallowing poisons like household cleaners by mistake (in the case of small children, this is a real problem); getting bumped, bruised and burned; drowning; and gun accidents. Here are some safety changes that are oh-so-easy and oh-so-very-worth-it!

17. Lock liquor cabinets, and remove all poisonous household items from accessible locations.

18. Keep medicine out of reach from small hands—and clearly marked for big ones!

19. Install lights in medicine cabinets so mistakes are not made when taking medicine.

20. If you have babies and tiny tots around, or visiting regularly, cover sharp edges with rubber cushioning.

21. Remove glass shower doors or replace them with unbreakable versions.

22. Set the hot water thermostat below 120° Fahrenheit to minimize the chance of burns—especially important if you have small children or elderly people in your home regularly.

23. Use faucets that mix hot and cold water, or paint hot water knobs or faucets red.

24. Install toilet guardrails or provide a portable toilet seat with built-in rails.

25. Store firearms in a locked cabinet, and keep bullets in a separate locked cabinet.

26. Cover outlets with childproof outlet covers to minimize the chance of shock. This may also minimize drafts in your home!

27. Keep very small sharp objects like tiny nails, razors, and pins out of reach of small hands (which are usually attached to curious mouths).

28. Make sure televisions and other large objects are secured safely to strong surfaces or the wall. (One great feature of flat-screen TVs is that they can be secured to a wall and out of reach of people who could bump into them or pull them down on top of them.)

29. Likewise, make sure pictures are secured to walls and out of reach of inquiring hands.

30. Keep knives on a knife rack high on the wall and out of children's reach or in a secure rack in a cabinet with a child lock.

31. When cooking, do not wear loose-fitting clothing or dangling sleeves that could catch fire on a burner.

32. Never leave food unattended while cooking—including food on the outdoor barbecue.

33. Keep space heaters away from curtains, furniture, and any other item that could catch fire, and unplug them when they are not in use and while you are sleeping.

34. Don't use electric appliances with frayed cords. Replace the appliance or the cord.

35. Keep one fire extinguisher in the kitchen and one near bedrooms, and know how to use them.

The Home

How safe are you? Taking this 5-minute, 10-question quiz helps you identify potential trouble spots quickly—and will get you thinking about emergency preparedness ahead of time. Any question that gets a "no" should be addressed immediately.

1. Do you have a NOAA (National Oceanic and Atmospheric Administration) Weather Radio or other battery-operated way (transistor radio or TV) to monitor news and weather in case of an emergency or a blackout?

2. Do you have a family emergency plan in place that includes two possible evacuation routes, a designated meeting place, and an alternative place to stay?

3. Have you created an emergency survival kit, the most basic of which should include a battery-operated radio (see question 1); drinking water; packaged, nonperishable food (like canned beans, tuna, and veggies); can opener; flashlight; flare; whistle; extra batteries; first aid kit; and a conventional land-line phone (cell and cordless phones don't work in blackouts)?

4. Is your house number clearly visible to firefighters, law enforcement, and other emergency workers? Reflective 911 emergency house numbers are available for low cost or free under some circumstances from all municipalities. If you are unable to install your own, your community will even send someone to do it for you.

Safety Quiz

5. Do you know how to turn off utilities including water, power, and gas?

6. Is your driveway accessible to emergency vehicles at all times—meaning that there is adequate clearance on both sides and a large vehicle like a fire truck would be able to make a wide turn into your driveway? Is there enough space to turn around?

7. Do you have a plan for covering windows and doors in the event of a weather disaster or other emergency? Likewise, do you have a way to cover or reinforce your garage door?

8. Are lawn furniture, children's toys, gardening tools, trash cans, and any other large, moveable objects stored away from stairs and exits? Do you have a secure place to store these items in case of high winds?

9. Have you cleaned leaves and debris off of or away from your walkways, roof, gutters, and air-conditioning units?

10. Are stair railings, both inside and out, secure and sturdy?

Dim Electricity Bills

So many of us take electricity for granted: We plug "it" in—whatever it is—and off it goes. Lights, heat, well pumps, washing machines, dryers, computers, televisions, stereos, treadmills, your stove, your fridge…virtually everything in your home runs on an electrical current, and this means big bills at the end of the month. The good news is that there are savvy ways for seniors to save, if you know what to do!

Low-Income Home Energy Assistance Program
Low on income and big on energy costs in the heat of the summer? No problem! The U.S. Department of Health and Human Services allocates federal funding to the Low-Income Home Energy Assistance Program (LIHEAP). Its primary focus is immediate assistance with home energy—whether it's a summer heat wave or the dead of winter—to seniors who have very low incomes. The LIHEAP Clearinghouse provides free telephone and e-mail referrals to people who need help applying for energy assistance. Call the National Energy Assistance Referral (NEAR) at 1-866-674-6327 from 8 a.m. to 6 p.m. (Eastern Time) or visit its Web site at www.liheap.org. You may also send an e-mail to NEAR at energyassistance@ncat.org, with your city, county, and state in your e-mail message.

National Fuel Funds Network
Hot enough for you? The National Fuel Funds Network helps eligible seniors find assistance with energy costs on a local level. Check out its Web site at www.nationalfuelfunds.org or call 1-866-674-6327.

Energy Star Ratings
If you change just one lightbulb in your home to an Energy Star approved bulb, it's as good for the environment as not driving your car for *two weeks*—and the energy savings is not only good for the planet, but it also adds up to dollars in your pocket. You can make significant changes in your carbon footprint and in your power bill by using products approved by Energy Star, a joint program between the U.S. Environmental Protection Agency and the U.S. Department of Energy. Using Energy Star techniques, advice, strategies, and approved appliances and lightbulbs, Americans saved $17 billion on their utility bills in 2009. Make sure you get your share of the savings! Check out the Energy Star Web site at www.energystar.gov for a wealth of hugely practical energy-saving techniques.

13 No-Cost Ways to Reduce Energy Bills

Small, inexpensive changes to the way you use energy around the house can significantly reduce your energy costs—from heat to hot water. Once you make these changes, the only thing you'll notice are lower bills.

1. **The big chill.** Our experts say that you can save up to $63 per year by washing all your clothes in cold water instead of warm or hot.

2. **Fully loaded.** Full loads of laundry and dishes result in maximum efficiency and help you avoid water waste. Air-dry dishes—and clothes, if you can—for even more savings.

3. **Lose the lint.** If you must dry clothes in a dryer, always clean the lint filter after every load to maintain peak drying efficiency (not to mention reducing the risk of fire).

4. **Separate heavy from light.** Dry towels, bedspreads, and other heavy items separately from lighter-weight items to increase drying efficiency.

5. **You're all wet.** Take showers instead of baths and install a low-flow showerhead to save on water and heat.

6. **No drips allowed.** Fix leaky faucets. Even a little drip can add up to a big-time water bill.

7. **Bundle up.** Insulate hot water pipes and water heater with approved insulation materials for efficiency. Your heating bills will be reduced up to 10 percent.

Film and Function

The summer sun streaming through your windows helps cut down on electric light usage, but it can also make your air conditioner work two to three times harder (that's a bill we don't want to see). Install non-light-blocking reflective window film over clear glass to reduce cooling costs by 5 to 15 percent (far more than the cost of the film)! Look for apply-it-yourself, high-tech, "spectrally selective" film that permits daylight to enter your rooms while blocking solar heat gains. Peel the film off around the time you turn the heat back on—in many parts of the country that's mid-October—or as soon as you no longer need the air conditioner.

8. **Turn it off.** Turn off lights, TVs, computers, and other electronics when they are not in use.

9. **Let there be (better) light.** Replace your most-used conventional incandescent bulbs with long-lasting, energy-saving compact fluorescent bulbs. Use the

sun as your main source of light during the day whenever possible—so open up those drapes and pull up the blinds!

10. **Filter savings.** Clean or replace air-conditioning and heating-system filters monthly for maximum efficiency.

11. **Air-dry for freshness and savings.** One of the cleanest, freshest, most frugal ways to dry your clothes is—you guessed it—outside on a line (weather permitting).

12. **Do the glow test.** Wait until after dark to walk around your house (with a flashlight!) to see what is "glowing." The results will amaze you: your power strips, your computers, your DVD player, your cable box, your microwave oven. Although you may not be actively using them, all of these items in your home are perpetually "on" and eating electricity, unless you pull the plugs when they're not in use.

13. **Keep your freezer full.** If your freezer is empty, you can be sure that it's working overtime to keep the space icy cold. Remedy this by filling it with a large stone, a bucket, a milk jug filled with water—anything that will take up space; the freezer won't work as hard and therefore will use less electricity.

Cut Cell Phone Costs

Buying minutes as you need them may seem like a good idea, but you almost always wind up paying more. By the time you've added in the cost of scrambling to use minutes before they expire, and the inconvenience of never quite knowing how many minutes you have or how many you just used up on a long-distance or "roaming" call, those pay-as-you-go phones aren't a good bargain. But don't do without: a cell phone is a necessity today. Check out these plans for great senior savings:

Verizon Nationwide 65 Plus Plans If you're 65 or older (age verification required), you can sign up for one of Verizon's 65 Plus Plans for $29.99 a month. That rate gets you unlimited calls with any other user on the Verizon cellphone network, 200 monthly anytime minutes, and 500 night and weekend minutes. You can also get a free senior-friendly cell phone such as the Samsung Intensity with a large keypad for visibility, dedicated 911 buttons, and special "In Case of Emergency" buttons. There's a $35 activation fee, and additional minutes beyond the plan are billed at 45 cents per minute (so don't go over your minutes!). There are no domestic roaming or long-distance charges within the United States or Puerto Rico. Find out more at www.verizonwireless.com.

Ka-Ching!

Save Energy,
Save the Planet, and
Save on Your Taxes!

Planning to do some renovation work on your home? Need to bring an old electrical or plumbing system up to date? Before you do, check out your opportunities to install federally approved energy-efficient systems in your home, and then sit back and reap the benefits when tax time comes. The recently enacted American Recovery and Reinvestment Act (ARRA) of 2009 contained a number of new or expanded tax benefits on expenditures to reduce energy use.

"These new, expanded credits encourage homeowners to make improvements that will make their homes more energy efficient," said IRS Commissioner Doug Shulman. "People can improve their homes and save money over the long run."

Homeowners now get bigger tax credits for making energy efficiency improvements or installing alternative energy equipment. Highlights of the new benefits include:

1. A uniform credit of 30 percent of the cost of qualifying improvements—such as adding insulation, energy-efficient exterior windows, and energy-efficient heating and air conditioning systems—up to $1,500. The uniform credit replaces the combination of a 10 percent credit for some property and a credit equal to cost for other property.

2. The limit on the amount that can be claimed for improvements placed in service during 2009 and 2010 was raised to $1,500 from the old $500 lifetime limit.

3. The cap on the 30 percent tax credit for alternative energy equipment installed in a home—such as solar water heaters, geothermal heat pumps and small wind turbines—has been eliminated, beginning with the 2009 tax year.

You'll need to file Form 5695 along with your receipts in order to claim these credits.

Details on the wide range of energy items is available in the special Recovery section of irs.gov, see Fact Sheet 2009-10.

AT&T Senior Nation 200 Plan If you're 65 and older, the Senior Nation 200 Plan, for $29.99 a month with 200 anytime minutes and 500 night and weekend minutes and unlimited minutes with anyone else on AT&T's network, may be perfect for you if your loved ones and friends are also AT&T subscribers. Both plans require a two-year activation and a startup fee ($36 for AT&T or $35 for Verizon), and your monthly bill, with taxes and fees, will likely be more like $35 to $40, rather than $29.99, but if you use your cell phone for all your long-distance calls, it might be a major savings. Visit AT&T at www.wireless.att.com.

Save on Those Phone Bills

Ever since 1876, when Alexander Graham Bell spoke those fateful words into his rudimentary telephone—"Mr. Watson, come here, I want to see you"—phone costs have only gone up. But seniors now have a wealth of ways to bring them back down, including the amazingly cheap world of Internet calls. Find ways to get your telecommunication bills back in line with reality with the discounts and tips below.

Internet Phone Service If you already have high-speed Internet service in your home (which we highly recommend to surf the Web for the very best senior deals and information), you can also use that connection for your regular home phone service. For an additional monthly fee, your Internet service provider can send you a small box that you plug into the back of your modem, and then you plug your regular phone into that. The phone will sound exactly the same as using a regular phone service, but now your voice is going out across your high-speed Internet line rather than your old phone line. What's the downside? If your Internet service goes down (which is rare but happens occasionally), your phone goes out, too. (It returns instantly when the Internet comes back up.) Also, using Internet service for your phone means that 911 dispatchers can't find your physical location if you dial 911 and are unable to speak your address. What's the upside? You'll get significantly reduced monthly costs on phone service and unlimited national long distance for one low price, usually around $20 per month.

Skype If you have grandchildren living across the country or even out of the country, here's a totally free, absolutely delightful way to see their faces and talk to them and let them see you. Skype is a free Internet program that you download onto your computer. The person you want to call must download the program, too, for free. Then, you both open Skype, one of you "dials" the other by hitting the green button on the Skype screen, and the other person

Ka-Ching!
Information Please?

Long ago, dialing Information was a free service from the phone company, but, like everything else, prices have crept up. It can cost as much as $3 to find a number! Don't ever pay for phone information again. If you have a cell phone (and if you don't, you should! See pages 76 and 78 for sweet cell phone deals for seniors), there are heaps of *completely free* services to help you out:

1-800-GOOG-411

Just dial this number from any phone, cell or regular, and you can ask for any listing across the United States and then be connected, all for free. You can also interrupt the computer voice to say "Details," and it will read you the listing, or say, "Text," and it will send the information directly to your cell phone.

1-800-FREE-411

This is another free information service, but it requires you to listen to a 20-second ad before giving you the listing you require.

1-800-2-CHACHA

Wonder when the Hoover Dam was built? Curious about the signs of a heart attack? Want to know what the temperature was in New York City on February 7, 2003? Call 800-2-CHACHA from your cell phone and ask. Thirty seconds later, you'll get a text message to let you know they received the question and are working on it. And in a minute or two, you'll get the answer as a text on your cell phone, along with a link to the Web page where the researcher found the info. You pay the fee, if any, that your cell phone provider charges for receiving a text—typically 10 cents—but otherwise it's a free service.

1-866-JOTT-123

First you have to sign up at www.jott.com, then Jott becomes your personal message service. Call it and say something like, "Remember to take the casserole out of the freezer," speak the date and time to send the message, and when you get home at 6 p.m., the text will appear on your cell phone, beeping you that a message has arrived. You could also have it call your relatives or friends—anyone whose information you've registered—and send any message at any time you like, at any time or day in the future. For free.

"answers" by hitting their green button. Lo and behold, you can hear their voice and see their face on your screen, and you can talk as long as you want for absolutely free. This service assumes you have a computer equipped with a camera and a microphone, as nearly any computer does these days, and also requires high-speed Internet access. Visit www.skype.com.

The Skinny on Car Insurance

You're a great driver, right? Of course! But just when you feel it's time you were due a nice discount on your premiums because you're getter older, the insurance companies start questioning your abilities because you're getting older! Nonetheless, there are insurance companies that understand that seniors with safe driving records deserve a discount.

Early Bird Secret

Extra Insurance Discounts

Whether or not the insurance agent mentions it to you, many insurers offer additional auto discounts if:

• you're retired from the military;

• you're retired from a government job;

• you complete a defensive-driving course;

• you're insuring multiple cars; or

• you have a completely clean driving record for 5–10 years or more.

If you fit the bill for any of these categories, be sure to ask about discounts, no matter which insurance agent you're talking to. And if you get the brush-off, there are plenty of other insurers in the sea! Ask around before settling on a policy that doesn't take any of these categories into account.

The Hartford In partnership with the AARP, The Hartford offers an AARP Auto Insurance Program that it says has potential savings of up to $402 in the first year alone. It also has a Six-Point Claim Guarantee that the company promises will make for fast, no-hassle claim payments. You can use the phone or make your claim online round the clock, with 24-hour claim service and an Online Customer Center to manage your policy. The AARP insurance plan offers Lifetime Renewability, which is important as you age because it ensures that, as long as you are able to meet some specific requirements, your policy will never be canceled. Since you are eligible to join the AARP beginning at age 50, this could be a good move. Visit www.thehartford.com (click on "Auto" under the heading "AARP-endorsed products").

Prime Time for Seniors at Geico If you're 50 or older and are not trying to insure any drivers under the age of 25 on the same policy, you can get a Prime Time contract for auto insurance with Geico. The policy offers guaranteed renewal, and it is only available to drivers who have had no accidents or violations in the previous three years. The vehicle being insured must be for personal use only and may not be used for any business purposes. Find out more at www.geico.com.

Make Your Wheels Roll Longer

There are some people who think of their cars as extensions of their personalities—and Early Bird, you are no exception. We all live in a car culture. A lot of us consider our drive time "our" private moment, and we really savor the freedom of being on the open road (whether it's a drive to the drugstore or a road trip down the Dixie Highway or Route 66), listening to our favorites tunes on the radio, or even doing a little singing ourselves. New car prices rise every year, so the key is to keep your vehicle roadworthy for as long as possible, and you want to take care of it at Early Bird rates! By making the effort to care for your car—lengthening its life and its mileage and maintaining the engine in optimal condition—you can save yourself some real money.

A fine finish. Drive your car through a car wash regularly to get rid of things like salt, mud, grit, grime, bug and bird splatters, and road gravel and tar. "Road dirt" causes permanent pitting and scarring, leaving open the possibility for rust and deterioration. And don't necessarily go for the bottom rate at the car wash. Some places put a polytetrafluoroethylene-based

(PTFE) product on as a final protective layer—the very same material used on Teflon frying pans. If you prefer to do this yourself, it's available under various brand names at automotive stores and in the automotive department of discount stores.

Keep it under wraps. When you are not driving, keep your car in a garage, underneath a carport, or in some sort of covered parking. If you must park in an open driveway, use a car cover—sort of like a water-repellant slipcover for your car. Left under the baking sun, a car's paint finish will oxidize—dark colors and red in particular are most susceptible to this kind of damage.

Stay in tune. Just like you need an annual physical, your car benefits from tune-ups. A well-tuned car runs better, consumes as much as 33 percent less fuel, and extends the life of all other car parts. By adhering to the manufacturer's recommended maintenance schedule, you can save up to $300 a year *over* the cost of a tune-up.

A Clean Discount

Go to an independently owned car wash rather than a national chain, and you're much more likely to get a discount just for the asking. In fact, if you call ahead and ask to speak to the owner or manager, you can probably get your own 10 percent senior discount simply for taking the trouble to request it. And if you become a regular customer, neither you nor the owner will ever have cause to complain about it!

Change is good. Most expert mechanics say regular oil changes—every 3,000 miles, no matter what kind of oil you use—keep your car's engine running smoothly. Heat, friction, and oil oxidizing over time result in sludge, otherwise known as "engine killer."

All tired out. Good, well-cared-for tires keep you safer and increase your gas mileage. Steel-belted radial tires with tread patterns chosen for the worst kind of conditions you regularly face (such as snowy, rainy, muddy, hot, or cold) are best. Make sure tires have the correct air pressure. Underinflated tires burn 5 to 10 percent more fuel. Overinflation causes wear to front-end parts. Get a wheel alignment, tire balance, and rotation once a year; unbalanced tires wear out suspension.

Go for heavy metal. Platinum plugs give you peak performance, and they do not need to be changed for 60,000 to 100,000 miles—three times longer than the life of standard plugs. They cost a bit more initially, but you save down the line on replacement parts and labor.

Fresh air fund. Have your air filter checked every month or two; a dirty one uses more gas and can shorten the life of your engine.

Put on the brakes. Your mechanic can check brake pads when you bring your car in for inspection. Otherwise, they need to be changed if you hear the squeal of the wear bar. An inspection process should include a check of your car's drums, rotors, and other brake parts to ensure they are in good working order.

Senior Discounts on Car Maintenance

While insurers might be a trickier bunch from whom to get a good senior discount, many national chains that provide car-maintenance service are delighted to make the extra effort for seniors. Even if your local shop is not part of a national chain, there's a good chance that you can get 10 percent off the cost of the parts or the labor or both, merely by asking. And let's face it: As you get older, even if you once knew how to change your oil, the thought of crawling under the car and doing it yourself gets less appealing every year! So take advantage of senior discounts, as well as special offers, promotions, and coupons at the following:

Make mine Meineke. Meineke Car Care Centers can put a new muffler on your car in about an hour or less, and if you're 60 or older, many locations will also offer you a 20 percent discount on the service. These car shops can handle oil changes, brakes, exhaust, and many other service issues. As with many national chains, the age requirement and the discount varies, so be sure to check when you bring your car in. At its Web site, www.meineke.com, you can type in your zip code and print out a variety

of coupons that are accepted at Meineke locations near you, such as 50 pecent off brake pads and shoes, or $10 off belts and hoses, or a free battery check.

Trust the Midas senior discount. Midas offers 10 percent off parts and services to seniors who are 60 and above, although the discount and age requirement can vary from location to location. Be sure to check when you take your car in, and be sure to visit its Web site to print out coupons, such as an oil change package for $19.99, which includes a tire inspection plus a courtesy check of brakes, filters, fluids, belts and hoses. You can also search for your car's make and model at its site, www.midas.com, and find the manufacturer's recommended maintenance schedule.

Take it off at JiffyLube. There are more than 2,200 locations of JiffyLube across the United States, and most of them will offer at least 10 percent off the cost of your oil change or tune-up for seniors age 60 and above. The age requirement and discount rate vary according to location, so be sure to ask, ideally *before* you get the service and not after. JiffyLube has a useful locator function at its Web site, www.jiffylube.com, and you can also sign up for special offers that may save you more than the discount, as well as find coupons and promotions, such as $5 off the price of an oil and filter change.

Gasoline Savings

In this time of continually rising gas prices, going to the pump can be expensive and alarming. Taking a trip to the store just for a quart of milk seems ridiculous when the cost for the gallon or two of gas it requires is many times the price of the milk. There are, however, a few things you can do to keep your gas costs as low as possible.

Pay the least amount possible. There are some terrific Web sites where rabid Web watchdogs obsessively track the price of gas at stations all over the United States. If you really want to know where the lowest gas prices are in your area, check one of them out and do a search for your street address, town, or zip code. You'll instantly get a listing, station by station, of the latest prices. Of course, make a decision about whether it makes sense to drive five miles out of your way to save 2 cents a gallon. Check out www.gasbuddy.com; www.gaspricewatch.com; or gasprices.mapquest.com.

Compare your car's mileage to other models. The U.S. Department of Energy has a list of all the current car models and the mileage they get, with information on common makes and models dating from 1985 to the present. This very helpful site, www.fueleconomy.gov, also includes a gas mileage calculator to help you figure out your own mileage; a Q&A section on current gas prices and the outlook for upcoming rates; information on alternate-fuel and super-efficient vehicles; and a very interesting, entertaining section on the future of automobiles. A sample: The 2006 winner of an annual competition for a fuel-efficient vehicle (the driver must be enclosed, there must be at least three wheels, and the vehicle must be powered by a small four-stroke engine) was the University of British Columbia, whose entry got a record 3,145 miles per gallon!

Get a tax credit for energy efficiency. If you buy an energy-efficient vehicle, you may be eligible for special state and federal tax credits on the car. Check out the Web site of the U.S. Department of Energy Efficiency and Renewable Energy at http://www.eere.energy.gov/afdc/incentives_laws.html. It has an interactive state-by-state map to let you search rules and regulations regarding tax incentives for fuel efficiency.

Early Bird Secret

Go Where the Trucks Go

One of the very few gas stations that offers an actual gas discount is Flying J, a national chain of truck stops, which you probably see regularly off the highway. Make a point to pull in—and sign up for one of its loyalty incentive programs. Once you've got a membership card in its RV RealValue Club or its Flying J Rewards Club, you won't want to buy gas anywhere else. Both clubs offer a membership card that tracks your purchases at Flying J. Spending anywhere from $10 to $400 a month on goods and services—such as restaurant and J Care service center purchases—can earn you anywhere from a penny to 30 cents off a gallon (generally there is a per-month limit on how much gas you can buy at the discounted rate).

If you've ever bypassed a truck stop looking for a "regular" gas station, think again! Find out more at www.flyingj.com.

The Fine Art of Hypermiling: Going Farther on Less Gas

If you can't get your hands on a hybrid, fear not. Here are simple steps you can take to go much farther in a regular car. In fact, simply maintaining your car can improve mileage by 19 percent. In its most extreme form, gas savings is called "hypermiling" or the art of wringing every last ounce of fuel efficiency out of any car. Many of the techniques embraced by hard-core hypermilers (who tend to be 20-something zealots who are obsessed with wringing every last ounce of performance from their cars) don't meet the average person's commonsense requirements in terms of comfort and safety (they coast down long hills with the engine off, for example). But many others are commonsense approaches to making your gas purchases good to the last drop. Here are a few to get you going.

Go forward. Always park so that you can pull forward rather than waste gas backing up. This can improve your mileage 25 percent (some experts say this might be an underestimate)!

Go the speed limit. The U.S. Department of Energy says that by following the speed limit and swearing off aggressive driving (rapid acceleration and deceleration), drivers can improve mileage by anywhere from 12 to 55 percent. Edmunds.com tested the idea and got similar results. They also found that using cruise control improved mileage by an additional 7 percent.

Stop idling. This leads to mileage improvements of up to 19 percent. If you're going to be at a standstill for 10 seconds or more, say at the drive-through lane at a fast-food joint or an outdoor deposit at a bank, it's better to cut the engine and do your business inside.

Warm up with a long drive. Modern cars don't become fully efficient until the engine is warmed up, so if you plan on running a series of errands, drive to the farthest location first and then work your way back—a series of short stop-and-start trips will never allow your car to reach maximum efficiency.

No junk in your trunk! For every 30 pounds of extra weight your car carries, miles per gallon decreases by anywhere from one-tenth to one-hundredth of a percent. That may not seem like much, but mile per mile it adds up. So de-clutter your car!

Avoid hard stops and starts. Rapid acceleration and hard braking, completely avoidable actions, just throw gas away. Instead of braking hard at a red light, coast from a distance. Come to stops slowly and gradually (if there is no one behind you, coast to the red light if you can).

4

Looking Good, Feeling Great

Cheaper Medicine, Cosmetics, Haircuts, Glasses, and More!

Get Thee to a Gym!

If you've never been to a gym in your life, get ready for some fun! Many national chains have special classes for seniors and physical trainers available to take you through an exercise routine or even a round of gentle weight lifting that's tailored to your needs. The result? You'll feel younger, fitter, more energetic—ready to go out there and enjoy all the other discounts that are available to you! Check out these examples, and don't forget to check with your local gym, fitness center, or recreation center, if a branch of one of these isn't nearby.

Curves This worldwide chain of fitness centers caters specifically to women, with special classes and exercise equipment that takes women's comfort into account, plus you never have to wonder if the man on the treadmill is gazing at your bared midriff when you stretch! AARP members can join Curves for an enrollment fee of $49, which is a savings of $100 from the usual fee. What's more, Medicare may cover the cost of your membership—check with your health-care provider. Type your zip code into the Curves Web site (www.curves.com) to find a branch near you, or call 1-800-848-1096.

Gold's Gym Senior discounts vary according to location since all the gyms are independently owned and operated, but a Gold's Gym representative in a Florida location said, proudly, of his center's discount: "It's pretty big!" Check with your nearest Gold's Gym and see how big your senior discount is. The Web site—www.goldsgym.com—can help you locate the nearest facility. AARP members can join Gold's gym for a $49 enrollment fee and save up to 20 percent off membership costs.

YMCA Many (many!) YMCA locations offer programs specifically geared to seniors, such as yoga or tai chi, and some also offer community-based activities such as lectures, social gatherings, and senior outings. Check with your local Y and find out what's on offer.

The YMCA is also a participating member in the SilverSneakers program, so you're in luck if there's a Y nearby! Check the Web site at www.ymca.net to find a Y near you, or call 1-800-872-9622.

Eyesight

Do those darn glasses not work as well as they used to? You have nobody to blame but yourself if you're not getting regular eye exams—vision can change, and you need your prescription to keep up. The days of bifocals that didn't let you see well either close up *or* far away are over. Modern optometry is keenly attuned to your changing vision needs, whether it's merely a pair of reading glasses or a high-tech pair of trifocals. Best of all, you can get your new glasses at a discount.

LensCrafters LensCrafters offers discounts to AAA and AARP members from 10 percent on contact lenses to 50 percent off specials on regular lenses. Check the Web site www.lenscrafters.com for their current discounts.

Pearle Vision It always pays to be a AAA member, and not only for your car: present your card and get a discounted eye exam, 30 percent off eyeglasses (frames, lenses, lens options), 30 percent off eyeglass accessories, and 10 percent off contact lenses. You can also get 30 percent off eye exams and 15 percent off partials. Present your AARP card and you can get a discounted exam, 30 percent off complete eyewear, 20 percent off non-disposable contact lenses, 10 percent off disposable contact lenses, and 20 percent off accessories. Visit www.pearlevision.com for the most recent deals and discounts.

The MD Foundation This little-known organization offers information on macular degeneration and the most recent scientific research into its causes and cures. You can read its regular newsletter, "The Magnifier," at its Web site, www.eyesight.org, where you can also listen to an audio version of the newsletter. You can also phone and ask for a free subscription at 888-633-3937.

Get a Salon Look for Less

As much as we might all wish for it, there is one basic truth about hair care: the wash-and-go cut, simple-and-easy hairdo is essentially a myth. Nobody rolls out of bed with perfect hair. Hollywood celebrities look the way they do because an entire hair and makeup team spent hours working before the celebrity ever set foot out the door. Most of us can manage without a team of stylists, but having someone else trim and style our hair now and then makes a big difference. We all know that to keep your hair looking good, you have to spend a little *time* on it. The good news is that you don't have to spend a lot of *money*.

Turn gray into gold! As hair grays, it becomes somewhat coarser than when it had its natural pigment, partly due to the natural loss of oils. Turn down the heat, if possible, on appliances such as curling irons, and use the low setting on blow-dryers because gray hair is more likely to be damaged, and damage on gray hair can take the form of a yellowish cast. Yellowing can also come from exposure to sun, smoking, hard water, and even from medication. Lavender- and blue-toned shampoos are an inexpensive way to counteract yellowing, but use them alternately with your regular shampoo to prevent the hair taking on that bluish tone.

Wash, rinse, repeat—not! Washing your hair twice in one session is an old marketing trick designed to make you use your shampoo up twice as fast. Double-shampooing strips all the natural oils out of your hair as effectively as paint thinner. Hair should never be "squeaky clean" because that's the same as "super-dry." Even people with naturally oily hair merely rev up their oil production by stripping all the natural oil from their scalps. One of our top experts, a partner and senior stylist at an upscale New York salon, recommends using shampoo on your hair not twice in one wash, but only every second wash. "Put in a little conditioner on your hair the days you're not shampooing," he says, "And be sure to rinse it out very well in warm water, so it doesn't start to build up on the strands. The days that you do shampoo, use about half the amount." The benefit to this system? Healthier hair with more body and shampoo costs that are cut in half.

Did You Know?

Don't use any clarifying shampoo, either store-bought or homemade, if you have just colored your hair, because it can remove some of the color and leave your newly coiffed head looking a lot less lustrous and evenly toned. But it's a great idea to use a clarifying shampoo just *before* you color your hair. Removing all traces of buildup allows the hair to take the color much better, and thus the color will last longer.

Baking soda for healthy hair! Your hair will look shinier and bouncier if you remove all traces of styling products and conditioner every six weeks or so. But do you need to buy a special clarifying shampoo? Not if you already have a box of baking soda in your cabinet. Mix a tablespoon of baking soda with two tablespoons of white vinegar and work it into your hair. Rub it in well all along the hair strands and then rinse thoroughly.

Stay away from too much of a good thing. Shampoo, conditioner, gel, mousse, hairspray—whatever you're putting on your hair, you're probably using too much of it. Try using half of the usual amount of everything you put on your hair, from shampoo and conditioner to gels and hairspray. You'll prevent (or slow) product buildup, allowing the products to be more effective, and you'll make a bottle or tube last twice as long— cutting the price effectively in half.

Ka-Ching!
Lace On Those Tennies!

The SilverSneakers Fitness Program is just what the doctor ordered if you're an in-the-know Early Bird. This terrific program offers:

CUSTOMIZED SENIOR WORKOUT AND HEALTH CLASSES

HEALTH EDUCATION SEMINARS

SPECIALLY TRAINED SENIOR ADVISER

The best part? It's *free* if you're a member of a participating Medicare health plan.

SilverSneakers provides a membership in a fitness center near your home. If no participating gyms or fitness centers are nearby, the SilverSneakers Steps program will provide you with a Personal Exercise Tracker, a recommended fitness program to get you started, newsletters, tracking logs, and a toll-free number where you can call for advice.

If your health plan covers the cost of SilverSneakers (and many do—just call the toll-free number on your health plan membership ID and ask), then all you have to do is take that ID to a participating fitness center and sign up. It's that easy to find a community of either like-minded exercise buffs or tentative beginners just like you! Find out more at www.silversneakers.com.

Sleep like a princess for Rapunzel-like locks. Your hairstyle rumples less if you sleep on a satin pillowcase. Cotton pillow covers (yes, even those 400 thread-count sheets) roughen the cuticle more, but satin allows the hair to slip smoothly over the surface as you roll and turn in your sleep. Satin allows you to preserve your do overnight. If you've spent a lot of time getting styled the day before, a night on the satin will help leave it magically preserved in the morning and ready to face another day.

Baby those tresses. Don't pay premium prices for high-end shampoos that are specially formulated for colored or permed hair. An inexpensive bottle of baby shampoo will treat your hair just as gently and will also allow the color or perm to last much longer.

Give it a natural shine. To bring out your highlights without a lot of expense, use an astringent rinse last thing while washing your hair. For lighter-colored hair, combine 1/4 cup of lemon juice with 1 cup of warm water and pour it over your hair. To bring out the highlights in darker hair, mix 1/4 cup of white vinegar with 1 cup of warm water.

Skin and Makeup Savings

Did you know that you can buy a skin cream that costs $600 an ounce (we're not kidding) and contains a chemical that's supposed to regenerate dead skin faster than normal, and it's only available at a few exclusive boutiques? Did you further know that this super-pricey skin lotion comes backed by "clinical trials" that assure you this product will change the way your skin looks in mere days? Further still, were you aware that these same trials are always paid for by the manufacturer of said cream? The truth? We never get to hear how a bottle of drugstore moisturizer measured up by comparison.

Fortunately, you can do far more practical and downright inexpensive things for your skin that will make it look just as good—and, probably, better—than that of the woman who's praying that her $600 worth of face cream makes her look like a 20-year-old. Here are some straightforward and inexpensive skin-care ideas that save time and money!

Borrow your grandmother's skin-care tool kit. What's the trick to great skin? Listen to your grandmother and pare down your supplies. According to a top dermatologist in New York, you can count on three fingers all you need for great skin health. What's in the arsenal? A moisturizing soap, moisturizer, and sunscreen. End of story. Anything else might make you *think* you're helping your skin, but the truth is you're just wasting time

Ka-Ching!

"Do" Discounts

Major national chains offer varying discounts for seniors, so be sure to check at your location. If all you want is the occasional trim, or a wash and blow-dry, check to see if you have a local barber training school or hairstyling school (most towns have some such institution—your hairdresser may be able to tell you where!). These places are glad to get willing models, and as long as you only want something simple—a color rinse, a trim, a blow-dry—they're usually worth the small fee you'll pay. Or you can get slightly more seasoned professionals to do your do for a nice senior discount at the following chains:

SUPERCUTS

Haircuts are $2 off the regular adult price for patrons 60 and older at this national franchise with over 2,000 locations. Discount and age requirements may vary by location so please call before you go. To find a salon near you, visit www.supercuts.com.

GREAT CLIPS

If you're 65 and older, you can get a haircut at a discount off the regular price (which differs with individual salons). Visit www.greatclips.com and click on Salon Locator for the GreatClips near you.

THIRD DIMENSION

Located in Washington and Oregon, these salons offer their clients 60 years and older, 10 percent off the regular price of any service that is performed Monday through Thursday, between the hours of 9:00 a.m. to 3:00 p.m. For salon locations, visit http://www.3dsalons.com.

and money on special eye or neck creams—moisturizer is moisturizer, so find one you like and stick with it.

Stay out of the sun. There's no such thing as a healthy tan. Tanned skin is effectively damaged skin, and nothing ages you faster or worse or puts you more at risk for skin cancer than cumulative exposure. As you age and your skin becomes thinner and more delicate, it's even more important that you use sunscreen on your face and neck (and ideally on your chest and the backs of your hands) *every day*, whether it's blazing hot summer or the middle of winter. Sun damage occurs year round, especially during hazy, cloudy days.

Get enough sleep. When you get a poor night's sleep, it shows on your face in the morning as surely as if it was written across your forehead in marker. Getting enough rest is one of the number-one beauty treatments, more important than any soap or moisturizer or makeup. Go to bed a little earlier and try not to worry—you're saving money *and* looking good!

Slice a cuke to lose those dark circles. While you're working on getting more beauty sleep, do what you can to lessen the effect of those telltale dark circles under your eyes. A slice of cold cucumber on each eye will reduce puffiness, as will a cold wet tea bag on each eye, but the best trick of all is cold, freshly grated potato. Wrap the damp shreds in one layer of cheesecloth (or one layer of a dampened, squeezed-out paper towel, if you're fresh out of cheesecloth). Recline and lay a potato packet over each eye, and rest for 15 to 20 minutes. When you discard the packets and rinse your face in cool water, eye puffiness will be noticeably reduced—as will fine lines around the corners!

Drink enough water. Skin hydrates from the inside out, so it doesn't matter what you're slathering on the surface if you're not drinking enough water. Researchers have backtracked a bit from the old recommendation of eight 8-ounce glasses a day, independent of any other beverages. Now we are told that the coffee or juice or soda you drink does count toward your daily water requirement, but nobody has backtracked from the fact that simple, unadulterated, really inexpensive water is still the healthiest drink there is.

Ka-Ching!

See a Celebrity Stylist for Pennies

Some of the top styling salons—the ones you see in celebrity magazines—charge up to $600 for a cut. Although their prices are insane, these people truly give you a terrific haircut and style that actually looks like you're a celebrity, so it can be well worth seeing one of them.

What?! The secret is to go to one of their modeling sessions. "Hair models" are the people whom salons use when training their staffs. Many upscale salons have very advanced hair-model programs, offering cuts, color, and styling—all for free. Some require you to come to an assessment session so they can see if you have hair they want to work on. Super-curly or super-short-haired clients, for example, probably will not qualify; some salons also won't color your hair if you have used certain coloring products within the last year.

Once you pass the test, you're usually in the door for regular cuts, color, and stylings as long as you meet all their criteria. Call the fanciest salon in your area and ask if they have a hair-model program, or do an Internet search for "hair model" and the name of your city. You'll feel like Dorothy sitting in the beauty salon in Oz!

The rules tend to be strict for getting these fancy and fabulous haircuts for free, even though nothing will be done without your consultation and approval. If you prefer the more traditional route of deciding exactly when you get an appointment and exactly what's going to happen while you're there, stay away. If you have some flexibility in terms of time, and you're willing to discuss various styles, however, you'll look like a million bucks for *free!*

Early Bird Secret

Say Hello to Sally

Sally Beauty Supply, the largest beauty supply store in the nation, also has stores around the world: in Ireland, Mexico, and Japan. They also have a very generous senior-discount policy, offering seniors 55 and older a discount of between 5 percent and 25 percent on non-sale items every day. The discount varies according to which product you're buying, and participation may vary according to location, but whether you need cocoa butter for your chapped hands or new hot rollers, the price may be just right at Sally! Visit www.sallybeauty.com for more information.

Exfoliate and glow! Especially in cold weather, skin can start to look rough, tired, and dull. The key to getting back your glow is to exfoliate, or rub off the dead skin cells clogging the surface of your skin, and you can do this once a month (but don't do it if your skin is already irritated or broken out). In a small dish, mix 1/4 cup raw rolled oats (either quick-cooking or traditional oatmeal is fine) with 2 tablespoons olive oil and 1 tablespoon of cornmeal. Add a few teaspoons of warm water until the mixture forms a paste. Wet your face with warm water and gently rub this mixture onto your skin with gentle circular motions. Stay away from the delicate skin around your eyes, but don't forget to massage the skin under and around your nose. Rinse well with warm water and pat dry very gently.

Have a facial. It's true: You don't need a lot of products for basic upkeep, but a once-in-a-while facial can leave your skin feeling soft and refreshed, and it's a great stress reliever. It promotes blood flow to the surface, and the whole process makes you feel and look more relaxed. And it doesn't need to cost more than a few pennies. An excellent facial for any skin type can be made from items that are already in your kitchen. Smooth one on, put your feet up, tip your head back, and let the stress flow out of you for 15 or 20 minutes. Whatever facial you use, be sure to moisturize your face generously after you're done.

Normal skin: Plain yogurt smooths and soothes almost any kind of skin, and it's the simplest mask there is. A full-fat yogurt feels creamiest, but even low-fat varieties give good results. (Nonfat yogurt is okay, but it won't feel as nice when you smooth it on.) Smooth a few tablespoons of yogurt directly on your face, or combine it with a teaspoon of honey, which moisturizes, and 1 or 2 drops of tea tree oil, a natural astringent. Allow to dry for 15 minutes, then rinse with warm water.

Oily skin: Clay masks are classic to help dry out oily skin, and you may be able to find facial clay at a health-food store. If so, combine 2 tablespoons clay with 1 teaspoon of honey and enough water to make a smooth paste. Smear all over your face, avoiding the eye area. If you can't find clay, smear unflavored milk of magnesia over your face (avoiding the eye area, as always). Whichever you choose, allow it to dry for 20 minutes before rinsing with warm water.

Dry skin: Mash half a ripe banana with half a ripe avocado using a fork, and blend in a tablespoon of warm olive oil (you can warm a bit in a cup in the microwave). Smooth it generously all over your face, avoiding the eye area. Leave on for 15 to 20 minutes, and then rinse well with warm water.

Skin with large pores: Put an egg white into a cup and beat it with a fork until it starts to get foamy. Smooth this over your clean skin and allow to dry. Rinse off with lots of warm water, buffing gently with a soft washcloth if necessary, and then moisturize.

Homemade Beauty and Health Products

The best discount of all might be the cost of making some of your beauty products at home. Most dermatologists agree that putting too many chemicals on your skin isn't good for it—especially as you get older and your skin is more delicate. Therefore, the best beauty products can be the simplest, without harsh alcohols and soap. In upscale beauty departments, the most natural products with the fewest chemicals are nowadays the ones that command the highest price! How have we come to this inverted way of doing business? Fortunately, homemade beauty products are easy to make, extremely effective, and can replace nearly every manufactured item in your bathroom cabinet. You'll look and feel better and keep your skin soft and smooth, your hair gleaming, and your cheeks and lips shining with health.

The "Spot Test" Rule

Before you put any homemade beauty product all over your face (or before you put any manufactured one that you've never tried before), do a spot test. Put a dab of it on the inside of your forearm. Leave for 10 minutes, then rinse off. If the skin is in any way discolored, reddened, or itchy, don't put that product on your face! You won't be surprised to find, however, that homemade facials such as yogurt and eggs tend to be much gentler on the skin than manufactured products, which often contain irritating levels of alpha hydroxy acids.

Bath products

"Soaking in bath salts" has a Victorian sound to it, but people have known for generations that a warm tub of water full of mineral salts helps relax the body and eases muscle aches, reduces inflammation, and can even soothe the skin. (We're not talking about table salt here.) Epsom salt, available in any drugstore, is in fact magnesium sulfate and contains no sodium chloride at all, but it can be used in place of "bath salt" in any bath soak recipe. Regular sea salt is usually damper and grayer than table salt and is full of minerals such as magnesium and calcium; it, too, can be used in the bath with good results. The amounts below are for one bath. You can either mix the ingredients in advance and package them for later use, or put the ingredients directly into the tub under hot running water.

Lavender Bath Soak

This bath is a classic soother of both mind and body.

> **1/2 cup bath salts**
>
> **1 tablespoon baking soda**
>
> **5 drops lavender essential oil**

Rosemary Bath Soak

This bright, herbally scented bath is invigorating and wonderful if you need a lift.

> **1/2 cup bath salts**
>
> **5 drops rosemary oil**
>
> **5 drops tea tree oil**

Rose Milk Bath

Ideal for irritated skin, the milk and baking soda in this bath make your skin feel soft and smooth.

> **1/2 cup powdered milk**
>
> **1/4 cup baking soda**
>
> **15 drops blended rose oil**

Oatmeal Bath

This is an extremely soothing bath for itchy, dry, or sunburned skin and perfect if you or a loved one has gotten into poison ivy.

1/2 cup oatmeal, ground to a fine powder in a coffee or spice grinder

1/4 cup powdered milk

1/4 cup baking soda

5 drops of your favorite essential oil

Bay Leaf Bath

This is a time-honored home preparation thought to ease strained muscles.

10 large bay leaves

1 pint of boiling water

Steep bay leaves in a boiling water for 10 minutes. Remove the bay leaves and pour the liquid directly into a hot bath.

Early Bird Secret

The Correct Epsom Salt

When you're looking for Epsom salt at the drugstore, don't buy the small box or bottle that contains about half a cup for $2 to $3. The small containers are for people who want to take their Epsom salt internally, a teaspoonful dissolved in water as a laxative. Look in the housewares section or ask in the pharmacy for the large containers—bags or boxes that hold a pound or more and that sell for $1 to $2. You need a lot more salt if you want to soak in it or use it as fertilizer in your garden.

Hand and body lotions, balms, and oils

Homemade hand lotion is more like the old-fashioned, thinner type of lotion our grandmothers used. It won't be as thick as a manufactured hand lotion, but it will generally be absorbed by the skin faster and feel much less greasy. A hand cream will be thicker and is better for dry skin or nighttime use. Whatever you choose, the active ingredients are usually the same: glycerin and/or petroleum jelly and maybe some beeswax or cocoa butter. All of these are available in their base form in nearly any drugstore, and you can combine them with various fragrances and other ingredients to make a truly personal body and hand moisturizer. For each recipe below, mix the ingredients in a small jar or tub and shake before each use. Store in the refrigerator and use each batch within five days.

Lavender Hand Lotion
- -
1/4 cup glycerin

1/4 cup rose water

4–5 drops lavender essential oil

Lime Body Lotion
- -
2 tablespoons glycerin

1 tablespoon fresh lime juice, strained

Lemon Body Lotion
- -
2 tablespoons glycerin

1 tablespoon fresh lemon juice, strained

Orange Body Lotion
- -
2 tablespoons glycerin

1 tablespoon fresh orange juice, strained

3 drops orange oil

Instant Hand Softener

- 2 tablespoons baby oil
- 3 tablespoons sugar

Rub and massage all over your hands, then rinse gently in warm water and pat dry.

Super-Soothing Hand Cream

- 1/2 cup oatmeal, ground fine in a coffee or spice grinder
- 1 tablespoon yogurt
- 2 tablespoons sweet almond oil
- 1 tablespoon rose water
- 1 teaspoon honey

Stir together and store in the refrigerator. Rub generously on itchy, dry hands and allow to soak in, then rinse with warm water.

Strawberry Foot Balm

- 1/2 cup fresh strawberries
- 3 tablespoons sugar
- 2 tablespoons olive oil

Mash strawberries (discard the stems first) with sugar and olive oil. Rub all over your bare feet and relax for 10 minutes. Rinse well with warm water and follow with Peppermint Foot Oil.

Peppermint Foot Oil

- 2 tablespoons sweet almond oil
- 1 tablespoon olive oil
- 12 drops peppermint essential oil

Lip balms and glosses

Making lip treatments at home is extremely appealing when you consider that this is the one cosmetic you actually tend to "eat," whether you mean to or not. The stickiest gloss eventually disappears off your lips, and it probably didn't get wiped off—you gradually ingested it. Taking that into consideration, wouldn't you rather know exactly what went in before you slather it on? With these simple versions, you can feel sure that your lip balms are simple and pure. Lip balms may require melting to get all the ingredients to combine, so use care if using the microwave.

Peppermint Lip Balm
- -
1 tablespoon cocoa butter

1 tablespoon beeswax

2 tablespoons sweet almond oil

5 drops peppermint oil

Melt the cocoa butter and beeswax in a small container in the microwave for 10 seconds, then stir in the oils. Pour into a small container and allow to cool.

Honey Lip Balm
- -
1 tablespoon petroleum jelly

1/2 teaspoon honey

Melt in the microwave for 10 seconds, then stir to combine. Pour into a small container and allow to cool.

Homemade Lip Gloss
- -
6 teaspoons sweet almond oil

2 teaspoons beeswax

1/2 teaspoon honey

7 drops peppermint oil

Melt the oil and beeswax together in the microwave for 10 seconds, then stir in the honey and peppermint oil. Pour into a small container and allow to cool.

Basic Toothpaste

The simplest mouth cleaner possible is to combine three parts baking soda with one part salt. Shake about a teaspoon of this mixture into your palm and dab your wet toothbrush bristles in it, and brush as usual. Your teeth will feel as smooth and freshly polished as if you had just left your dentist's office.

Mint Toothpaste

If the salty taste of basic toothpaste isn't to your liking, make a slightly fancier, minty, and equally effective cleaner.

2 tablespoons baking soda
1/2 teaspoon salt
1 tablespoon glycerin
10 drops oil of peppermint

> Combine all ingredients. Add a few drops of water, if you like, to achieve the correct paste consistency, and store in a tightly covered container.

Natural Teeth Whitener

1 teaspoon baking soda
1/2 teaspoon table salt
hydrogen peroxide

> In a small container (or in your clean palm) combine baking soda, table salt, and a little hydrogen peroxide, just enough to make a paste. Dip your brush in this mixture and brush as usual, paying special attention to the front teeth.

Basic Mouthwash

Nearly all commercial mouthwashes contain alcohol as a major ingredient. If you use one daily, you may find that eventually your mouth starts to dry out more and more, becoming uncomfortable and, paradoxically, increasing the likelihood of the very bad breath that mouthwash is supposed to combat. Homemade mouthwashes are a much gentler rinsing agent and can be infused with a bit of herbal or spicy flavor. Make them in small quantities and use each batch within a week. Gargle with 1/4 to 1/2 cup a day, as you like. For added refreshment, store your homemade mouthwash in the refrigerator.

Basic Mint Mouthwash

2 cups water

2 teaspoons baking soda

2 drops oil of peppermint

Combine in a small bottle, cover, and shake.

Basic Cinnamon Mouthwash

2 cups water

2 teaspoons baking soda

2 drops oil of cinnamon

Combine in a small bottle, cover, and shake.

Fresh Mint Mouthwash

3 cups water

1 handful fresh mint leaves

1 teaspoon fresh rosemary leaves

1 teaspoon anise or fennel seeds (optional)

Boil the water and drop in the leaves and seeds. Steep for 10 minutes, then strain, bottle, and store in the refrigerator.

Saltwater Dental Wash

This is particularly good at removing stray food particles and helping ward off gum disease.

1/2 cup warm water

1 teaspoon salt

Combine warm water with salt, swish and gargle. Mix each batch fresh as needed.

Department Stores That Discount

Department stores are a reliable source of senior discounts because so much of their goods are discretionary as opposed to necessity. It's worth the while of these retail outlets to court the patronage of a group of customers who wield, by some estimates, nearly 80 percent of leisure spending. So you'll often find a slightly higher percentage off—15 percent or 20 percent, say—than you might at a grocery store. Look out for good sales at your favorite department store, and then breeze in and get your additional discount on top. You'll be glad you asked! Here is just a selection of discounts you get.

Early Bird Secret

Secondhand Discounts

You might think that secondhand clothes at Goodwill and the Salvation Army are inexpensive enough, but don't forget to ask for your senior discount when shopping there as well!

Goodwill offers a 10 percent to 20 percent discount to customers 55 and above, depending on which location you're shopping.

The Salvation Army offers seniors 55 and older discounts that range from 15 percent to 50 percent off, depending on the location. Some stores offer these discounts to seniors every day, while others only offer them on Wednesdays. Check with your nearest store and don't forget to ask!

Banana Republic Nearly all Banana Republic stores offer a 10 percent senior discount every day, but check with the cashier before your purchase is rung up. Find a store near you at www.bananarepublic.com.

Bealls If you're 50 years or older, you'll save 15 percent on all your purchases on the first Tuesday of every month, 20 percent if you use a Bealls Credit Card. You need to sign up with a sales associate. For details of Club 50 Plus, visit bealstx.com and click on Customer Rewards.

Belk This chain of upscale department stores across the South and the Midwest has a Seniors Day the first Tuesday of every month. If you're 55 or older, take an extra 20 percent off all sale purchases storewide and 15 percent off Home and Shoes with your Belk Rewards Card.

Bon-Ton Check with your closest Bon-Ton store to find out which day of the month is Senior Day (it's often a Wednesday). If you're 55 and older and using a Bon-Ton credit card, the discount is 20 percent. It's 15 percent off if you use any other type of payment. All purchases from the home department (sheets, towels, curtains, etc.) are 10 percent, no matter what payment type you use. Visit its Web site at www.bonton.com.

Dress Barn Customers 62 and older can take an additional 10 percent off their entire purchase every Tuesday, although the day and the percentage may vary at some locations. Check out details at www.dressbarn.com.

Goody's Customers who are 50 and older can save 15 percent off their purchases on the first Tuesday of every month, 20 percent off if you use a Goody's Credit Card. You need to sign up with a sales associate. To find out more, go to www.goodysonline.com and click on Club 50 Plus "Customer Rewards."

Kohl's While Kohl's does not offer a standard senior discount, every December they advertise several senior days when seniors can take an extra discount off their purchases. The percentage and the days vary from store to store, so be sure to ask, especially when you're doing your holiday shopping! They offer senior days occasionally throughout the rest of the year, but you'll have to check with your individual store. Kohl's Cash may be an even better deal than a senior discount: for every $50 you spend, you get $10 in Kohl's cash, effectively giving you back 20 percent of the purchase price to spend on your next visit. (The senior discount and the Kohl's Cash are not mutually exclusive, but you'll receive the "cash" reward based on the discounted final amount, not the base price.) Find out more at www.kohls.com.

Lord & Taylor If you're 62 and older, Lord & Taylor may give you a 15 percent discount on Wednesdays, but this may vary from store to store, so visit customer service to confirm, and then shop happily!

Meijer One day a month (the day varies according to the store but generally on a Monday or Tuesday), Meijer has a Senior Discount Day offering customers 55 and up 15 percent off all general merchandise purchases. Get details at www.meijer.com.

Peebles If you're 50 or older, you can apply with any sales associate at Peebles (find a store near you at www.peebles.com) for a Club 50 Plus card, which allows the holder to save 15 percent on all purchases on the first Tuesday of every month, 20 percent if you use a Peebles Credit Card. Proof of age is required.

Ross Ross Stores have a Tuesday ClubDiscount Day for customers 55 and older. By becoming a member of the program, customers are entitled to 10 percent off their purchases on Tuesday. Sign up at the customer service desk during store hours and show ID with your age or date of birth and the store will issue you a card. Visit their Web site at www.rossstores.com.

Welcome to Senior Discount Village!

La Grange Park, a town in Illinois that bills itself as "The Village of Roses," is also the Village of Senior Discounts. In 2001, they formed a commission on Aging Well that has not only led to a series of initiatives to make the town senior friendly, such as free 911 cell phones for seniors and a Walk for Health program, but they have also coordinated local businesses in offering senior discounts.

If you're 65 and older, you can enjoy a minimum of 10 percent off a wide range of goods and services in the town each Wednesday. There are nearly 30 businesses participating, and each one displays an "Aging Well" discount sign. That's a town that knows how to live well. Find out more at www.lagrangepark.org.

Outlet Shopping

"Outlets" used to mean a decrepit wholesale store attached to a factory, such as bread outlets offering overstock and day-old goods. Nowadays an outlet is more likely to be an upscale complex of high-end stores, and the prices don't always seem *that* much lower than what you'd pay at the same store in the mall. But outlets are also eager to build their status as "destination" shopping—and if they want you to make a day trip out of it, then an added discount can only help.

Chelsea Premium Outlets

This parent company of outlet complexes has stores across the United States, and the names vary: Woodbury Common Premium Outlets is near New York City, for example, and Napa Premium Outlets is in California. You can locate the one nearest to you through the map on its Web site, www.premiumoutlets.com. You can get an additional 10 percent discount off your purchases at participating outlet stores (ranging from Old Navy to A/X Armani Exchange) every Tuesday with their 50 Plus Shopper Perks Program. Show a photo ID when paying and you *automatically* receive your discount. You can also join its VIP Shopper Club at its Web site and receive exclusive online coupons and e-mail updates for sales and special events.

HSN Outlets This chain of outlet stores offers Senior Discount day every Tuesday in all the outlet stores of the complex. If you're 50 or older, you get an additional 10 percent off your total purchases—with a maximum savings of $50. (That means, once you spend $500, you should put your credit card away until the next Tuesday!)

Prime Outlets Prime Outlets are mostly east of the Mississippi. You can pick up a Senior Savings Guide near the food court in each outlet complex and figure out what your savings potential is at every store. Find out more at www.primeoutlets.com.

Don't Re-buy Your Clothes: Clean Them!

Found the linen suit of your dreams that will need professional pressing every time you wear it? How about a gorgeous silk blouse marked "Dry-Clean Only"? We feel your pain, because a lot of dry-cleaning is not only bad for your pocketbook, but it can actually damage your clothing, and do a lot worse to the environment. More and more cleaners are attempting to switch to "healthier" chemicals, but the fact remains that most dry cleaning is still accomplished by powerful solvents that are potentially toxic. Here's how to cut down on your dry-cleaning bill and those solvents' impact on the environment, and maybe make your clothes last a little longer in the meantime.

Spot clean. If you get a spot on a "dry-clean only" item, remove it yourself, instantly, with a portable spot cleaner. Before you ever wear the item, test a spot on an inside seam with a bit of the cleaner, and make sure it does not leave a visible mark on the fabric. Then carry your spot cleaner with you and use it, fast, as soon as you dribble a drop of coffee or spill a little ketchup.

Air it out. Refresh a dry-cleanable garment each time you wear it rather than rolling it in a ball to take to the cleaners. Put it on a hanger and allow air to circulate around it rather than tucking it in an overpacked closet or throwing it in a pile. Hang it in the bathroom while you shower, and let it steam a bit to relax wrinkles and allow odors to dissipate.

Press it. You *can* iron a "dry-clean only" outfit without harm if you keep the heat low and don't iron too much. Avoid any obvious stains and try not to iron over areas where stains may emerge, such as under the arms or over the chest and belly.

Make your own home dry-cleaning kit. There's no need to spend a lot of money on those kits, which will provide you with a solvent and a "freshener," also known as a "dryer sheet." Put the garment in the dryer with a regular dryer sheet for 10 to 15 minutes, on medium heat, and you'll find that it's nearly the same as taking it to the cleaner: freshened, sweeter smelling, and with most of the wrinkles released. (Don't overdry, and be sure to remove the garment and hang it up promptly, or you'll set the wrinkles back in.)

Hand wash. Why should a silk cardigan be dry-cleaned when silk is supposed to be one of the toughest natural materials on earth? Knitwear, linen, and silks are especially likely to be hand-washable. (Men's suits, not so much—it's not that it will ruin the fabric in most cases but it *will* ruin the shape.) Use cold water and a delicate detergent. Lay knitwear flat to dry, or reshape the garment on a hanger to dry; be sure to use a wide hanger that reaches to the shoulder seams, so that the item doesn't end up with little marks at the shoulders where the hanger caught it.

The Top 12 Heart-Happy Foods

When you put wholesome, unrefined, unprocessed foods into your body, you are helping to promote glowing health and reducing all sorts of health risks like obesity, diabetes, high blood pressure, and stroke. That in turn can reduce doctor visits, improve your good mood, and lower stress. Best of all, ounce for ounce, pound for pound, real "whole" food costs a lot less than packaged junk. You get a much bigger bang for your buck, and it tastes better, too. Eat a balanced diet full of a variety of fresh foods, like these 12 superstars, and you'll have plenty of reasons to smile.

1. Almonds Vitamin B2 (riboflavin), vitamin E, magnesium, and zinc all help to make a handful (about 1/4 cup a day) of crunchy almonds good for your heart and your mood. B vitamins and magnesium help produce serotonin, which helps regulate mood. Zinc has also been shown to fight some negative effects of stress, while vitamin E is an antioxidant that

5 Smart

Where to shop? Super-sales at major department stores can yield discounts much deeper than what the store offers you as a senior, especially if it's end of season. You can also get creative about the places you buy things and think outside the big-name box—there are serious savings in shopping a bit off the beaten track, in the best possible way, such as vintage stores or designer overstock.

1. CHAIN BARGAIN STORES

Places such as Ross and T.J. Maxx not only offer senior discounts but can also offer treasures if you're willing to plunge in up to your elbows and pick over the bargain racks. The racks at the front of the store have become less of bargains over the years, offering full-price merchandise from lesser labels. Move straight on back to the "Clearance" sections and start to sort. This is where you can often find real designer goods at major discounts. Subtract your senior discount from the rock-bottom price, and you've got a real deal!

2. OUTLETS

Outlets used to be the first outpost of the bargain hunter, but as this business has become firmly entrenched, outlets sometimes sell their own brands, such as the Gap Outlet label, offering clothes that never make it into actual Gap stores. Full price at outlets is suspiciously like full price at the regular store! Happily, the senior discount at a large outlet center is usually for all the stores in the entire outlet, and it's usually a higher discount than the stores might offer individually.

3. OVERSTOCK WEB SITES

Here's where you can get real bargains on designer labels. Type into a search engine (such as Google) the name of the item or designer that you want and the word "overstock." You'll find a range of sites selling brand-new stuff, usually with tags still on, at complete bargain-basement prices.

4. VINTAGE, CONSIGNMENT, AND THRIFT STORES

Like any store, these eclectic selections can be hit or miss. They're not the types of places to find something highly specific, along the lines of, "I need a blue raincoat right now," but they are the place to find a true bargain on some very distinctive pieces: a Gucci handbag, hardly used, for $15; a pair of Chanel shoes never worn, for $5; perhaps a velvety suede coat, tags on, for $20. Basics can be found for literally cents on the dollar, such as a skirt for 50 cents or a stretchy top for a quarter. These types of stores offer the thrill of the serious bargain and the hunt for the unexpected (and unexpectedly inexpensive) in exchange for giving up control—you never know what you might get on a given day, but it will likely be fabulous and cheap!

5. TAG SALES, YARD SALES, GARAGE SALES

Sometimes a risky place to buy clothes because people are inclined to overprice something that means a lot to them. They know they paid $200 for that winter coat two years ago, so they put it in their front yard for $45, when to you it's only worth $5 or $10. Bargain gently in these situations, and you might end up with a really good deal. Ask, "Do you have a senior discount?" and you'll probably make the owner smile and give you one!

destroys the free radicals related to stress and heart disease. They're the perfect snack—so much better than a bag of chips. Or, add some slivered beauties to your morning oatmeal.

> *Early Bird Buy:* Buy roasted and unsalted almonds from a bulk bin, and get just what you need at a lower per-pound price than packaged nuts.

2. Asparagus

Asparagus contains heart-healthy anti-inflammatory nutrients like folate and vitamins C and D. It is also low in calories and quick cooking. Sauté it with sugar snap peas and toss with whole wheat pasta, olive oil, lemon juice, and a bit of freshly grated Parmesan cheese and pepper for a meatless meal fit for a (very healthy) king or queen.

> *Early Bird Buy:* Buy it fresh during spring and early summer, when local crops are harvested. Canned asparagus lose something in translation, so they are best left on the shelf, but frozen make a passable substitute for the fresh stuff.

3. Beans

These versatile legumes contain more protein than any other plant food—just one cup provides a quarter of what we need each day. They also provide heart-healthy and stress-busting B vitamins, iron, and all-important calcium. Plus, they are considered "nature's scrub brush" because one serving's 15 grams of fiber goes through the intestines and sops cholesterol and takes it away (you know where). Use beans in soups and stews or create a vegetarian chili with kidney beans, tomatoes, carrots, celery, and a little bit of hot pepper. Puree a rinsed and drained can of white beans with two tablespoons of olive oil, a small clove of garlic, and salt and pepper for a Mediterranean-style veggie dip.

> *Early Bird Buy:* Stock up on canned beans when they are on sale; dried beans are always less expensive than canned but take longer to soak and cook.

4. Blueberries

Almost all fruit is good for you—cherries, strawberries, mangos, peaches—yum! But these blue-hued beauties work overtime to provide you with antioxidants and vitamin C, both potent stress busters. They're low in calories and sugar, so you can snack on them to your heart's content without an ounce of guilt (or fat). Blueberries are also a good source of fiber, which can help relieve the cramps and constipation that can occur when you're stressed out. Pile 'em on cereal, eat them fresh from the basket, or blend them with some plain yogurt, a banana, and some ice for a fabulous smoothie.

> *Early Bird Buy:* Summertime is berry time; otherwise frozen berries are a better bargain in winter (and may be fresher than imported berries that have traveled many miles to get to your store).

Ka-Ching!

Farmers' Market Senior Discounts

If you tend to drive right on by all the jewel-toned produce on roadside stands or avoid visiting green markets and farmers' markets because you're afraid the prices will be all over the map (whereas you know for sure what an apple will cost you at the grocery store), then a program called **Senior Farmers' Market Nutrition Program** (SFMNP) is perfect for you. The SFMNP is a program that provides qualifying senior citizens with coupons for certain foods at farmers' markets, roadside stands, and community-supported agriculture programs. It ensures that low-income seniors have access to healthy and delicious produce direct from the grower.

Congress authorized $20.6 million for the SFMNP through 2012. Here are examples of how some states administer the program:

Florida offers 10 coupons worth $4 each (redeemable from April 1 through July 31) to low-income seniors 60 and older living in Alachua, Bay, Jackson, Leon, Sumter, Suwannee and Union counties.

Washington State provides low-income seniors 60 and older with $40 in assistance. The maximum gross monthly income for eligibility for an individual is $1,669. The program runs from June through October.

Alabama offers low-income seniors of 60 and above a book of $4 vouchers to use between April 5 and November 15. For a single-person household, the annual income must be $18,200 or lower. For couples, the annual income must be $24,500 or lower.

Who qualifies? Low-income seniors are generally defined as individuals who are at least 60 years old and who have household incomes of not more than 185% of the federal poverty income guidelines—which are posted anew every year. If you already qualify for food stamps or other food assistance, you may already qualify for this program. You can get more information and help defining your status at the USDA Web site, www.fns.usda.gov/wic. Click on "SFMNP State Agencies" for a full contact list, state by state.

5. Broccoli Broccoli is packed with B vitamins and folic acid, which has been shown to help relieve stress, anxiety, panic, and even depression. Steam broccoli in the microwave (rinse and chop it, place it in a glass or other nonreactive bowl, and cover it with a damp paper towel, not plastic wrap) for a few minutes for optimal nutrition. Add a squeeze of lemon juice, a drizzle of extra-virgin olive oil, and, if you dare, a sprinkle of red pepper flakes for punch, and you've got yourself a sublime yet simple side dish.

> *Early Bird Buy:* Fresh stalks are available all year round, and you can stock up on broccoli when it is on sale. Just blanch in boiled, salted water for 3 to 4 minutes, then freeze for up to two months.

6. Chocolate Dark chocolate (at least 75 percent cocoa; 85 percent is best) is not only a stress reducer—who doesn't love a piece of chocolate?—but it is heart-healthy, too! One study, conducted by researchers at the University of Scranton in Pennsylvania, showed that eating 6 ounces of dark chocolate a day lowered bad cholesterol. And that's not all. Another researcher found that cocoa contains phenols—antiseptic, anti-inflammatory compounds that reduce your risk of heart disease by keeping fat-like substances from oxidizing in the blood and clogging your arteries. Do you really need a serving suggestion for chocolate?

> *Early Bird Buy:* After-holiday sales are one way to find good buys on this good-for-you confection.

10,000 Steps a Day Keep the Doctor Away

Research has shown that taking 10,000 steps every day helps you lose weight, lower your blood pressure, fight off depression, and stay fit and active. And no wonder: 10,000 steps is the equivalent of five miles! There's no need to reach that upper limit. Many of us could simply double the amount of steps we take and achieve big results without ever coming near the 10,000 step level.

But how in the world can you tell how many steps you're taking? Buy a pedometer, an inexpensive device that attaches to your shoe or waistband, so that the vibration registers each step throughout your day. If you're only taking a thousand steps, you need to get out more!

7. Leafy greens Spinach, kale, dandelion greens, turnip tops, and Swiss chard—they're all amazing foods that provide iron plus lots of vitamin C, both good for strong bones, teeth, and hair, and vitamin A and magnesium, both of which are excellent at helping you maintain calm. Sauté one or more type of greens with lemon or orange juice and garlic, or purée with a little low-sodium chicken or veggie broth and white beans for a satisfying soup.

> *Early Bird Buy:* Fresh, loose greens are generally less expensive than washed and bagged. Frozen spinach is a fabulous bargain. Stock up when it's on sale and store in the freezer for up to three months.

8. Lean beef

Surprised this is on the list after hearing admonitions from experts about avoiding the red stuff? Don't be. Beef is a substantial stress buster. It's loaded with zinc, iron, and B vitamins (not to mention protein), all known for keeping us calm and happy. It is also satiating, meaning you feel fuller longer (hunger pangs can cause irritability and anxiety). Avoid fatty cuts, and stick to lean cuts like flank and skirt steak, and 95 percent lean ground beef. Or, look for cuts marked "round" or "loin," such as top sirloin, bottom round (great for pot roast), and tenderloin—they are the kindest cuts in terms of fat content. And limit your intake to 4 to 6 ounces when you do enjoy it.

> *Early Bird Buy:* Meat can be pricey, but luckily the leanest cuts are also the least expensive. Supermarkets have weekly specials on cuts like London broil (perfect for quick grilling or slow pot roasting) and bottom round. If you have room in the freezer, unwrap the meat and rewrap it in freezer paper or wax paper, then place it in a freezer bag to reduce the chance of freezer burn.

9. Salmon and other fish

Most kinds of fish are loaded with B vitamins, particularly the renowned stress fighters B6 and B12. In fact, B12 is one of the most important vitamins in terms of serotonin production; a vitamin B12 deficiency can even lead to depression. Omega-3 fatty acids are prevalent in salmon (Alaskan wild is the best; farm-raised is the least desirable) and tuna—even the canned stuff. Grill or pan-roast fish, and serve on a bed of leafy greens with a side of lentils and carrots for a true power meal. Or, toss rinsed and drained water-packed white albacore tuna with a tablespoon of extra-virgin olive oil and a teaspoon of drained capers and serve on a bed of salad greens. You'll be doing swimmingly after meals like those!

> *Early Bird Buy:* Canned salmon and wild Alaskan tuna are great buys, especially when they go on sale. They last almost indefinitely in your pantry.

10. Sweet potatoes

Talk about a nutritional powerhouse! The more color a veggie has the better it is for you, according to nutritionists—and sweet potatoes might be the brightest of all. Potent antioxidants found in sweet potatoes help to shield our hearts. Plus, their sweet taste makes them delicious enough to eat for dessert. But if you don't want to go that far, try chunking them up into 1-inch squares, roasting them at a high heat (400 degrees) for

10 Ways to Have a Healthy

We all know eating right and getting regular exercise is good for you and helps you live longer (regular exercise alone can extend your life by 1 1/2 years according to some experts), but did you know that it can also save money by reducing medical and medication bills, reducing your risk of heart disease, and lessening the risk of catching cold? Here are 10 ways to start getting active that are so cheap—free, in fact—that they're like money in your pocket:

1. ADOPT A DOG.

And then take him or her for daily walks. In the long run, it's less expensive than joining a gym and a lot more fun. It also helps broaden your social circle (very healthy!) by putting you in contact with other animal lovers.

2. FIND A WALKING PARTNER.

Same theory, only this time we're talking human, not canine. Sharing activities with a friend makes it more likely you will stick to an exercise regime.

3. WALK THE MALL.

Your mall provides a traffic-free, climate-controlled area to take a healthy stroll—for free. Some malls encourage walkers by opening early to accommodate them. Inclement weather will never stop you from stretching your legs again!

4. GO OUT OF YOUR WAY.

Take the stairs instead of the elevator if you can, park farther from the store entrance, use the self-serve line to check out and pack your own groceries—whatever you can do during the day to add movement to your routine will get you going, build strength, and burn calories. And it's free.

Lifestyle

5. GO DANCING!

If there is no place in your town (like a swing-dance society or square-dance club) that offers free dancing venues, then turn up the radio and dance at home.

6. WATCH TV.

FitTV is just one cable station that offers free exercise programs all day. Some public television stations include early morning yoga, tai chi, and stretching programs you can follow along with.

7. BABYSIT THE GRANDCHILDREN.

When was the last time you ran after a toddler? Uh-huh. That burns a lot of calories, not to mention the free resistance training you get every time you pick up the little princess (or prince) and put her (or him) down in another room.

8. VOLUNTEER.

Many communities offer property tax reductions to people—usually those 60 and older—who work for the community a certain number of hours. Find out if there is something active you can do, like planting bulbs in the town square or substitute teaching.

9. WORK.

Get a part-time job. Again, think of it as getting paid to exercise. Even working a few hours in a department store, florist shop, or grocery store can give you the activity you crave, some extra cash, and an employee discount to tack on top of your senior discount!

10. FOOL AROUND.

Canoodling with your partner is a free, fun way to add some calorie-burning movement to your daily routine—and it will certainly cheer you up and brighten your day!

about 30 minutes, and then tossing them with some chopped dried plums (better known as prunes) for a tempting and unique side dish next to roasted chicken or turkey—or as a vegetarian meal on its own.

> *Early Bird Buy:* Sweet potatoes are available all year round. Cut down on waste by storing sweet potatoes in the fridge away from onions; unlike white potatoes, sweet versions deteriorate quickly when they are not kept chilled.

11. Walnuts Another powerful nut! Walnuts contain alpha-linolenic acid, or ALA, an omega-3 fatty acid that is similar to the one found in salmon and herring. A handful of walnuts a day as a snack is an easy way to get this important nutrient. Or, scatter a few on top of a salad for a satisfying crunch. Or, add some to your oatmeal along with raisins or dried cranberries for a power breakfast.

> *Early Bird Buy:* Like almonds and other nuts, walnuts are cheapest when bought from bulk barrels. Keep them in the freezer for the longest shelf life.

Freeze Nuts for Freshness

Store nuts in the freezer to keep them from going rancid. They last several months this way, and you won't end up throwing them away.

12. Whole grains Cracked wheat, barley, faro, millet, and quinoa are just a few of the 19 whole grains you can cook with and enjoy in all sorts of dishes. Whole grains digest slowly, keeping you feeling fuller, longer. Plus they boost serotonin levels and make you feel happy—and they brighten your mood because they're so delicious! A half-cup serving size of any whole grain alongside a serving of veggies and lean protein should have you strolling on the sunny side of the street in no time. Follow packaging directions for preparation, but realize that most whole grains don't require any special technique. However, toasting them in a dry pot for a few minutes before adding water adds depth of flavor.

> *Early Bird Buy:* Purchase in bulk at health food stores and freeze for freshness.

Saving at the Drugstore

You're getting exercise, and you're eating healthy and staying fit (not to mention the fact that your clothes are stupendous bargains!), but still, everyone needs prescriptions filled from time to time. Not everyone, however, can get the discount on prescriptions that you can get. And in today's climate of increasingly high-priced medication, that senior discount is something to be especially thankful for. Here's a roundup of your best bets when it comes to knocking a few dollars off your prescription prices:

A&P Supermarket If you sign up for an A&P Club Card, customers 60 and over can get a 10 percent Senior Citizen Prescription Discount. Get details at www.apsupermarket.com.

CVS/Longs Drugs At CVS or Longs Drugs, (which is now a part of CVS), you can sign up for a CVS/pharmacy Health Savings Pass for $10 per year per person. With the pass, you can get a prescription with a 90-day supply of over 400 generics for $9.99 and 10% savings on MinuteClinic services at over 6,300 CVS/pharmacy locations nationwide. You can fill prescriptions online for home mail delivery or pick-up in-store. Stop by your local store to sign up or visit www.cvs.com.

Hannaford This grocery store chain does not treat its pharmacy like an afterthought. There are significant drugstore sections in Hannaford branches, with pharmacists available for consultation. They offer an R_x Healthy Saver Program, which is not only for seniors and is well worth joining. Anyone can apply, either with or without insurance, and you'll receive a Healthy Saver card to present when paying for drugs. If your drug is one of 400 in the program, you'll receive your prescription for $4. You can also receive a 90-day supply for $9.99. Visit Hannaford's Web site at www.hannaford.com (click on "Be a Hannaford R_x Healthy Saver").

Kmart If you're 50 and over and uninsured, you can sign up for Kmart's GoldK Program, which is free. You get a GoldK card, which lets you save 5 percent on diabetes prescription items (not all items apply), up to 10 percent on brand-name drugs, and up to 20 percent on generics. If you have an 80/20 prescription deductible plan, where you pay first and submit receipts later for reimbursement, you can still use the GoldK card. Visit the Web site at www.kmart.com (click on "Pharmacy", then on "GoldK Program").

Kroger Although it's not just for seniors, Kroger offers a generic drug discount program that lets you buy a 30-day supply of a list of generic drugs for $4, or $10 for a 90-day supply. Find details at www.kroger.com.

Osco Pharmacy at Shaw's Supermarket Depending on the location, the Osco pharmacy of Shaw's Supermarket offers approximately 10 percent off your prescription, depending on the drugs. The discount will likely be higher for generics. The age requirement can vary so check at your location. Visit its Web site at www.shaws.com.

Rite Aid Eckerd and Brooks have been absorbed into the Rite Aid family, which offers a Living More program for customers 60 and older. When you apply for a Living More card, which is free, you get 10 percent off prescriptions for which you pay cash. Your card also gets you 20 percent off your purchases the first Tuesday of each month, with 10 percent off on the other Tuesdays of the month, and 10 percent off Rite Aid brand products every day, with other occasional special offers and discounts for Living More members. Find details at www.riteaid.com (click on "Pharmacy," then "Living More").

Stop & Shop If you use your Stop & Shop card, you pay only $9.99 for up to a 90-day supply of a list of generic drugs. Find out more at www.stopandshop.com.

Target Target's in-store pharmacies now offer more than 400 generic drugs for $4 per 30-day supply or $10 for a 90-day supply. The pharmacist will give you a print-out of the list of drugs, or you can search for your drug's availability at its Web site (www.target.com and click on "Pharmacy") or stop by your local branch.

Walgreens If you do not have prescription drug coverage or your insurance does not cover all your prescription drug needs, you can sign up for a Walgreens Prescription Savings Club. There is a fee of $20 a year for individuals or $35 a year for families, and then members can receive a three-month supply from a list of about 400 common medications for $12.99. Find out more online at www.walgreens.com, and visit your local store to sign up.

Early Bird Secrets

Good Health Info

AARP and Walgreens have a partnership to provide health-care information specifically for seniors. For free, you can download brochures on topics such as how to manage your medication, generic vs. brand-name drugs, traveling with medication, caregiving resources, and much more. You can also order through the Web site printed copies to be sent to you for free: www.walgreens.com/aarp/resources.jsp.

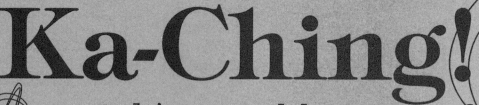

Ka-Ching!

Taking Health Costs Off Your Tax Bill

Even when you have insurance, it can be surprising what you have to pay out of pocket—a co-pay here, a test bill there, an unexpected supplementary cost on a prescription, and suddenly it all adds up. Keeping detailed records of the money that you spend on health care may seem like a bit of a hassle day by day, but you'll be glad you did when tax time comes! Unreimbursed medical expenses that add up to more than 7.5 percent of your total income are fully deductible from your year-end taxes.

Here's a list of the kinds of medical expenses that the IRS will let you deduct from your year-end taxes. Again, keep all your receipts carefully for every medical expense, and remember that you can't deduct over-the-counter medicine and most cosmetic surgery. Check with your tax preparer or go to www.irs.gov to confirm this year's deductible expenses. During tax season, you can get live help from the IRS on the phone at 1-800-829-1040.

- Visits to dentists, doctors, chiropractors, acupuncturists, therapists, and other medical practitioners
- Laser eye surgery
- Hearing aids
- Prescription drugs
- Lab fees
- Prescription eyeglasses and contact lenses
- Crutches, walkers, wheelchairs, and other mobility devices
- Dentures
- Guide dogs
- Health-care premiums and long-term care policies
- Some health-related transportation, such as trips to doctors' offices

Wal-Mart Wal-Mart offers the same deal: $4 for a 30-day supply, $10 for a 90-day supply on a similar list of generics. They also have good prices on items such as mobility aids, diabetic supplies, blood pressure monitors, and more. Learn more at www.walmart.com (click on "Pharmacy").

Getting Free Medical Advice

Medical costs are rising by the day, but there are still plenty of good deals out there—if you know where to look. It's always better to prevent a medical condition than to treat one, so take the opportunity to accept the free screenings and advice offered on many fronts to keep yourself as healthy and well as possible. Many drugstores and in-supermarket pharmacies offer screening services for free or for a small fee. While screenings are usually offered by health professionals, generally they are not run by doctors, so don't hesitate to follow up with your regular physician if a screening uncovers any abnormalities or concerns.

Osco Pharmacy at Shaw's The pharmacies at Shaw's Supermarkets offer regular free and low-cost screenings, ranging from diabetes, blood pressure, and bone density, to flu and pneumonia vaccinations. Visit the web site www.shaws.com (click on "Pharmacy," then "Health Screenings" to find a schedule).

Publix Publix grocery stores have low-cost health-care checkups such as an osteoporosis screening for $15, free blood pressure screenings, and cholesterol screenings ($20 for total lipid; $15 for non-fasting screening). Get details at www.publix.com.

Target Target Clinics are available in Minnesota and Maryland and provide treatment for patients ages 18 months and older for many common illnesses and injuries with most services costing in the $59 to $69 dollar range. To find locations, go to www.target.com and click on Pharmacy and Target Clinic.

Wal-Mart Health and Wellness Centers It's hard to drive far in the United States without passing a Wal-Mart somewhere in your vicinity—and that's a good thing when it comes to low-cost clinics. Wal-Mart now offers 68 low-cost clinics across eighteen states, where a typical visit costs about $65. (The Web site, www.walmart.com, has a clinic locator to see if there's one near you. Click on "Pharmacy," then "Health and Wellness Center.") They generally assist with minor health issues, not emergency care, but they're a good place to go if you need help with earaches, flu, respiratory infections, and other basic concerns.

Enjoying Your Free Time

5

Indulging in Life's Little Luxuries without Spending a Lot of Money

Deep Discounts on Hobbies and Crafts

Whether you've been pursuing a hobby all your life, or just wished you could find a few minutes each week to begin one, now is the time to turn your attention to the activities you love. And there are added benefits to having a hobby: it fosters creativity and community, it helps you relax, and it keeps your mind keen and actively engaged. What you began as a leisurely pastime can sometimes take on a life of its own. If your hobby actually produces something—whether it's paintings, summer tomatoes, or needlepoint pillows—you might find that the demand for what you produce outstrips the supply. Whatever you create, there's always the opportunity to enjoy the outcome yourself, to give the item as a gift, or possibly even sell it at a craft fair or church bazaar.

Strum and Toot Without Spending a Dime

It happens to all of us—life gets in the way of something that we used to do (or want to learn), like playing an instrument, and it falls by the wayside. It's only when we sit down to it that we realize how much we loved doing it after all! You may not be a Liberace or Chet Atkins, but if your hobby involves a musical talent, then put it to good use, and reap the benefits.

Play it again, Sam. If you love to play the piano, go ahead and make it part of your life again! Church choirs, grade school shows, dance schools, senior centers—they're all wonderful places to offer your skills and talents tinkling the keys. If you volunteer, your offer will almost always be accepted (assuming you're not a beginner).

That old six-string. Always wanted to learn to play the guitar but never found the time—or money!—for lessons? Forget the extra cash. All you need is an Internet connection and a guitar. There are dozens of sites on the Web that offer step-by-step videos and lessons to teach you to play *all for free*. Check out sites such as www.justinguitar.com or www.guitarmasterclass.net to get an idea of what's out there. And then get ready to strum along!

Gimme (sheet) music. Dust off your instrument, whatever it is, and treat yourself to some new music. Don't worry if you can't get to the music store to buy a paper copy. The Internet can give you music to just about any song you can remember and everything else as well. Sites such as www.freesheetmusic.net or www.findfreesheetmusic.com have countless scores and arrangements available to download for free. If you're looking for a lovely arrangement of "Danny Boy"—be it for the accordion, the violin, or the bagpipes—you can find it for free on the Internet.

Practical Crafts...Practically Free

There are few things as satisfying as making something useful by hand, whether it's a handmade book, a quilt, or an heirloom piece of furniture. Supplies can be specialized and tools can be expensive to purchase, so consider ways to try out a craft, such as taking a class or learning from a friend, before you splash out on something that you may not want to continue. When you do find your calling, whether it's smocking handmade children's clothes, nature photography, or throwing pots, don't hesitate to get yourself the necessary professional implements you'll need. Your loved ones will treasure your efforts, and you'll have the deep satisfaction of a project well done.

Say cheese! Taking digital photos frees you up to shoot like a professional, and you get instant results. First, you're not wasting film by snapping photos over and over to get just the perfect shot. Then, you can download them to your computer and print only the ideal picture. Printing at home can get expensive since you have to buy photo paper and those expensive color ink cartridges that run out so quickly. Instead, compare prices and see if it's a better deal, depending on your printing habits, to print from a photo site such as www.snapfish.com or www.shutterfly.com. You upload the photos to the site from your computer, and they make prints and mail them to you.

Be sew-cial and join a bee. Love to partake in this treasured, practical hobby of American women everywhere? There's no more social way to sew or quilt than to join a bee, and while you can piece together quilts at home by yourself whenever you have the time, there's real pleasure in joining a quilting class or club and putting the whole shebang together with your peers. Ask about local clubs at your favorite fabric shop, or log on to your favorite search engine, type in "quilt club" and the name of your town, and you may be surprised to find how many quilters are stitching away near you.

Got feet of clay? Throwing pots is addictive. It may not sound exciting at first, but wait until you put your hands on a damp mound of clay spinning on a wheel. It spins and hums and shapes into a pot beneath your palms like a living thing, and the results can be magnificent, even for beginners. Because pottery requires specialized tools—such as a wheel and a kiln—that aren't easily available to home users but are more readily found in classes or clubs, pottery can be a surprisingly social hobby as well as an immensely satisfying way to work with your hands. Visit your local community college or pottery shop and just ask, "Where can I learn this art?" and they'll be happy to guide you.

Make an heirloom. Woodworking creates instant family heirlooms, whether it's an inlaid tabletop or a plain wooden spoon. Develop your woodworking skills with classes at community colleges, or ask at your local lumberyard if there are any woodworkers' groups you can join. Woodworkers are a passionate bunch, eager to share knowledge, and the only thing they like more than creating beautiful items with wood is talking about the process and showing off their handiwork. There are also a lot of community Web sites where you can get advice and learn advanced techniques, such as www.woodweb.com.

Did You Know?

The Statue of Liberty–Ellis Island Foundation, in partnership with the National Park Service, not only preserved and restored the Statue of Liberty and Ellis Island, the main entry port for millions of immigrants to the United States, but also created the American Family Immigration History Center. This is a terrific place to visit if you're in New York and go to Ellis Island, but you don't have to make a trip to get the records of your forebears who may have passed through Ellis Island when they first came to America. On the Web, at www.ellisisland.org, you can search millions of passenger records for free to find your own ancestors who made the brave journey from their home countries. If you're looking to find out how you came to be who you are today, Ellis Island may be the place to begin. And make sure to ask for that senior discount when you visit!

Sew fabulous! If you've got a way with a needle, you can turn your hand to many crafts, besides quilting, embroidery, and needlepoint. You can also make stunning baby clothes, napkins, and pillowcases, and decorative tablecloths, towels, and runners that will be treasured by you and your family for years. Ask at your local fabric shop or community center about

Ka-Ching!
Saving at the Craft Store

Retailers of crafts and hobby supplies are less inclined to offer discounts to seniors because seniors make up a big part of their customer base in the first place. Jo-Ann Fabric and Craft Stores, for example, one of the largest chains of fabric and craft material in the United States, no longer offers a senior discount. (They do, however, offer special preferred customer coupons for patrons of any age, so be sure to ask at your nearest Jo-Ann's.) You're more likely to find a senior discount at your little local mom-and-pop fabric store, where the service tends to be more personal and the management is more concerned with the needs and opinions of the customers. If you're an avid crafter and a discount is not readily apparent, try this:

1. **Patronize a smaller craft or hobby shop** instead of a major national chain. If the owner or manager is the person ringing you up, that person also has the power to give you your own personal senior discount on the spot.

2. **Ask for a senior discount**—or ask why there isn't one! Some fabric and quilting shops, for example, may offer 10 percent off for seniors on Tuesday mornings or another day, but they may not post a sign to that effect. When the cashier is ringing up your fat quarters and roll of batting, say, "Do you have any senior discounts?" You might pay full price for that particular transaction, but you can come back on Tuesday if you need more supplies.

3. **Buy it online.** If you need a regular source of materials, whether you make stained glass or homemade paper, or build wooden ships or birdhouses, you can compare prices and probably find it cheaper online—including shipping.

If you *don't* happen to live near Red Bank, New Jersey, the site of Hobbymasters, which bills itself as the oldest and largest hobby store in the United States, you can still access it for orders online and receive its senior discount of 20 percent—far more generous than most craft stores! Visit www.hobbymasters.com or call 1-877-MR-HOBBY.

classes and sewing groups, and join up with experts to refine your art to its highest level. The Internet is also a rich resource for the needle arts, from free patterns and designs to contacts with other needle workers in your area.

Plant your family tree. Just because your children or grandchildren haven't asked doesn't mean that they don't want to know about their family history. We all like to know where we came from, and it becomes all the more fascinating when you begin to uncover fun facts and details about your forebears. If you know a few basic facts about where your family came from, there are a number of places you can start searching for free, including www.genealogy.org and www.familysearch.org. You can also find downloadable trees to print out and share with your family members.

Low-Fuss, Low-Cost Gardening

Growing a garden these days has become more than the simple pleasure of working the soil. A vegetable or herb garden can make a significant difference to your food bill, and a package of perennial seeds will provide years of annual color! Early Bird gardeners in the know are attuned to tons of ways to do what they love without spending a fortune in seeds or plants, bending over in the hot sun, or canning for hours in the kitchen.

Plant in containers, eat what's fresh while it's fresh, and give away the rest—to your family, your neighbors, your church, or a local soup kitchen. A bag of seasonal homegrown veggies is a gift worth its weight in gold to a non-gardener. You can also plant other gardens that don't require you to find recipients.

Throw it in, watch it grow. Forget about pricey annuals, and, instead, plant what will give you years of pleasure. Two of our senior gardening experts agree that the bright blues and purples of Nepeta (otherwise known as catmint) and varying yellow hues of coreopsis make a garden pop in the most persnickety of soil conditions. The best news is that all you have to do is sprinkle the seeds along the ground before a light rain, and you'll have color for years, without fuss.

The Early Bird, no-maintenance lawn. Wait! Don't kill that moss that's creeping across your lawn. Dig up the grass nearby and let the moss grow instead. Moss gardening is a steadily growing trend, because it's lush, velvety, and beautiful to walk on and look at, and it requires absolutely no mowing. All it needs is shade, a bit of moisture, and, ideally, poor quality, acidic soil. The EPA estimates that the average suburban grassy lawn requires 10,000 gallons of water annually, while a moss lawn requires about 1 percent of that. Check out www.mossacres.com or call 1-866-GET-MOSS for tips on moss gardening and to buy a moss starter kit.

Herbs for a song, with parsley, sage, rosemary, and thyme. An herb garden doesn't require quite the same commitment level as a vegetable garden. You don't need to work the soil as deeply or tend the herbs as much. But the results are delightful, colorful, and fragrant. Many herbs, such as chives and cilantro, bloom with bright flowers as the growing season progresses. And what could be nicer than walking through your herb plants in the evening, trailing your hands across the leaves to release the fragrance of a rosemary bush, a bed of peppermint, a tangle of delicate thyme, or a bunch of basil? And whether you make pounds of pesto or dry some sage to enrich your Thanksgiving stuffing, an herb garden can enrich your life all year.

The No-Bend, Ouch-Free, Early Bird Garden

6 WAYS TO CULTIVATE WHAT YOU LOVE FROM AN UPRIGHT POSITION

Even if you love gardening, it's strenuous work. Our experts came up with the following six ways to grow great grub, herbs, and flowers without ever bending over.

1. Install window boxes on your front and back deck railings or sills, and plant everything from cherry tomatoes to baby carrots, radishes, herbs, and flowers (anything lightweight).

2. Invert a large planter and put another planter on top of it, at waist height, for visual design interest and elevation.

3. If you must sit, borrow a child's tricycle to wheel from one growing area to the next.

4. Sharpen and use your long-handed tools, like scuttle-hoes, rakes, and border shovels.

5. Extend the handles of your shorter tools by duct-taping them to full-length broom handles.

6. Cultivate easy-to-grow perennials immediately after a rain, when the ground is still workable. Rake up the soil to loosen it, sprinkle in perennial seeds, rake back the soil, and walk away.

Cultivate a cutting garden. If you've only ever bought flowers from a store, you may be surprised at how easy it can be to grow a "cutting garden" of flowers. Hardy brown-eyed Susans or Michaelmas daisies, bright zinnias or snapdragons can grow in a season and be ready to fill vases, bouquets, and photographs by midsummer. Heavy-headed peonies or heirloom roses may take a year or more to establish before they start to bloom, but once they get started, they'll bring you joy for seasons to come.

The (new) Victory Garden. When food prices are as high as an elephant's eye, it's time to grow some food! A vegetable garden isn't expensive to begin, but it does require a fair amount of effort. Get the grandkids to come help you turn the soil and break up the clumps, or, even better, see if you can find a helpful neighbor with a tiller. Once you've dug your plot, it's easy and inexpensive to grow many, many veggies from seed, from beans and squash to pumpkins and lettuce. Other plants, such as tomatoes, are often best grown from bedding plants. If you've never planted a garden before, give it a try—nothing tastes as sweet as a pea you grew yourself!

Find your inner Johnny Appleseed. There are plenty of fruit trees and plants that will produce in a year or two—and blueberries are high on that list. Blueberries are now grown commercially in 38 states, so you've got a good chance of living in a climate that will support these luscious little jewels. Invest in a couple of blueberry bushes at a local nursery, and you may find yourself making blueberry pancakes and muffins with your own supply before summer is out. You can also find apple, pear, and peach trees of medium size that will produce by the following season—just be sure to plant more than one for cross-pollination, and be sure to keep a close eye out for pests.

Early Bird Secret

Serious Sales on Fruit Plants and Trees

If you're serious about putting in a fruit garden, wait until the end of the season and buy all the plants you like at the local nursery, where they'll be going cheap. Ask for advice from the experts at the nursery on whether the plants can winter over in your climate zone when they're going in the ground so late in the growing season. Most plants can survive but may need special mulching or covering. And the upshot is that you'll have gotten a terrific deal on your garden, sometimes as much as 75 percent off!

Senior Perks at State and National Parks

America's great national parks are so senior-friendly that you might think the government has just been *waiting* for you to retire in order to welcome you with open arms into the park system! From free passes to special packages and discounts, the park services of the nation and of each state offer an enormous wealth of advice and assistance to Americans over 50. Get outdoors and enjoy your national parks—at greatly reduced rates, with lots of special benefits thrown in.

State parks have varying senior discounts from park to park and state to state, but below are some of the best deals around for getting into parks and enjoying amenities at the best possible rates!

Alabama State residents are eligible for discounts on a park-by-park basis. For more information, visit http://www.alapark.com.

Blue Springs State Park
2595 Hwy. 10
Clio, AL 36017
334-397-4875
$1 admission fee for those age 62 and older (normally $3 for adults)

Chewacla State Park
124 Shell Toomer Pkwy.
Auburn, AL 36830
334-887-5621
Seniors 62 years of age and older: $1 (normally $2 to $3 for adults)

Frank Jackson State Park
100 Jerry Adams Dr.
Opp, AL 36467
334-493-6988
Senior Citizens age 62 and older get in for 50 cents ($1 regular admission)

Lake Lurleen
13226 Lake Lurleen Rd.
Coker, AL 35452
205-339-1558
Seniors 62 years of age and older can enter for $1 ($3 regular admission)

Meaher
5200 Battleship Pkwy. E.
Spanish Fort, AL 36577
251-626-5529
Senior citizens age 62 and older get in for 50 cents ($1 regular admission)

Monte Sano
5105 Nolen Ave.
Huntsville, AL 35801
256-534-3757
Seniors 62 years of age and older: $1 (normally $2 to $3 for adults)

California's Early Bird Park Bargain

California offers to those 62 years of age or older a $1 discount for vehicle parking and a $2 discount for family camping in state-operated parks, year round. Its even better deal, however, is the Golden Bear Pass. It's available to anyone receiving Aid to the Aged, Blind, or Disabled, or to any person 62 years of age or older with income limitations, so an application with income verification is required. It provides free entrance to all parks.

There's also a Limited Golden Bear Pass for those 62 years of age or older, which costs $10 and provides free parking between Labor Day and Memorial Day. Contact:

California Department of Parks and Recreation
1416 Ninth St.
Sacramento, CA 95814
800-777-0369, 916-653-6995
www.parks.ca.gov

Colorado Aspen Leaf Pass. This $30 pass, for all Colorado residents 64 years or older, provides unlimited access to all Colorado State Parks for one year. It has the added bonus of 50 percent off camping, Sunday through Thursday, excluding holidays. Visit: www.parks.state.co.us.

Connecticut The Charter Oak Pass is free to any Connecticut resident age 65 and older. Free admittance is also provided for the Charter Oak pass holder when visiting Gillette Castle, Dinosaur or Fort Trumbull State Parks, or fishing at the Quinebaug Valley Hatchery, as well as free parking at these places. It can be obtained through the mail or in person. Visit: www.ct.gov.

Delaware Delaware residents 62 and older get free entrance to most parks with a $12 pass which can be ordered online at egov.dnrec.delaware.gov.

Florida Florida residents who are over 65 pay only half the camping fees at state parks. Silver Springs Park is not a state park, but it offers an annual Silver Pass to adults 55 and over for $44.99, with free admission and parking and VIP entry for concerts. The daily admission is $29.99.

Georgia Seniors 62 and older get half off the usual fee of $50 for the annual ParkPass or they can join the Friends of Georgia State Parks & Historic Sites, and get both the annual Park Pass and the Historic Site Pass for $30, a $15 savings. Visit: www.gastateparks.org.

Hawaii Seniors pay no fees for the state parks in Kauai, Oaho (except Diamond Head Monument), Maui, Molokai, or Hawaii.

Idaho Those 62 or older will receive 50 percent off camping fees within the following Idaho State Parks:

Dworshak, Heyburn, Winchester, Lake Cascade, Three Island Crossing, Bruneau Dunes, Bear Lake, Lake Walcott, Massacre Rocks. Discount is valid midweek on stays Monday through Thursday (excluding holidays).

Illinois Adults 62 or older who are state residents receive camping fee discounts, the amount depending on the site. Generally, Monday through Thursday campers receive 50 percent off the fee.

Indiana Just $18 gets you a Golden Hoosier Passport, when you're an Indiana resident at least 65 years of age. It admits the driver and passengers of noncommercial vehicles to state parks which charge a gate fee. Visit: www.in.gov.

Kansas Kansas resident seniors 65 and older pay half of the regular price, which can vary from park to park. Visit: www.kdwp.state.ks.us.

Kentucky Residents age 62 and older receive a 10 percent discount on camping and lodging fees with valid ID.

Louisiana Admission to state parks, historic sites, and preservation areas is free for all seniors age 62 and older, with these exceptions:

Hodges Gardens State Park
$4 for seniors (62 and older)
Rosedown Plantation SHS Fees
$8 per senior citizen (ages 62 and over)

Maine All citizens 65 and over receive free admission to parks for day use with proof of age. Visit: www.maine.gov.

Did You Know?

Maryland's Golden Age If you're 62 or older and a resident of Maryland, you can apply for a Golden Age Pass that's good for your lifetime. It allows free entry to all state parks as well as half off the fees for camping from Sunday through Thursday. The pass is available via application online or at any of the park offices, and proof of age is necessary. Once you've got it, you're ready to hit the trail! Visit: www.dnr.state.md.us.

Massachusetts The Massachusetts Senior Pass, which is for state residents 62 and older, allows free parking at state parks for the vehicle occupied by the pass holder. Visit: www.mass.gov.

Michigan Those 65 and older can get a permit for $6 that admits you free into all state parks, and a hunting or fishing license for $6 a year. Visit: www.michigan.gov.

Montana Residents age 62 and older receive free fishing and conservation licenses and pay reduced fees for hunting licences and camping. Visit: www.fwp.mt.gov.

Nevada Residents of Nevada for at least five years who are 65 and older pay $15 a year for a permit that provides entrance to all parks and use of camping and boat launch facilities. Visit: www.parks.nv.gov.

New Jersey Residents who are 62 or older can get free passes from Parks and Forestry Division, allowing free admission and parking at all state parks and historic sites. Visit: www.state.nj.us.

New York New York residents over 62 are allowed into all state parks for free except on holiday weekends. Visit: www.nysparks.com.

NO KIDDING?

The Golden Buckeye

Any Ohio residents with a driver's license or state ID automatically get their Golden Buckeye card mailed to them for their 60th birthday—and it's quite a gift. Accepted by more than 20,000 businesses in the state, it offers seniors in Ohio discounts on everything from food and prescriptions to entertainment and clothing. Among other things, Golden Buckeyes receive 50 percent off camping fees at all state parks from Sunday to Thursday, 10 percent off the rest of the week, and 10 percent off all cottage and lodge rates. Visit: www.goldenbuckeye.com.

Pennsylvania Adults 62 and older get $4.50 off the base campsite rate with valid ID. Visit: www.dcnr.state.pa.us.

Rhode Island If you're 65 or older and a resident, you're entitled to half off beach and golf fees. Visit: www.riparks.com.

South Carolina Those 65 and above receive 35 percent off entrance and amenity fees (for fishing, camping, golf, etc.), and residents of that age may buy a Palmetto Passport for $25, half the standard price, which is good for free admission for one year. Visit: www.southcarolinaparks.com.

Tennessee Resident seniors 62 and older receive varying discounts according to the park. Visit: www.state.tn.us.

Texas Residents 65 and older who meet certain eligibility requirements can receive a free Texas Parklands Passport which admits them to state parks for 50 percent off the usual price. Visit: www.tpwd.state.tx.us

Utah A $35 Utah Senior Adventure Pass is available online or by mail, allowing free day-use entrance to all state parks (a savings of $40 off the regular pass price) and $2 off camping fees. Visit: www.stateparks.utah.gov.

Vermont Residents 62 and older can buy a Green Mountain Passport from their town clerk for $2 that allows the holder free entrance into any state park. It is valid for the holder's lifetime. Visit: www.vtstateparks.com.

Early Bird Secret

Senior Pass to National Parks

If you're not yet 62, the America the Beautiful – National Parks and Federal Recreational Lands Pass is available for $80 and admits up to four adults and one noncommercial vehicle to any national park for one year. But if you're 62 and older, you can get the same pass for $10, and it's good for your lifetime! The Senior Pass admits three adults besides the pass holder, and children under 16 are free. The pass also provides 50 percent off many amenities requiring additional fees, such as camping, swimming, boating, and special interpretive exhibitions and tours (the 50 percent discount is not available at all parks). The pass must be purchased in person at a park, and you must show proof of age (your driver's license is just fine).

Virginia The Lifetime Naturally Yours Passport is available to residents age 62 and older for $110, allowing admission and parking for free at all state parks, but there are varying packages, such as the one for boaters, including launching fees, which includes lifetime launching fees and costs $314. Seniors may also buy annual passports for less, such as the one-year Passport Plus for $33. Visit: www.dcr.virginia.gov.

Washington Qualifying residents 62 and above can get a Senior Citizen Limited Income Pass for free, which offers half off camping and moorage fees. Visit: www.parks.wa.gov.

West Virginia Admission to all state parks is free to all users, but residents over 60 receive a Golden Mountaineer discount card, that entitles the holder to discounts at retail businesses all over the state, including camping fees at parks. Visit: www.wvstateparks.com.

Wisconsin Residents over 65 pay half-price for licenses and annual admission permits. Visit: www.dnr.state.wi.us.

Wildly Low Admissions to Zoos and Aquariums

And yes, it really is true! Zoos (and aquariums) are no longer the musty places they once were. In fact, they offer incredible learning and educational programs and opportunities to volunteer. The best part? They're not just for kids anymore. Check out the Early Bird savings at these worlds of wonder, and you'll become a regular.

Atlanta Zoo Adults 55 and older can get $10 off an annual membership card that allows express entry into the zoo for the cardholder and one other named beneficiary, with 10 percent off admission for all other friends and family. Visit: www.zooatlanta.org.

Brandywine Zoo (Wilmington, Delaware) Senior citizens pay half price, or $2, from October 1 to May 31, and pay $4 instead of $5 from June 1 to September 30. Visit: www.brandywinezoo.org.

Dallas Zoo Seniors age 65 and older are admitted for $9 instead of the regular admission price of $12. Visit: www.dallas-zoo.org.

Indianapolis Zoo Seniors 62 and older are admitted for $9.50, instead of the regular admission of $14.50. Visit: www.indyzoo.com

Monterey Bay Aquarium Seniors 65 and above get $2 off the standard admission of $27.95, and get free admission for two seniors with a senior membership for $50, all tax deductible, compared to the standard membership for $75. Visit: www.montereybayaquarium.org.

National Aquarium (Baltimore, Maryland) If you're over 60, you get $1 off the standard admission of $28.95. Visit: www.aqua.org.

Oakland Zoo The regular adult admission is $11, but seniors 55 and above get in for $7.50. Visit: www.oaklandzoo.org.

San Diego Zoo For $50, a Single Senior Membership entitles the holder to one year of unlimited admission to the Zoo, the Wild Animal Park and Skyfari Aerial tram, a $29 discount over the Individual memberships. Residency requirements apply. Visit: www.sandiegozoo.org.

Early Bird Secret

Become a FONZ!

Being a Friend of the National Zoo (FONZ) can have significant benefits whether or not you live near the nation's capital. Although the National Zoo is always free to everyone, the Senior Membership, for $40 annually (instead of $45 for an Individual Membership), also gives you free or discounted admission to 100 zoos around the United States. It also provides the following benefits, plus the knowledge that you're supporting the zoo in its mission of being a leader in conservation, research, and education:

• Free parking while visiting the zoo

• Up to twenty percent off at in National Zoo stores

• *Zoogoer* magazine and Wildlife Adventures newsletter

• Annual member event

• Discounts on tickets to popular zoo events

• Invitations to previews of new exhibits

Find out more at www.nationalzoo.si.edu, or call 202-633-3038.

Shedd Aquarium (Chicago, Illinois) Seniors 65 and up get in for $21.95, reduced from the usual $24.95 for the day admission Shedd Pass. Visit: www.sheddaquarium.org.

South Carolina Aquarium (Charleston Harbor) Seniors 62 and older get $1 off the adult $16.95 admission. A better deal, if you live in the vicinity, is the Grandparent membership level, which is $80 for two senior adults plus all grandchildren free, compared to the Family

membership of $90 for two adults with all children free.
Visit: www.scaquarium.org.

Scoring Savings on Spectator Sports

If you love to watch or play sports, you're a lucky Early Bird. While the cost of tickets and equipment continues to rise, there are great deals out there just for you. So step up to the plate, and swing for home!

Pro Ball for Less Dough

Ka-ching, indeed! Professional league sports have become unbelievably pricey. (They have to be to pay all those incredible salaries.) The fact is that going to watch a baseball game on a Saturday afternoon or a seeing a basketball team in all its tall glory used to be an entertainment within reach for regular joes, but these days you might have to take out a second mortgage to get courtside seats or sit somewhere other than the farthest part of the outfield—and that's before you've paid for parking, bought a T-shirt or pennant, or even had your first $6 soda and $8 hot dog! Still, there's nothing like the thrill of a live game. So what's a sports fan to do? As they say in the big leagues…punt!

Seniors Have a Ball at Big-League Games

The National Football League, National Hockey League, and National Basketball Association do *not* offer specific senior discounts, but some teams hold special senior days at specific games. The schedule changes each season, so you'll need to check specifically with your team. You can find your way to every team's season schedule and their ticket prices through each league's main Web portal:

www.nfl.com

www.nhl.com

www.nba.com

Take me out. Baseball is your best shot for a discounted game, if you insist on the major leagues. Senior discounts are not available to every game or every team in Major League Baseball, so it's important to check with your team. Many teams offer special senior citizen appreciation days, when the tickets are discounted, and there are special events, such as a "Senior Stroll the Bases Night." What's pretty constant is this: Baseball fans 60 and older can usually get half off of non-premium seat prices on certain days during the regular playing season. The days vary according to each team's schedule, but you can check your team's schedule at www.mlb.com.

Games That Are Less Pricey, but Just as Exciting

If the major leagues can't be bothered to offer you a special discount, you can leave the major players to their multimillion-dollar contracts and look around for other exciting and less expensive options to indulge your love of the game—any game. Local sports teams offer the best bet for the thrill of a roaring crowd without the chill of the roaring ticket prices.

Friday night lights. There's nothing like the drama of a hotly contested game between two local high school rivals, and many communities turn out in force to support their teams, whether they're related to the players or not. Sit in the bleachers like everyone else and wave a pennant for your favorite youngsters.

Conference me in. Check out your local college's prices on basketball and football games. If your team is in the top of the NCAA or a major conference, it might cost nearly as much as a professional team. But if your guys are mid-list, season tickets will bring all the excitement of live games—cheerleaders and marching band included!—for a fraction of the cost of the big leagues.

Watch the women. Women's sports have become very popular, but the ticket prices still aren't as high as those of the top men's teams. Even if you're bemoaning the injustice of it, buy a ticket to the big game—you can show your support *and* get a bargain on some serious sports.

Watch something new. Colleges and universities offer a wealth of sports to watch. Check out your local college's offerings and try something new—soccer, lacrosse, rugby, tennis, ice hockey, field hockey, or even snow boarding, if you live in northern climes. Check out a sport live that you've only ever seen while flipping through the TV channels on a Saturday afternoon. You may find you're a real rugby fan!

Take me out to the (minor league) ball game. Farm teams offer all the fun of an old-fashioned baseball game at a pittance. You'll have enough money left for hotdogs *and* popcorn *and* peanuts if you're sitting in the bleachers of your local baseball team—and you might see a star in the making, just waiting to be called up to the big leagues.

Special Offers for Sports Participants

Now we're talking! If you want to go sit and watch a major team, there aren't a lot of discounts. But if you want to get off your duff and actually *play*, there's a whole world of bargains and special offers to entice and welcome you into participating.

Old Folks on Spokes? That's how this Senior Cycling company bills itself, even though nothing could be further from the truth! It caters to cyclists 50 and above, and its tours are arranged according to difficulty level, from beginner to intermediate to advanced, so there's something to suit every rider, along with good food and a support van. Recent tours included Bike the Florida Keys, Bike the Great Allegheny Passage, and Bike the Erie Canal! Find out more at www.seniorcycling.com, or call 540-668-6307.

Elderhostel bike tours. This remarkable organization that also has educational, hiking, and travel programs counts among its many great activities the opportunity to tour with similarly minded senior cyclists all around the United States and Europe. Depending on the tour you choose, you'll pedal about 30 miles a day. Bikes are provided, along with all food and accommodations, and a support van to carry the luggage and you, if you can't go another mile. Visit www.elderhostel.org or call 1-800-454-5768.

Women on wheels. The average age of Woman Tour cyclists is 54 on shorter tours and 59 on longer cross-country tours. According to this organization, its oldest cyclist so far was 79. So you'll be in good company as a senior in this group specifically devoted to organizing bike trips for women. You can get a 5 percent discount if you're one of the first six to sign up for a tour, or a 10 percent discount on the second tour if you take two tours within 180 days. Bring a friend on her first trip with the group and you get 5 percent off your trip. Find details at www.womantours.com or call 1-800-247-1444.

Tennis, anyone? Joining the United States Tennis Association (USTA) for $40 a year allows you to participate in the many senior tournaments it organizes throughout the year and all around the country (often for an additional fee). Tournaments are broken up by age, and the Senior Division

Ka-Ching!

Batter Up, Peewee!

One of the best, cheapest, most thrilling, delightful, and true-blue American ways of enjoying the best in sports is going straight to where it starts—the peewee leagues. Yes, Little League is right up there with the big league for excitement. Not only do you get to watch and cheer for kids who are proud as punch to be out there on a Saturday afternoon with the promise of sliding into home, but you get to watch future champs in the making, for free. Gather up a few friends and neighbors, bring some lawn chairs and a tube or two of sunscreen, pack a cooler with some homemade sandwiches, and make a day of it. It'll cost pennies. Our experts made a list of the top 10 items to bring to a Little League game to keep the costs down and the pleasure up:

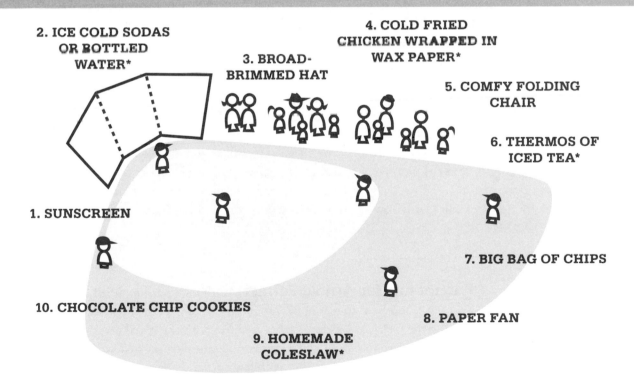

2. ICE COLD SODAS OR BOTTLED WATER*

3. BROAD-BRIMMED HAT

4. COLD FRIED CHICKEN WRAPPED IN WAX PAPER*

5. COMFY FOLDING CHAIR

6. THERMOS OF ICED TEA*

1. SUNSCREEN

7. BIG BAG OF CHIPS

10. CHOCOLATE CHIP COOKIES

8. PAPER FAN

9. HOMEMADE COLESLAW*

These are traditional. Pack them on ice in a cooler, and make sure they stay cold until consumed.

includes women's tournaments for players 85 and above, while the men's group has tournaments for those older than 90. Tennis is truly a lifelong sport! You also get discounts on tennis supplies, tennis camps, and tennis resorts. Visit www.usta.com or call membership services at 1-800-990-USTA (8782).

Squash: more than just a vegetable. Aficionados promise that, despite its fast pace and highly competitive nature, squash—traditionally known as squash racquets—is the game of a lifetime. This means that once you're hooked (one of our experts is a die-hard fan), you'll play for life. The United States Squash Racquets Association (USSRA) holds many age-appropriate competitions all over the country, on both public and private courts. Most universities have at least a few public courts on the premises, and a simple call to the team coach is a great way to get in the door. For more information, visit www.ussquash.com.

Early Bird Secret

There's Gold in Senior Golf

The National Senior Golf Association is the original and oldest provider of amateur golf events in the United States, and it exists to make the game as pleasant, enjoyable, and accessible as possible to seniors.

The organization defines senior as 50 and up, but it welcomes any age members, although only those over 50 can win awards at its tournaments. Membership costs $35 a year, and a new membership brings with it a $50 gift certificate for use at a Senior Golf event.

Membership provides access to its senior tournaments at golf courses around the United States and the world and assistance in booking reduced-rate travel, as well as discounts on computerized golf club fitting or a discounted rate on shipping your clubs ahead of you to any course around the world. Visit www.nsgatour.com or call 1- 800-282-6772.

It's not just for Arnold Palmer. With membership billed at just over $4 a month for singles or $7 a month for a couple, the benefits of owning the Golf Card includes free green fees with the rental of a power golf cart for two rounds of golf a year at 600 participating golf courses. You also get up to 50 percent off the combined cart and green fee for two rounds per year at an additional 2,400 courses, as well as savings at Stay and Play resorts, chances to test products, discounts on car rentals, and free copies of *Golf Traveler* magazine. Find out details at www.golfcard.com or call 1-800-321-8269.

Walking the world over. Walking the World is a group for walkers 50 and older who take trips from 10 to 14 days through different regions. Upcoming walks include Costa Rica, Utah, and the wild outback of New Zealand. For details, visit www.walkingtheworld.com or call 970-498-0500.

Lace on those trekking shoes. If you want adventure on your walk, look no further. ElderTreks specializes in the far-flung for those over 50, whether it's hiking the Silk Road through Pakistan, exploring Mongolia on camelback, or hiking to the stunning ruins of Angkor Wat. Visit www.eldertreks.com or call 1-800-741-7956.

Hiking with America's mountaineers. The Appalachian Mountain Club, America's most famous hiking organization, runs a number of programs specifically for those 50 and above. Recent offerings include moderate hikes of three to six miles to examine the June flowers in bloom along the Appalachians, as well as five-day trips to Adventure Camps, which include hikes to special huts deep within the mountain range. Find details at www.outdoors.org or call 617-523-0655.

Move Over, Mark Spitz

The National Senior Games Association is the umbrella group overseeing all the individual states that host Senior Olympics, for competitors 50 and above, and it hosts the National Senior Games, which take place every year ending in an odd number (2011, 2013, etc.) in the fields of archery, badminton, basketball, bowling, cycling, golf, horseshoes, race walk, racquetball, road race, shuffleboard, softball, swimming, table tennis, tennis, track and field, triathlon, and volleyball. You must qualify at the state or local level competition, held in even years (2010, 2012, etc.) to take part in the national competition. For more information on Senior Games held in your state, check out the Web site at www.nsga.com.

Ski (and more) with The Over the Hill Gang. Founded as a ski club, this group for adventurous and hardy seniors over 50 has expanded into learning golf in Arizona, biking in Europe, treking coast-to-coast in Costa Rica and sailing in Turkey. And its skiing options include St. Moritz, British Columbia and Spain. The Over the Hill Gang International does not run vacations for folks who mostly want to put their feet up! But if you crave the powder or the call of the wild, these are your guys. Membership is $60 a year, and that gives you discounts on lift tickets at 100 ski areas in the United States and Canada. Visit www.othgi.com or call 719-389-0022.

Going Back to School Without Going Broke

Learning keeps your brain active and keeps you young! Colleges and universities welcome seniors back into their hallowed halls because mature students bring a lot to the party when it comes to learning and classroom discussion. Nearly every college and university has a continuing education program that allows seniors to attend classes for credit or to audit them for no credit. State schools are a wonderful place to start if you're looking for low-priced classes; some states have particularly good programs that offer seniors free tuition. Even if you don't see your state in the list below, it's worthwhile to contact your closest state-funded university or college and ask about its requirements for senior students. The university may offer you a deal even if it's not mandated by the state legislature, as it is in most of the cases below.

Alabama The Alabama Commission on Higher Education has a free tuition program for any resident 60 or older who meets the requirements to attend any two-year post-secondary educational institution.

Audits Can Be Fun!

To audit a class means literally to "listen" to it, rather than taking the class for credit. Auditing doesn't mean that you only have to sit and listen, however. You can take part in the class just like any other student. The difference is that you're there merely to enjoy and educate yourself, and auditors don't have to do the homework, write the papers, or take the tests (although some professors may allow you to do so if you wish).

Alaska Any resident eligible to receive full Social Security retirement benefits has been able to attend state-funded colleges for free, but the recent leap in oil prices and the financial instability of the Alaska state college system has led officials to temporarily halve the waiver.

Arkansas Residents of Arkansas 60 and older may attend Arkansas State University for credit and for free. All tuition is waived.

Colorado Residents 60 and older may enroll tuition-free at UC-Denver on a no-credit audit basis.

Connecticut Citizens 62 and older may attend any public university or college in Connecticut for free.

Delaware Residents of Delaware 60 and above may attend the University of Delaware for credit tuition-free.

Hawaii The University of Hawaii-Mānoa has a Senior Citizen Visitor Program that allows senior citizens to audit classes for free, but those wishing to attend for credit must pay full tuition.

Indiana Purdue University waives tuition for Indiana residents 60 and older taking undergraduate courses.

Kansas Wichita State allows residents 60 and above to audit courses without tuition.

Kentucky The University of Louisville waives tuition for residents of the state who are 65 and older.

Maine Residents 65 and older for whom tuition would be a financial hardship may apply to have their tuition waived at any University of Maine campus.

Did You Know?

Even if you can't go back to school for free, you *can* go back to school near you with the Osher Lifelong Learning Institute (OLLI, formerly Learning in Retirement), designed specifically for seniors. The Bernard Osher Foundation was founded in 1977 to support higher education, and the foundation now supports senior learning programs on 115 campuses across the United States, at universities such as Harvard, Penn State, and the University of Southern Maine, which hosts the OLLI program's National Resource Center. Contact the center or surf its comprehensive Web site (www.osher.net) to find an OLLI program at a college or university near you. You may also call 207-780-4128 or write:

OLLI National Resource Center
University of Southern Maine
PO Box 9300
Portland, ME 04104-9300

Ka-Ching!

There are heaps of free and inexpensive courses available on the Internet. If you want to go back to school in the privacy of your own home, give it a whirl!

FREE ED!

A site wholly devoted to education for education's sake, this site provides courses in a huge range of topics, all entirely free. The upside is that you can range as far and wide as you like, never even completing a course if you find you prefer a different one. You don't have to register, you don't have to do homework, and you don't get a grade. The downside is that you won't have a live teacher or fellow students with whom to discuss anything. But if you want to travel widely in the realm of self-education, this site is waiting with open arms. Get going at www.free-ed.net.

SENIOR SUMMER SCHOOL PART I

Travel programs with a strong educational bent are the focus of Senior Summer School, which takes place on campuses and at universities across the United States, allowing seniors to immerse themselves in the local culture with tours and events in different cities. Enjoy Burlington, Vermont, from the base of St. Michael's College, or get to know America's heartland at University of Wisconsin-Madison. Find out more at www.seniorsummerschool.com or call 1-800-847-2466.

Online Higher Learning

SENIOR SUMMER SCHOOL PART II

The online part of the Senior Summer School program is made up of courses from a number of schools, generally in a six-week online class and offering a wide range of topics, from art history and accounting to math, marketing, and Web design. The online courses are complete with class (online) discussions, quizzes, and final exams—and all for $99 a class. Sign up at www.ed2go.com/ssschool.

OPEN CULTURE

At www.oculture.com, you'll find a site that is essentially one-stop shopping for continuing education, from podcasts of lectures and courses at great universities around the world to thought-provoking essays and videos. Nearly all the content is free, but it also points you to sites such as www.extension.harvard. edu where you can register for online courses at Harvard for a fraction of the usual cost.

MIT

The Internet offers some amazing things, but it's really remarkable that it will let you take classes at the Massachusetts Institute of Technology for *free*—in any subject that interests you. Go to http://ocw.mit.edu, find a subject, and you can either read the course or download some mp3 files of lectures and listen to them just like any student sitting in the lecture hall. Many of the courses also include class notes to help you catch up, along with lists of the course reading.

Massachusetts State residents who are 60 and older may register tuition-free for credit courses any of the state-funded colleges or universities.

Missouri Residents 65 and older are exempt from tuition at Missouri state schools.

Montana State residents 65 and above may have their tuition waived at any publicly funded Montana college.

Nevada Students 62 and older who are state residents may register for courses at the University of Nevada-Reno without paying per-credit registration fees.

New Hampshire Residents 65 or older who are not enrolled in a degree program may take two for-credit courses per academic year tuition-free.

New Jersey Rutgers allows residents 62 and older to audit courses without paying tuition on its Camden, Newark, and New Brunswick campuses in the spring and fall only.

Did you know?

Wisdom Wins the Race! Recent studies have shown that our brains take in information differently from those of younger people. One study found that young people in a test group could all plow quickly through a text, ignoring the words or concepts that they didn't understand, and could parrot back the major ideas with speed. Thus young people appear, superficially, to be getting the ideas faster and more easily. The older people in the study group, faced with the same material, worked far more slowly, stopping to take in, understand, and fully integrate any unfamiliar concepts and words. Researchers concluded that this phenomenon might actually be the visible sign of...wisdom. Only age can bring that level of concentration and understanding, so never think that a return trip—or a first-time visit—to school won't be worth your while!

New Mexico Each public, post-secondary, degree-granting institution in New Mexico may only charge senior citizens $5 per credit hour, on request by the student.

North Carolina The Senior Student Tuition Waiver allows North Carolina residents 65 and older to attend classes for credit (or take online courses for credit) at all North Carolina public universities and state community colleges for free.

Ohio Residents 60 and above can take classes for free at Ohio State University.

South Carolina Senior citizens 60 and above may enroll at the University of South Carolina-Beaufort for free, provided they wait to register until the third day of class. (Registering prior to that will incur the usual tuition.)

Texas Any Texas resident 65 or older may audit classes at any publicly funded university or college for free. Residents 55 to 64 may attend classes at a reduced tuition.

Utah State residents 62 or older can audit any University of Utah class numbered 1000 or above for $25 per semester.

Virginia Any resident age 60 or older may audit any class in any publicly funded Virginia college or university for free. You are only guaranteed free classes for credit if you made less than $15,000 the previous year.

Volunteering for a Cause

Volunteering during your retirement may turn out to be the most rewarding work that you have ever done. Senior volunteers are always in great demand because they bring a lifetime of wisdom and experience to every project they undertake, and that's an immense benefit for everyone involved. Because of this, there are dozens of organizations coordinating senior volunteering on a national level, as well as state and local organizations, that can help pair you with the volunteer work that best suits your needs in terms of interest, time, and expertise.

Although many seniors have the time and energy to volunteer, a lot of them don't do it simply because *nobody asks them*! If you don't know that you're wanted, it can be intimidating to go look for a volunteer position. Most volunteers age 55 and older find their volunteer positions through their church or religious institution because they attend on a weekly basis and the opportunities arise. Many, many nonprofit and charitable organizations are eager for your assistance but don't know how to reach you, so you can be sure that you'll be received with open arms.

Ka-Ching!

Take a Vacation with the National Trust

The *British* National Trust, that is, an organization overseeing the cultural heritage of the United Kingdom. It offers "Working Holidays," many specifically limited to volunteers ages 40 and older, which allow you to live and work for a few days or a week on the grounds of one of its national historic houses or estates. It's like getting a dream vacation for nearly nothing: You pay a minor fee, about $150 a week, for food and accommodation, which might be austere hostel-style dormitories, but, then again, might be an extremely comfortable gardener's cottage on a grand estate. Each working vacation group usually includes about a dozen volunteers, and in the evenings, the volunteers prepare dinner together.

You can choose your working holiday at the National Trust's Web site by selecting the region of the United Kingdom you wish to visit and the approximate dates you're available, and the site will offer you a selection of possible holidays. Some recent offerings included:

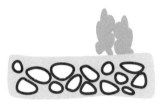

Repairing dry stone walls and upgrading Lakeshore paths for wheelchair access in the countryside around Wasdale.

Managing woodlands and wildlife habitats on the banks of the Menai Straits as you earn your John Muir award.

Learning tree identification while you help wardens run the countryside education program for local primary schools.

Each Working Holiday tends to fill up quickly, so you may have to plan far ahead. But for the price of a plane ticket and a little hard work, you can have an extremely inexpensive holiday and a truly unique experience. To find out more, go to www.nationaltrust.org.uk (click on "Get Involved with the National Trust").

The American branch of the National Trust is called The Royal Oak Foundation, at www.royal-oak.org, and you can join from the United States. Membership gives you free admission to all the properties of the National Trust, which you can visit when you're done with your Working Holiday!

National and International Volunteer Organizations

Many venerable institutions such as the Peace Corps and Senior Corps exist to help match knowledge with service, but there are also plenty of places that exist for the sole purpose of pairing you up with the right opportunity. If you don't find what you want at one place, check another. Positions, openings, and opportunities change frequently, so search around to find the one that suits you.

Peace, baby! Interesting enough, you can still, all these years after Camelot, answer President Kennedy's call to service and join the Peace Corps, which defines "Older Americans" as anyone age 50 and beyond (there is no upper age limit for Peace Corps volunteers). Couples must apply separately and each qualify as a volunteer, but once that happens, there are joint postings for couples at Peace Corps sites around the world. Forget traveling in an RV—if you want *real* adventure, learn to speak Swahili under the Peace Corps' auspices and go teach schoolchildren at a remote outpost in Kenya!

Even if you feel a bit less adventurous than that, there are countless opportunities all around you for volunteering.

Peace Corps
Paul D. Coverdell Peace Corps Headquarters
1111 20th St., NW
Washington, DC 20526
1-800-424-8580
www.peacecorps.gov

Corpsman, Corpsman! The Senior Corps is an independent federal agency dating back to 1965, when the Foster Grandparent program was founded to help seniors with limited incomes give something back to their communities. It was so quickly successful that it expanded into the three main parts of the organization that are still active today:

- Foster Grandparents, which hooks up volunteers age 60-plus with children who need the stabilizing influence of older adults;
- Senior Companions, which lets volunteers age 60-plus assist older adults with daily activities; and
- RSVP, a volunteering clearinghouse with a wealth of opportunities for community and local work available to Americans age 55 and over.

Senior Corps
1201 New York Ave., NW
Washington, DC 20525
1-800-424-8867
www.seniorcorps.org

He ain't heavy; he's my (little) brother! For as little as four hours a month (or as much more time as you have), the Big Brothers Big Sister program can make a huge difference in the life of a child who may have a home environment that's less than ideal. This program involves pairing you with a child in your area and allowing you to get to know that child and spend some quality time with him or her. Whether you go to a baseball game or have a picnic in the park, the benefits are incalculable.

Big Brothers Big Sisters National Office
230 N. 13th St.
Philadelphia, PA 19107
215-567-7000
www.bbbs.org

Did You Know?

Senior Environmental Employment Program A program of the Environmental Protection Agency (EPA), the Senior Environmental Employment (SEE) Program is a unique setup that pairs retired Americans with EPA labs and regional EPA offices around the country. Once there, generally on a short-term stipend or contract, they bring their specialized skills to bear on environmental issues. The SEE Program is for retirees age 55 and above, and mostly requires professional qualifications for participation (engineers, scientists, accountants, grant writers, technicians), but if you have a profound interest in working on environmental issues, some of the work is clerical and requires only your passionate interest rather than your lifetime of professional experience. Contact the SEE Program or check out its Web site to see if it's right for you.

SEE Program
U.S. Environmental Protection Agency
1200 Pennsylvania Ave., NW, MC: 3605A
Washington, DC 20460
202-564-0420
www.epa.gov/epahrist/see/brochure/backgr.htm

If you build it... Don't think that volunteering for Habitat for Humanity will require you to cart around wheelbarrows full of bricks. There are many volunteering jobs with Habitat that don't require physical labor—but if you would like to build, or just wield a paintbrush, Habitat is happy to teach you how. Check out its program called Women Build, which teaches women the skills they need to go out safely on a job site. Call 1-800-422-4828 (1-800-HABITAT) or visit the Web site at www.habitat.org.

Smokey says...join the National Park Service. If you're fortunate enough to live near a national park—and many of us do, even in urban areas—you can volunteer to do practically anything. The parks are frequently in need of help in a huge variety of ways, from excavation and construction to making an inventory of plant life. The National Park Service has a wonderful Web site that lets you find your closest park and all the upcoming events requiring volunteers, with the specific contact information for each event. Visit www.nps.gov (click on "Get Involved").

Early Bird Secret

Start Close to Home

When you're considering what kind of volunteer work you want to do and where, it can help to think local before you think national (or international!). While major programs that involve travel with the Peace Corps or Habitat for Humanity can be exciting, it can be just as rewarding—and a lot less tiring—to do lower-key but equally vital volunteer work in your own community or neighborhood. Consider places such as these in your own town:

• Schools, colleges, youth groups, sports teams, preschools, day-care centers, after-school programs

• Retirement and assisted-living communities, Meals on Wheels, church- or community-sponsored soup kitchens, Neighborhood Watch organizations

• Prisons, halfway houses, drug rehab centers, shelters for the homeless or battered women and children

• Community theaters, bands, choirs, orchestras, dance troupes, art museums, civic clubs

• Local parks, monuments, battlefields, historical homes and markers

Assistance with Volunteer Opportunities and Placements

If you're not sure where you want to volunteer or what exactly you want to do, you'll find a huge range of ideas and opportunities from these organizations.

Experience Corps Experience Corps is specifically designed to utilize the talents and accumulated knowledge of Americans over the age of 55. It currently has branches in 19 major cities across the country. Check out its Web site at www.experiencecorps.org to see if there's an Experience Corps opportunity near you.

Network for Good If you don't have a lot of time for volunteer work but still want to be involved in assisting charities and the needy, Network for Good can help you, with a few simple clicks, direct your money to places where it will be put to work for you. The network vets the organizations and charities that they help benefit to be sure that your funding is getting into the right hands, and they also provide a network of places where you can actively volunteer, not to mention a useful list of questions to ask yourself when considering volunteer work.

Network for Good
7920 Norfolk Ave., Ste. 520
Bethesda, MD 20814
1-888-284-7978
www.networkforgood.org

Volunteer Match This is another clearinghouse to put people together with the best volunteering positions for their skills and talents. At its Web site, you can type in your location and a keyword of what interests you, such as "health care" or "children in need," and it will search opportunities for you from its database of more than 60,000 non-profit organizations.

VolunteerMatch
717 California St., Second Floor
San Francisco, CA 94108
415-241-6868
www.volunteermatch.org

1-800-Volunteer.org This is a national database organized by the Points of Light Foundation that allows users to search, in English or Spanish, for volunteer opportunities all over the United States. The site works in partnership with more than 75,000 organizations across the country. To use the site, you must first register for a free account, and then access to all information is free. Visit www.1-800-volunteer.org or call 1-800-VOLUNTEER (865-8683).

6

Keeping Cultured

Amazing Ways to Go Out on the Town—on a Shoestring

Big Savings at the Big Screen

The price of movie tickets has been climbing steadily since the first silent movie thrilled the public more than 100 years ago, and don't we feel it! In New York and Los Angeles, movie tickets are headed for $12—and that's evenings *and* matinee. If you live anywhere in between, you've got a much better shot at saving a little money for some scrumptious popcorn. In addition to a rundown of the standard senior discounts at the major cinema chains, here are some cinema-tastic tactics that will fulfill your craving for the silver screen. Are you ready for *your* close-up? We thought so!

Always on a Tuesday (never on a Sunday). It might be because it follows one of the busiest days of the work week (when most folks just want to head home), but Tuesday nights are notoriously slow movie nights——so slow, in fact, that many theater chains slash their ticket prices by 20 to 50 percent. Call your local theater to make sure it's on board, and if not, ask why. Inquiring minds generally get favorable responses.

(Never say never.) Sometimes on a Sunday. Three cheers all around for that great American institution, the Sunday matinee. Tickets are usually 30 to 40 percent lower than at other times, and if you get a senior discount, you may be entitled to even more off the discount.

Be artsy. Independent theaters—the ones that show foreign and short-run films—generally price their tickets 10 to 15 percent lower than chain theaters. Why? Independent theaters are usually smaller, as are their audiences, so it's important to them to draw more viewers.

Early Bird Secret

Free Movie Passes Online

A number of Web sites offer access to free movie screenings. Some of the showings are promotions by the studios hoping to stir up advance buzz; others are actual passes you can print out and take to the cinema with you; and some are discounted tickets (although the discount rarely reaches higher than the 35 percent you may already get on a senior ticket). Some sites also allow you to purchase packs of tickets at a reduced fee, which is generally lower than the senior price. Visit these sites to find bargains: www.iscreenings.com, www.freemoviescreening.net, and www.wildaboutmovies.com.

Use your rank. Are you active-duty military personnel? If so, you can gain entry to all National Amusements theaters for $7 (general admission) or $5 (during matinees).

Be a star! Many theater chains, like National Amusements (in Connecticut, California, Iowa, Kentucky, Massachusetts, Michigan, New Jersey, New York, Ohio, Pennsylvania, Rhode Island, Virginia, and as a far away as Wales, Russia, and Argentina) offer special rewards programs that result in free tickets, free snacks, and more. The StarPass Membership (http://www.nationalamusements.com/programs/star_pass.asp) is free. Each time you make a purchase at a participating theater, you will earn 10 credits on the dollar, redeemable for tickets and much more.

Enjoy the classics. If you love the best of the silver screen (from the 1930s to the 1980s), you may be in luck. Many theaters show classics during off hours (usually in the early afternoon), at a deep, deep discount. One of our experts in New York discovered a Long Island-based program called Silver Screen Classics, for which the price of admission is $2 per ticket.

Lights, camera.... Some of us who would never ask for a senior discount anywhere else are thrilled to get one at the movies. Maybe that's because the movies tend to post the discount price clearly, up high, behind the cash register—why can't everyone else do that? In any case, there's nothing better than sitting in the cinema, enjoying your popcorn, with the knowledge that *your* ticket came at a discount, often as much as 35 percent off. Actual discounts vary all over the country, as do base ticket prices, and the age restriction may vary as well, but this is the general rundown of senior discounts at a sampling of the major movie chains.

- AMC Loews: Senior discount for ages 60 and older (62 at some locations).
- Carmike: Seniors age 55 and above get a discount.
- Clearview: Ages 62 and above get a senior discount.
- Imax: Discount for ages 65 and above.
- Regal: Seniors age 60 and above get a discount.

Theater Discounts On, Off, and *Way Off* Broadway!

Think that you can't afford the luxury of live theatrical performances? Guess again! We discovered that actors don't like empty seats, but more important, neither do producers and theater owners. The result? There are heaps of special discounts to help fill the house when it comes to showtime. You won't find actual senior discounts to a Broadway or West End of London show, but there are plenty of other ways around paying full price. (And that's a good thing, because box-office ticket prices for top Broadway shows can run as high as $200.)

Make friends with Craig. Craig's List, that is! Go online to www.craigslist.org and search in New York, Boston, Chicago, and Los Angeles for half-price tickets. Make sure you proceed with caution, and verify the tickets are legit. Most are fine, as people whose schedules have changed offer them as a way of trying to make up their losses.

Taking stock. If a trip to a big city isn't in your future, don't forget about regional theater and summer stock. Many plays headed for Broadway travel to one of the country's 1,800 regional theaters for tryouts. Ticket prices are much less than they will be once they hit the big time. According to *Time Magazine*, the five best regional theaters in the country are: Goodman Theatre, Chicago, Illinois; Oregon Shakespeare Festival, Ashland, Oregon; American Repertory Theatre, Cambridge, Massachusetts; Guthrie Theater, Minneapolis, Minnesota; and South Coast Repertory, Costa Mesa, California.

TKTS, get your TKTS. Why do people line up in all weather at the Times Square branch of TKTS in New York City? Because it's the place to get same-day tickets to nearly everything on Broadway for 50 percent off. The Times Square location of the Theater Development Fund's ticket booth opens at 3 p.m., and the long, twisting rope of a line starts to form hours before that. You can generally get anywhere from 20 to 50 percent off nearly everything on the Great White Way, and on lots of other shows around the city. TKTS is cash only, and there's a small handling fee of about $4.00 per ticket, but it's worth it for the major savings. Visit www.tdf.org/tkts for more information.

The Early Bird Who Heads South Gets First Crack at Bargain Tickets

If you're visiting Manhattan, skip the lines in Times Square for the TKTS booth and hop on a subway to the South Street Seaport TKTS booth. This one opens at 11 a.m., and the lines tend to be much shorter and faster-moving—it's where the locals go to buy tickets. If you're in Brooklyn, you can also take advantage of the recently opened Brooklyn branch. The outlying branches are selling the same tickets at the same discounts, but without the staggeringly long lines. You can get to South Street Seaport, buy your tickets, have lunch, even, and be back uptown before the Times Square branch even opens!

Visiting London? The best way to score half-price tickets is to check out the British version of New York's TKTS. In London it's known as tkts, and the kiosk is in Leicester Square. You must turn up in person and have an open mind—there's no telling what plays or musicals will be available. Popular shows that are sold out in advance are likely unavailable.

Get online, wherever you live. Wherever you live in this country, virtually every metropolitan area and university town offers great theater for less. While you may not be able to find a TKTS booth for half-price tickets, you can find similar bargains by logging onto the Internet and going straight to TheaterMania.com. This site lets you buy tickets in advance at up to 40 percent off for plays in New York, Boston, Chicago, Dallas/Ft. Worth, Washington, D.C., Las Vegas, Los Angeles, Philadelphia, San Francisco, and more. Registration is required but free, and there are special sections and discounts on shows specifically for children, if you're trying to introduce young grandkids to a love of the theater. Visit www.theatermania.com for more information.

To be or not to be...free! More than 400 years after the great Bard sharpened his quill, Shakespeare would be delighted to know that we can all enjoy his plays for free. Many metropolitan areas have theaters that offer free Shakespeare in the summer, not least in Central Park, where New Yorkers in the know wait in line to get free tickets to world-class productions at the Delacorte Theater, some of which later even transfer to Broadway. Many smaller communities offer free Shakespeare, usually in the summer. If you don't live near one of these places, check your own arts pages to see if there are any upcoming performances.

Boston, Massachusetts: www.citicenter.org
Cleveland, Ohio: www.cleveshakes.org
Louisville, Kentucky: www.kyshakes.org
New York, New York: www.publictheater.org
San Francisco, California: www.sfshakes.org

Take it play by play, and fill a seat. Apply for membership to the private organization Play by Play, which helps to fill seats that might otherwise go empty, and you can see top Broadway shows for $4.00 a ticket! There's an online membership fee of $99 a year, as well as an $8 processing fee, and you must apply by phone. Once you've been accepted as a member you can find out what shows are available online, choose one, and reserve two tickets for it—for $4.00 each. For your annual fee and the per-ticket fee, you can see as many shows as you can possibly sit through. The rules are clearly defined, if strict, but the benefits are nothing short of fantastic. If you live anywhere near New York City, it's the sweetest ticket deal imaginable. Visit www.play-by-play.com or call 212-868-7052 (phone membership is $125, plus $8 processing fee).

Usher in great savings. If you love theater, volunteer to be an usher and odds are you'll get to see every play you work for free. Even if you truly love the lights of Broadway and you live in New York City, you can be an usher and see all the shows you like, while helping patrons get seated and get their Playbills. The task is not onerous, and usually these positions are filled by theater-loving seniors. This is not an option for visitors since there's a certain commitment level expected of volunteers. If you're interested, inquire at the theater where your favorite show is playing, and ask for details on how to volunteer.

Attend a festival. A great way to see upcoming world-class plays while they're still at bargain-basement prices is the Summer Play Festival at the Public Theater in New York City. The Public's festival, which runs throughout July, offers cutting edge new drama for the rock-bottom price of $10 per play. Check out this year's offerings at its Web site. If you miss the thrill of live theater in your hometown, $10 a show might just lure you to NYC! Note: The SPF is on hiatus in 2010 but plans to return to the Public Theater in 2011. Visit www.spfnyc.com for more information.

Go back to school. If you live in or near a university town, you're in luck. Some of the best, most enthusiastic young actors and actresses take part in university theater, often with the help of one special star who shows up to draw the crowd. University theater companies also usually offer a senior discount as well, so make sure to flash that driver's license!

Stage your own play. Want to be on the other side of the stage? ArtAge's Senior Theatre Resource Center helps seniors fulfill their theatrical aspirations with a big selection of plays; all the tips and advice you could ever need to stage a play, including help with production design, publicity, and marketing; and even professional consulting on how to write a grant proposal if, for example, you are looking for funding from your arts council to aid with a local production. Some productions take place in retirement homes and communities, others through religious groups or social organizations, and some troupes have taken on a life of their own with advertising that brings together seniors who didn't even know one another prior to putting on a show together. Look for details on how to get a theatrical production started with your own friends—or find out where seniors are performing near you and go support a Senior Theatre production! For more information, visit www.seniortheatre.com.

Be an extra. Not in the show—in the audience! For an $85 annual fee and a $30 reserve fund to start (for a total setup fee of $115), you can help "paper" a house—fill the seats—of events all over New York City, from top Broadway shows (less likely) to concerts and experimental theater (often lots of seats available!), anything that needs an audience. Once you've applied, you receive a password for online access to find the list of shows on offer, and each ticket costs $3.50. You can get one or two tickets, based on availability. For an additional donation of $50 when you sign up, you can get up to four tickets per show, when available, for a year. For more information, go to www.audienceextras.com or call 1-212-686-1966.

Money-Saving Museum Deals

Love art, history, horticulture, animals, rock 'n' roll, Harley-Davidsons, robots, bananas, or even hats? You're in luck! Museums of *all* sorts, galleries, and botanical gardens offer deeply discounted admission for seniors (and sometimes free admission on certain days during the week—usually weekdays or weekday evenings). If there's something that interests you, there's probably a museum dedicated to it, so let your fingers do the walking.

Get (free) culture at the Met... New York's Metropolitan Museum of Art, that is. Like many cultural institutions, its entry fee is not a requirement; it's a "recommended" admission fee. So if you're in the Big Apple and feel like spending a few glorious hours at one of the nation's most magnificent museums—home to everything from a colossal Egyptian sphinx to a priceless Stradivarius violin to the portrait of George Washington that eventually wound up on our dollar bill—then march up to the counter and lay down any amount you like, from two cents to the suggested admission of $20, and you'll be admitted with a smile and no questions asked.

Are you named Isabella? If so, you're in for a pleasant Beantown surprise: the Isabella Stewart Gardner Museum, located a few blocks from Boston's Fenway Park, offers you free entrance for life if you share the name of the mansion museum's original owner and resident. If you're not named Isabella but you are a senior, you can get in for the senior discount rate of $10 instead of the regular admission fee of $12.

Go corporate. Many corporations—from Chase Bank to *Forbes* magazine—have stunning art collections that the public can visit for free at the corporate headquarters. If you live near the national headquarters of pretty much *any* major company, call its main information number and ask if it has a gallery that's accessible to the public. You'll likely see some delightful sculpture (and some very large paintings)!

Ka-ching!
Free Cultural Events in Your Own Backyard

You don't need to travel to major cities to find museums and theaters. Check your local newspaper listings for events such as these—nearly always free and delighted to see you.

BOOKSTORES:

Authors travel the country pouring their hearts out in bookstores, whether reading from their newly published tomes, talking about them, or signing them. Most bookstores that host regular events have newsletters and Web sites, but you can get a better scoop if you get to know your local bookstore employees. Find out what visiting scribe they're excited about and show up in time to get a ringside seat. And if you're the only one who comes? You'll get a private show, and the author and employees will be eternally grateful that you bothered!

GRAND OPENINGS:

Art galleries, exhibitions at your local museum or civic center, new shops and stores—whenever something new is opening, there's usually a public party to lure you in. Scan the newspapers, look for banners, ask your friends to come along. Opening celebrations often include free food, free drinks, and sometimes live performances. Who can resist? And the price is right.

POETRY READINGS, OPEN-MIKE NIGHTS:

For the price of your latte at a comfy coffee shop or perhaps a gin-and-tonic at a slightly wobbly table, you can get a ground-floor view of what today's upcoming talents are up to. The really bad performers are entertaining in their own way, and on any given night, there are always a few gems.

LIVE MUSIC PERFORMANCES:

Depending on where you live, there's probably nearly free live music and concerts happening all the time. From practicing choirs to jazz guitar to indie singers and string trios, musicians, like any artists, like to share their stuff, and generally the price of admission is not high.

LOCAL THEATER:

At a high school near you, dozens of teenagers are preparing to act their hearts out in *No, No, Nanette*; *Godspell*; or *Hamlet*; and they'd love it if someone was in the audience besides their parents. There are also community theaters and one-off performances of small, traveling troupes. Get one of these usually inexpensive tickets and give it a whirl. If it's opening night, community theaters may serve free cheese and wine!

STREET SINGERS, PARK PERFORMERS:

This is how to catch music on the run, without sitting down for it. If you live in an urban area, chances are someone is singing or playing an instrument in a pedestrian passageway or in your local park. And sometimes they're enormously talented. Take the time to stop and listen. When virtuoso violinist Joshua Bell played his Stradivarius at an entrance to the Washington Metro (as a little experiment for the *Washington Post*), only seven people of more than a thousand who went by paused to listen.

Borrowed admission. Most public libraries offer *free* passes to selected museums and other area attractions. These are kept at the library's circulation desk and are available to card-holding library patrons. Below you'll find a mere sampling of the offerings available at the libraries where we inquired—ask at your local library and see what's on offer:

- The Boston Public Library furnishes numerous free and discounted passes at its main and branch locations.
- The Chicago Public Library issues Kraft Great Kids Museum Passports for up to four family members.
- The Mill Valley (California) Public Library offers free museum passes.
- The Huntingdon County (Pennsylvania) Public Library offers museum passes to its patrons.
- In Michigan, public libraries offer patrons a free Museum Adventure Pass to over 25 museums, and nature, art, and histroric sites.
- The Minneapolis Public Library offers patrons passes to museums, zoos, and other attractions.
- The Ottawa (Canada) Public Library furnishes passes to more than 30 Canadian museums and historic sites.

The Modern for free. The Museum of Modern Art (MoMA) in NYC does *not* offer a suggested admission: $20 is the price, take it or leave it, unless you're a senior 65 and older, with ID, in which case you only pay $16. Or you can take advantage of Free Friday Nights, sponsored by Target, which allow visitors into the museum for free between 4 and 8 p.m. These "tickets" cannot be obtained in advance, so you have to line up with everyone else and wait your turn for admission. If you want quiet, go for a morning admission at the senior discount price, because even these spacious galleries are jam-packed on a Friday night, but it's a cheerful hubbub and will convince you more than anything that art still matters!

Go to Washington, DC. The Smithsonian Institution consists of 19 museums, including the delightful National Air and Space Museum, the National Portrait Gallery, the National Museum of American History, the National Museum of African Art, the Hirshhorn Museum and Sculpture Garden, and many more. Admission to all of the museums that are located in Washington, DC (which is everything but the Cooper-Hewitt in New York) is free.

Our Nation's Most Offbeat (and Inexpensive) Museums

For mere pennies on the dollar, you can gain entry into any of the following museums, which run the gamut from the sublime to the, well, just plain kooky.

American Clock & Watch Museum, Bristol, Connecticut

Burlingame Museum of Pez Memorabilia, Burlingame, California

Circus World Museum, Baraboo, Wisconsin

Cuba Cheese Museum, Cuba, New York

Frederick's of Hollywood Lingerie Museum, Los Angeles, California

The Hat Museum, Portland, Oregon

Haverstraw Brick Museum, Haverstraw, New York

Kansas Barbed Wire Museum, LaCrosse, Kansas

Liberace Museum and Foundation, Las Vegas, Nevada

Lizzie Borden Museum, Fall River, Massachusetts

Marvin's Marvelous Mechanical Museum, Farmington Hills, Michigan

Museum of Bad Art, Dedham, Massachusetts

Mütter Museum, Philadelphia, Pennsylvania

New York Museum of Water, New York, New York

Sing Sing Prison Museum, Ossining, New York

World Kite Museum, Long Beach, Washington

Check out great design at the Cooper-Hewitt. For the New York City branch of the Smithsonian, filled with wonderful examples of design past and present, the regular admission is $15, but seniors are $10—unless you're already a member of the Smithsonian Institution, in which case admission is free.

Get a City Pass. A City Pass allows substantial discounts on many museums and other attractions and also allows you to skip the long lines in many places and march right in through special entrances. Whether you're visiting Atlanta, Boston, Chicago, Hollywood, Houston, New York, Philadelphia, San Francisco, Seattle, Southern California, or Toronto, a City Pass can be a wise investment in terms of money and time. You don't even need to prepurchase: a City Pass can be bought at the main ticket window of any of the attractions included. Visit www.citypass.com or call 1-888-330-5008.

When in the Apple, stop in at the Whitney.
Regular admission to this stunning collection of American art is regularly $18, but seniors 62 and older with ID can get in for $12.

Go to the Guggenheim.
If you only know what the famous spiraled shell-like exterior looks like, treat yourself to an interior view as well with a senior discount price of $15, down from the regular admission of $18. On Saturdays from 5:45 until the 7:45 p.m. closing, you can visit the Guggenheim in Manhattan on a donation basis, paying what you wish for admission—the tickets are not "free," since you must pay something, but the amount is up to you. The final tickets that night are issued at 7:15 p.m.

Get to the Getty.
Admission is free to this Los Angeles collection of Western art dating back to the Middle Ages, but you must have a timed ticket to visit the Getty Villa in Malibu, with its unparalleled collection of ancient Greek, Roman, and Etruscan art. (Note that parking is $15, but free after 5 p.m.) Save yourself the hassle by checking for availability online at www.gettymuseum.us, where you can order your free ticket and print it yourself. You can also call 310-440-7300 to book your visit.

Climb those famous steps like Rocky.
The Philadelphia Museum of Art is $16 regular admission but seniors 65 and older with ID can get in for $14. The first Sunday of every month is pay what you wish. For more information about membership and current exhibits visit www.philamuseum.org.

Visit the Windy City's Art Institute of Chicago.
Entry to the Art Institute is $12 for seniors 65 and older with ID, a savings of $6 off the regular admission. You can also enter free from 5 to 8 p.m. on Thursdays, sponsored by Target.

Way out west at the Los Angeles County Museum of Art. Seniors 62 and older with ID get in for $8 instead of $12 to visit the world-class collection of LACMA.

Did You Know?

Many Museums Only Suggest an Entry Fee Most museums in the United States have a "suggested" admission fee for entry? This means that if you can't pay the suggested senior rate (which is likely already discounted), or you'd simply rather pay less, you can do so. Museums nearly always have discounted admissions, from free admission for children to special student prices and senior discounts, because they're eager for you to attend. To find out more information on rates, including info on museums close to you or on museums you plan to visit while traveling, check out the Web site Museums of the World at www.museum.com, which gives you admission hours and prices on literally thousands of museums and galleries throughout the world.

Concerts, Opera, and Live Music Festivals on the Cheap

Do you crave the transporting sounds of classical music, yearn for the sweet-hot swinging vibes of jazz, or pine for a moving and memorable aria? Don't stay home because live music prices seem out of reach! Early Birds have awesome options when it comes to getting their fix of live music. While it's true that drink minimums and cover charges can add up at big-city nightspots, and concert tickets can range anywhere from $25 to more than $100, you can still hear world-class musicians perform for very little and sometimes even nothing! Many churches, universities, and colleges offer free or very low-cost concerts that are open to the public. Government art grants or private foundations generally subsidize these concerts—lucky for you! A random search on the Internet turned up loads of fascinating performances. For example, the Old Church in Portland, Oregon, (www.oldchurch.org) offers free "Sack Lunch" concerts on Wednesday afternoons and low-priced jazz and classical concerts for less than $15 a ticket, with a senior discount for music lovers 65 and older.

How do you get to Carnegie Hall? With a discounted ticket! (And, of course, it never hurts to practice.) While concert prices vary greatly depending on the venue within Carnegie Hall and who's playing what, there are senior discounts for certain shows. Senior discounts are available at the box office and only sold up to one hour before showtime. To find out when senior discounts will be available, visit Carnegie Hall's Web site and sign up for its biweekly e-mail newsletter, "At a Glance." You can also call the box office on the day of the event to see if discounted tickets will be available. Visit www.carnegiehall.org or call 212-247-7800.

Stay in tune with the Boston Philharmonic. Seniors can get discounted tickets to most shows as well as "rush" tickets on the day of the show, only at the box office. Rush tickets are also available to students, so you'll need ID, and you may need to stand in line! Get details at www.bostonphil.org or call 617-236-0999.

When in Beantown, shop at BosTix. Hear the Count Basie Orchestra or listen to classical music under the stars; catch an Elvis tribute band or hear a moving performance of *Carmen*—all for half-price when you shop at BosTix. Run by the nonprofit organization ArtsBoston, BosTix is one-stop shopping for any cultural event happening in Boston, from bands and orchestras, operas and musicals, to dance and theater, too. They operate two ticket booths, one in Faneuil Hall, the other in Copley Square, which open at 10 a.m. daily (11 a.m. on Sundays) and sell discounted day-of-show tickets. All tickets are cash only, but the savings are 50 percent off. You can also buy half-price tickets in advance at its Web site: www.bostix.org.

Early Bird Secret

RUSH Over to Carnegie Hall

The cheapest way to hear world-class music at Carnegie Hall is to come to the box office clutching a crispy new $10 bill on the day of the concert you want to hear. That's when a limited number of Public RUSH Tickets are available for concerts in the Stern Auditorium and Perelman Stage. It's best to get there (at 57th Street and Seventh Avenue) when the box office opens (at 11 a.m. Monday through Saturday and at noon on Sunday) because limited means when they're gone, they're gone. Visit www.carnegiehall.org for upcoming events.

From jazz to opera at Lincoln Center for less. The Lincoln Center in New York City is actually a complex of 12 resident organizations: Lincoln Center for the Performing Arts; the Chamber Music Society of Lincoln Center; the Film Society of Lincoln Center; Jazz at Lincoln Center; the Juilliard

School; Lincoln Center Theater; the Metropolitan Opera; New York City Ballet; New York City Opera; New York Philharmonic; the New York Public Library for the Performing Arts; and the School of American Ballet. Each organization has its own policy on senior discounts, but they are indeed regularly available for many performances and presentations. The best way to find out for sure is to contact the box office about what you want to see and reserve your discounted ticket directly through them. Visit www.lincolncenter.org for more information.

Opera Carolina. The vibrant opera community of Charlotte, North Carolina, which tends to offer classics such as *The Marriage of Figaro* and *The Barber of Seville* during its regular season, offers seniors a standard discount of 10 percent off the base ticket price, and proof of ID may be required. An even better deal, if you qualify, is the military discount of 15 percent. Find out more at www.operacarolina.org.

Long Leaf Opera Festival. Based in Chapel Hill, North Carolina, Long Leaf is the only opera company in the United States dedicated to presenting fully staged operas that were originally written in English. If you want to understand exactly what's going on onstage without reading subtitles (or "supertitles," as used at New York's Metropolitan Opera and many other opera houses), then Long Leaf is for you. They are also committed to making opera as affordable and comfortable as possible, with audience members encouraged to wear anything they like to performances, other than hats and big hair! Ticket prices are as low as $20 per performance. Get details at www.longleafopera.org.

SPTs at the Kennedy Center. SPTs, or specially priced tickets of 50 percent off, are available at the Kennedy Center in Washington, DC, for seniors 65 and older with valid ID. (They are also available to military personnel, those with disabilities, and those on a fixed income.) The tickets are subject to availability and can be ordered in advance except for any Saturday night events or Friday night *Shear Madness* performances. (When ordering in advance, ID must be shown at pickup.) Go to www.kennedy-center.org or call 1-800-444-1324 for information.

Grand deals for the Grand Ole Opry. There are a number of ways to get several dollars off your ticket to a performance at the Grand Ole Opry, both at the current Opry House and the old Ryman Auditorium, where the Opry was held from 1943 to 1974. The best bet is to book online, either with a tour group, which will give you a few dollars off your ticket and may include round-trip transportation to your hotel as part of the price. Visit www.opry.com/fancoupon.aspx or call 1-800-733-6779.

Branson for less. The Ozarks have always been known for music, and with the huge variety of shows available in Branson, Missouri, you can find far more there nowadays than foot-stomping country. The Branson Tourism Center, while not offering specific senior discounts, has mountains of discounts on everything from food and lodging to last-minute show tickets. The site claims to have sold more than 1,000,000,000 tickets to Branson shows, so they ought to know what they're doing by now! Log on to www.branson.com or call 1-800-785-1550 for more information.

Summer Folk Festivals

THEY'RE NOT LIKE WOODSTOCK ANYMORE!

One of the most underrated ways to enjoy live music inexpensively is to visit a summertime music festival. They're comparatively inexpensive, and you get to listen to fabulous music, usually while surrounded by like-minded people. All over the United States each summer, people congregate for weekends of music and dance, staying in local hotels, RVs, or campgrounds, and enjoying the delights of music in an outdoor setting. Many of these festivals, true to the family atmosphere most of them engender, offer a senior discount. Here is a list of some of the biggies:

- **Augusta Heritage Center Bluegrass Week**, Elkins, West Virginia
- **Beartrap Summer Festival**, Casper, Wyoming
- **Bitterroot Valley Bluegrass Festival**, Hamilton, Montana
- **Cumberland Dance Week**, Nancy, Kentucky
- **Falcon Ridge Folk Festival**, Hillsdale, New York
- **Founders Title Company Folk and Bluegrass Festival**, Salt Lake City, Utah
- **Kerrville Folk Festival**, Kerrville, Texas

For more information about what's going on in your neck of the woods, log on to festivalfinder.com where you can search by your favorite genre or use the Find By feature to locate festivals by date, location or name.

Live (and Free) Television Show Tapings

Live TV tapings can be a real thrill—the lights, the camera, the roar of the crowd all make for a fabulously free experience! Getting tickets to a live show used to be a rarity, but these days there are plenty of shows shot before a live studio audience and plenty of ways to get them. From David Letterman and Rachael Ray to Jon Stewart, Stephen Colbert, and Jimmy Kimmel, talk shows are the first line of tickets. You might have to win the lottery to see Oprah, but someone has to fill those seats, so you might as well throw your name into the hat. And if you don't get tickets to anything else, you can always go by Rockefeller Center if you're visiting New York City, and say "good morning" to the hosts of the *Today Show*, who regularly come outside to greet their guests on the plaza outside Studio 1A at NBC. Here are some leads to getting your free TV tickets. If you manage to get into *Saturday Night Live*, your kids will be thrilled!

TV sitcom tickets. Ever dream of being in a live studio audience? If you live in Los Angeles, here's your chance! Go to TVTickets.com, a direct hookup to a plethora of sitcom tapings of current network shows, nearly all of which are taped in studios in and around Los Angeles. You can search among the listings of currently taping shows; read all about each sitcom, its stars, and cast of characters; and check out the schedule of shoot dates. Then you can submit your request for tickets up to 30 days prior to the tape date you wish to attend. When you click "Submit," your map to the studio and your free ticket will be generated for you to print. Recent shows available included *The New Adventures of Old Christine* with Julia Louis-Dreyfus and *According to Jim* with Jim Belushi.

Watch a pilot taping. Pilots, which are essentially a "sample" of a new show for the networks, often require live audiences for their shoots. You can get tickets to see new shows being shot through Audiences Unlimited, which reminds visitors to the site that, once upon a time, *Seinfeld* and *Friends* were both just pilots before they were massive hit shows! The free tickets from this site are all for studios in and around Los Angeles, so if you're just visiting, they ask that you provide them with a working cell phone number so they can contact you with any changes. Maybe you'll get lucky and be there for the birth of a winner. Go to www.audiencesunlimited.com to learn how.

Saturday Night Live. The days of John Belushi and Chevy Chase may be long gone, but tickets to *Saturday Night Live* are among the most sought-after in TV tapings, and tickets are given out by lottery once a year. In August, you can submit a request via e-mail to snltickets@nbcuni.com. You can only send one e-mail per household, and you cannot select the date you would like to attend. If your request is successful, you receive two tickets for a randomly selected date. Alternately, you can try for a standby ticket at 7 a.m. on the morning of a taping. Tickets are distributed on the 49th Street side of 30 Rockefeller Plaza, and you can choose between the 8 p.m. dress rehearsal or the 11:30 p.m. live taping. Standby ticket holders are required to keep their places in line until the taping, with only minimal breaks allowed. Get more info at NBC's Web site: www.nbc.com/Tickets.

Take a Seat at Your Favorite TV Show Tonight

Want a quick way to get onto the set of a television show? If you're flexible—not to mention available during the daytime, when most of these shows tape—you can get tickets at Free TV Tickets for that same day or during the next week or so for anything taping in Los Angeles. This Web site (www.tvtix.com) is both a clearinghouse for those who want tickets and a seat-filling machine for the show's producers, who never want their stars to be talking to a half-empty house. Even if you're just visiting LA, you can visit the Web site in the morning and be sitting in a studio in Culver City that afternoon. Tickets are free and must be printed directly from your computer. Certain dress codes apply. These are always specified and usually include things like, "No shorts, no hats, no white shirts" (which don't look good when the camera scans the audience). Recently available tickets included: *Let's Make a Deal, Dr. Phil, Mike & Molly,* and *Pair of Kings.*

Oh, Oprah! Getting tickets for *Oprah* is much like winning the lottery—and if you do manage to get on, you may really feel that way, since who knows what she'll be giving away that day. Oprah's show tapes in Chicago from August to November and January to May, and while the show is on hiatus, no reservations are given out. Visit the Web site for information on how to call for a reservation when the show is taping: www.oprah.com. You'll also find information on how to send an e-mail request for a last-minute ticket.

The Daily Show with Jon Stewart. If you're going to be in New York City for any stretch of time, this is one of the hottest free tickets in town. Send an e-mail request to requesttickets@thedailyshow.com.

Late Show with David Letterman (and other CBS shows). Forty-five years after the Beatles made their infamous appearance onstage at the Ed Sullivan Theater on Broadway at 53rd Street in New York City, funnyman David Letterman calls the historic space home. Representatives are available in the lobby of the theater to take ticket requests and let you know if any seats are available for that day's or week's tapings of the *Late Show with David Letterman*. Those tickets are awarded randomly, and requests are taken Monday through Thursday, 9:30 a.m. to 12:30 p.m., and Saturday and Sunday, 10 a.m. to 6 p.m. You can also request a standby ticket starting at 11 a.m. on the same day you wish to attend by calling 212-247-6497. To submit a request online, go to the CBS Web site, choose David Letterman from the Shows listing, and click on Tickets—which is how you get information on tickets to other CBS shows such as *The Price Is Right*. Visit the CBS Web site at www.cbs.com for complete instructions.

Theme Parks and Attractions at Bargain-Basement Prices

It might seem unlikely that theme parks would be the place to find seniors, but in fact we make up a big part of the visiting audience. We may not necessarily be there to ride the roller coasters, but many of us visit a lot of major attractions every year both to take our families along (roller coasters are for grandkids) and to be entertained ourselves.

And what a way to be entertained! America is filled with thrilling theme parks, some time-honored, such as Cypress Gardens, and others, such as the planned Wizarding World of Harry Potter, thrillingly new. Many, many attractions offer senior discounts, which are usually clearly posted when you buy tickets. If you're buying on the Web in advance of your visit, you may find even better prices or specials that won't be available at the front gates, so be sure to check before you go.

Early Bird Secret

What a sweet deal! Hershey Park, the wonderful chocolate-themed playground in Hershey, Pennsylvania, has a two-tier senior discount that saves you a significant amount. The regular admission ticket for one day is $52.95, but seniors 55 and up can get in for $31.95. And if you're 70 or older, it costs $20.95. The two- and three-day passes are also enticing—$52.50 instead of $70.50 and $77 instead of $99, respectively. What's more, Hershey Park has a special "Sunset Admission" price structure: If you enter the park after 3 p.m. on days when the park closes at 6 p.m., or after 5 p.m. when it's closing at 11 p.m., regular admission is $26.95, discounted to $22.95 for those 55 and above, and all the way down to $15.95 for those over 70. For more information, visit www.hersheypark.com.

A "berry" nice farm. California's Knott's Berry Farm offers deep discounts to seniors 62 and older. A regular adult ticket for one day costs $53.99, but the senior price for one day is only $23.99—less than half the price. Knott's is affiliated with Soak City water parks, with locations in San Diego, Orange County, and Palm Springs, also have senior pricing: $19.99 for those 62 and older instead of the regular admission of $25.99. Annual passes to Knott's with unlimited admission are also favorable to seniors: $59.99 instead of $64.99 for the regular pass. Go to www.knotts.com and let your fingers find you savings!

Visit Shamu and Flipper's digs for less. There are three locations of Sea World—Orlando, San Diego, and San Antonio—and the senior discounts are not consistent across all locations. In San Diego, the park offers "Terrific Tuesdays" for guests 50 and above, with special activities just for seniors, including a complimentary breakfast and special symposiums, for $61 for one day (which is, in fact, the same as the regular admission for a day but with added activities). San Diego also offers those 50 and older a discount on a Silver Passport, good for a year of free Sea World admission, for $89 instead of $99. If you buy your ticket to the Orlando park online, you can get $10 off the standard $69.95 admission. Get details at www.seaworld.com.

A universe of savings for seniors. At Universal Studios in Orlando, there is not a senior discount, but there is special pricing for Florida residents who buy their tickets online. You get a two-day, two-park ticket for $75, a savings of $59.99 over the regular two-day, two-park ticket price. It also saves you time because you print your tickets out at home and go straight to the front gate. And Universal also includes a coupon book with $150 in savings. Go to www.universalorlando.com and watch your savings add up.

The Early Bird's Garden of Eden. There is not a specific senior discount for either Busch Gardens locations in Williamsburg, Virginia, or Tampa Bay, Florida, but AARP members can present their cards for discounts at the parks. A regular tickets at Williamsburg is $61.95 and Tampa is $74.95, but Williamsburg offers special pricing and promotions for Virginia residents as does the Tampa Bay location for Georgia and Florida residents. Visit www.buschgardens.com for more information.

Super Savings on Other Points of Interest

Not everything classifies as a theme park, and there may nary be a Van Gogh in sight or a Chopin étude within earshot, but plenty of other cultural attractions offer a lot of thrills and informative excitement and senior discounts at the same time.

Move over, Henry Kissinger. Talk about excitement! At its gleaming, imposing headquarters on the East River in New York City, the United Nations is a fascinating tour, especially if you've ever seen Alfred Hitchcock's

Ka-Ching!

10 Absolutely Free and Peaceful Things You Can Do to Amuse Yourself

Don't want to go out to some big event? Not looking for a show or a spectacle but merely to enjoy the quiet company of a friend or spend a few hours communing with yourself? These kinds of quiet amusements often lead to the most pleasurable hours that we spend in life, either alone or with others, so, hey, don't forget about the small stuff when you're looking for something to do.

1. Go for a walk. Whether it's a beautiful, sunny day or there's snow falling, dress appropriately for the weather and go outside. Your neighbors may have never before seen you strolling around the block rather than driving around it, but what's especially nice about walking around your own neighborhood is how quickly people get used to the fact and start waving or stopping to chat. They might never come ring your doorbell, but they may be glad to see you as you go by.

2. Read a book. It sounds simple, but some people may recall that in the days before TV, books were a major source of entertainment. And they can be again. Pull out a classic, or borrow the latest number-one best-selling novel from the library. Surf around on Google, which is working on scanning the libraries of the world, and you can read the full text of hundreds of thousands of books (and plenty more to come) all for free.

3. Listen to a book. Audio books can be a terrific way to reacquaint yourself with your favorite classics or to get into a brand-new novel. Sometimes the performance by the reader is truly outstanding and can bring out nuances in the text that you might not even have noticed while reading. If you listen to one while driving or doing housework, you can tell yourself you're using a bit more brain power. Audio books can be checked out at the library and many can be downloaded free on the Internet (try www.freeclassicaudiobooks.com).

4. **Join a book club.** One of the pleasures of a good book is talking about it with others afterward. Start a book club with like-minded friends or join a group of interesting strangers. If you have no idea where to start, ask at your local library—they can hook you up.

5. **Watch a movie.** If you've got cable TV, you probably have more movies than you'll ever want to see. But, ideally, you also have Turner Classic Movies (TCM), which is showing something good at this very moment. They have all the golden oldies in black and white; it's a rare film on this channel that's in color. From all-day tributes to Cary Grant and Greta Garbo to Westerns that run all day Saturday to the earliest silent movies on Sunday nights to documentaries about filmmakers from the Golden Age of cinema, they've got it all, and it's all commercial-free. Watching this channel is a film education.

6. **Go to a movie.** From half-price matinees to second-run cinemas for a buck or two a pop, going to the movies can be really cheap. Just don't be suckered into paying 10 times as much for popcorn and a soda as you paid to get in.

7. **Watch TV.** Have you given up regular TV because the advertising has become so pervasive on the network channels? Are you tired of watching the umpteenth reality show about nothing? If you have a computer with a high-speed connection, you can stream your favorite network shows directly off their Web sites with no commercial interruptions. And find free classic episodes from the Golden Age of TV on http://video.tvguide.com/episodes.

8. **Listen to music.** So many of us treat music like a background noise. But real music lovers sit down and give their favorite CDs as much attention as any reader gives a book. Put on your headphones, close your eyes, and really listen to your favorite recording.

9. **Learn to speak a new language or play an instrument.** Gave up French after high school? Found your son's old guitar in the upstairs closet? You can get language and music training tapes, videos, and DVDs at the library, or, perhaps even better, you can learn on various Web sites: www.youtube.com has video guitar lessons from various masters (as does www.ultimate-guitar.com), and www.livemocha.com is a site where you can study languages completely free and be tutored by native speakers.

10. **Build a puzzle or play a game.** People might laugh if you tell them you love puzzles, but put one out on a card table and most people set to without hesitation. Puzzles are very absorbing, as are crosswords, Sudoku, and anything else that challenges your brain and keeps it active. Play chess with an old friend, or better still, teach your grandkids to play backgammon, Scrabble, or dominoes, for a little bit of old-fashioned excitement.

classic film, *North by Northwest*, where Cary Grant suddenly finds himself in the UN holding a knife in the back of a newly deceased diplomat. Trust that your visit will be far less eventful, and pay the discounted rate of $11, as opposed to the regular admission price of $16.

Run for the roses—and the savings. Our experts considered putting this listing in the sports chapter, but in fact, Churchill Downs is one of Kentucky's greatest cultural spots of interest. On regular racing days at the home of the Kentucky Derby, general admission at the front gate is $3, but seniors are admitted for $1. Place your bet wisely and maybe you can move your seat to Millionaire's Row instead!

Honk if you love a deal! One part educational, one part recreational, and two parts fascinating fun, the Henry Ford Museum in Dearborn, Michigan, offers a discount to visitors 62 and older. Seniors save $1 off the regular $15 Museum and $22 Greenfield Village tickets. For more information, see www.thehenryford.org.

Safe and Savvy Travel

Amazing Seniors-Only Deals on Excursions and Lodgings

Getting the Best Deals on Airfares

In the early days of commercial air travel, people used to dress up, dine sumptuously in midair, and arrive rested and refreshed. Nowadays, with skyrocketing fuel costs and increased expenses at every turn, the skies just aren't quite as friendly as they used to be. In an attempt to lower their costs and save money, airlines are cutting corners right and left—no more pillows, no more food, less legroom, checked baggage fees—and, more to the point, senior airfare discounts have become a lot scarcer than they used to be.

Because so much travel is now booked by individuals on the Internet and airlines no longer need to wait to publish fares in a newspaper, for example, speed rules when it comes to the airlines' response to fuel prices and passenger demand. Fares can change, quite literally, from minute to minute on the Internet, and so can the availability and/or existence of senior discounts. Fear not! This can all be turned to your advantage. With a little flexibility, patience, and savvy, there are still plenty of ways that seniors can get those skies feeling a little friendlier again.

Start shopping well in advance of your trip. Good news if you're Internet savvy: It's hard to beat online prices when you're booking a flight. If you're planning a big trip, or even a holiday break to see the grandkids, check out fares a few months in advance to get an idea of the going rates. Many of the largest travel sites, such as www.orbitz.com, have features that will automatically "fare watch" for you and send e-mails when the fare for your route goes up or down significantly.

Get on the phone. Most airlines' Web sites do not publish senior fares, which usually kick in at age 65. Delta Airlines, for example, specifies that senior fares are not available through online bookings, so you'll have to get on the phone. Ask the reservations agent specifically about senior pricing, which, when available, is generally about 10 percent off the base fare. That amount, however, will often be higher than the airline's special offers. Don't hesitate to ask the agent if there is a lower fare than the senior discount, and if so, whether it can be booked for you over the phone.

Visit the zoo. Travelzoo, that is! Spectacular deals are to be found at a Web site called Travelzoo.com. Sign up for the Travelzoo Top 20 newsletter (www.top20.travelzoo.com) and receive a weekly email with the twenty best travel deals for that week. Two recent postings had a 6-night trip to Ireland including air and a rental car for $599, and a suite at the 5-diamond Venetian resort in Las Vegas with breakfast for $159.

Ka-Ching!

Seven Travel-Savvy Ways to Save Time, Money, and Your Back

Gone are the days of loading up two "rollerboys" to take on a weekend excursion for you and your sweetie, or of dressing up as though you were embarking on a transatlantic journey on the *Queen Mary*. Here are our experts' surefire ways to make air travel as smooth as possible for yourself and your wallet.

Invest in a lightweight, microfiber, rolling carry-on: You'll be less inclined to overpack and less likely to go over the airline's allowed weight limit.

Pack one pair of shoes. Make the ones you wear on-board slip-ons, like loafers. The Transportation Security Administration (TSA) and your fellow passengers will thank you when it comes time to remove them.

Decant your shampoo. No need to pack whole bottles into your checked luggage. Buy inexpensive 3-ounce plastic bottles at your drugstore, and decant at home.

Stay away from salty snacks. The TSA now demands that any snacks brought on board be purchased after security check-in. Stick with fruit and cheese, and beware salty chips: you'll get dehydrated faster once aboard and be forced to pay premium prices for bottled water.

Pack one lightweight sweater suitable for day or night. Unless you're visiting the Arctic, there is no reason to travel with your entire winter wardrobe. Choose carefully, and pack lightweight clothes that can be layered.

Stick with one color scheme. Our experts uniformly agree that packing clothes that are black or white is the wisest way to travel. Everything will always match, black can be very dressy (or not), white always looks crisp, and you can brighten up outfits with a simple, lightweight scarf.

Avoid checking luggage. Packed intelligently, a carry-on rolling bag can work for trips as short as a weekend or as long as a month. Another reason to go this route: airlines are all starting to charge for checked luggage.

Did You Know?

During the holiday season, you'll get the best, cheapest seats if you travel on, not before, a holiday. You can reap significant savings if you book your flight for Thanksgiving or Christmas Day. Most people want to be there in advance of a major holiday, but if you're planning to spend time with your family for several days or weeks after the event, why not travel the day of the holiday and reap the benefits? It will give you even more to celebrate.

Look before you leap at a super-sale price. The hot sales are generally the first thing you see on the home page of an airline or travel site, but surf around and compare prices first. Be sure to read the fine print on the super-sale price to make sure it doesn't have restrictions you find too onerous. It can be tempting to jump at the lowest fare you see, but you may discover it has taxes and fees that raise it higher than the next price up from the "sale," or even that it's only a one-way price, cleverly worded to make that fact hard to figure out until you're already typing in your credit card number!

Fly on Tuesday, Wednesday, and Saturday. Airfares tend to be lower midweek and on Saturdays, a fact that is driven largely by the needs of business travelers, who typically pay more on the other days while traveling for work because their companies are paying. Because airlines generally have a slightly lower demand for Tuesday, Wednesday, and Saturday, you can save anywhere from $10 to $100 off the price of the same domestic destination on Monday, Thursday, Friday, and Sunday.

Spending Less on Lodging

Hotels rooms are a commodity that can be even harder to pin down than airfares, because Internet rates can change, if possible, even faster. But a little research in this field can pay off big because hotel rooms are very much a business of supply and demand. A large booking for a convention might make the price on the remaining rooms in a hotel go sky-high, no matter that you saw them the day before at a much lower rate. Conversely, booking on the Wednesday before a slow weekend may see rates plummet through the floor, with the hotel delighted to get you in to fill all that empty space! If you're a senior, however, all those convention-goers can step aside while you claim your special rate, no matter what the demand, since it's hard to find a hotel, motel, bed-and-breakfast, or inn that *doesn't* have a senior discount of some sort. The standard rate, even at the most basic motel, is usually

10 percent off. With plenty of advance notice or a little bit of last-minute wrangling, you may be able to get 15 percent or even 20 percent off. The caveat: These rates are rarely posted, so be prepared to ask.

Check the Internet rates first... Go to your chosen hotel's Web site and check all advertised prices and special promotional deals. Then type in your specifics (dates, arrival times, king, queen, suite, etc.) and see what rates you're offered for the time you want to stay. Search "senior discount" if it's not obvious where to find that rate (and if there's a site-specific search box). Write down the rates but don't book anything on this research visit.

...and then call the hotel directly... If you dial the toll-free national reservation number for a major chain, you'll be duly quoted the rack rate, along with standardized promotional offers and senior discount. But if you want the best possible rate—and why wouldn't you?—call the actual hotel in the city where you want to stay. The hotel's on-site reservations clerk has the most updated information on supply and demand in that hotel and can potentially offer you a much better rate than you'll ever get from the operator at the national switchboard—and may even quote you a better senior discount.

...and *then* make the best deal. If the hotel's own reservations clerk can't beat the rates you researched on the Internet, ask why not—and then see if you can book at the better rate you already found. If it's a published deal, you should be able to book it via phone or Internet, even though you had to check both to find it!

Go against the grain. If you're heading to a unique bed-and-breakfast in a prime countryside location, its weekends are likely booked while its weekdays may be surprisingly quiet. If your goal is a national chain's city-center hotel in a major metropolitan area, business travelers likely stream through all week while the corridors echo on weekends. If you're traveling for leisure and can be flexible, get much lower rates by doing a "reverse commute" on visits, and try to make reservations to stay when everyone else is not.

Bring all your ammo to bear (politely!). Ask for the senior discount, then ask if there's a AAA discount or perhaps a separately negotiated AARP discount for card-carrying members. Don't forget to ask if there are any other discounts for military or government employees, if that applies to you, and then ask if you can double up on any of these discounts! Depending on demand for the dates you want, you may find a reservations operator who can do you a particularly sweet deal.

Staying Off-Season Yields Big Savings

One of our experts visited a major ski area in Colorado, midsummer, midweek. Instead of staying at a motor inn, she called the area's premium resort, which was virtually empty. The result? She was able to book a four-star room for the price of a basic room in a motor lodge. Remember: It always pays to use your noodle.

Plan well in advance. If you're going for the straight senior discount at a major hotel—as opposed to a special promo rate or last-minute deal—be sure to book well in advance. Some hotels impose restrictions such as a 21-day advance notice or a non-refundable credit card deposit.

Always confirm. Once you've asked for and received the senior discount, be sure to confirm again when you check in and *before* the bill is prepared when you check out. "There's many a slip," as they say, and you may find it more difficult to insist on your senior discount if you've already been presented with a final bill that doesn't include it.

Make your own senior discount. A hotel may set aside a limited number of rooms that can be booked at a senior discount price. If you find that you can't get the rate you want for the date you want, ask about the following weekend, or month, or another date that's convenient to you. If not, ask if the hotel can do something else for you instead: Upgrade to a bigger room or suite at the basic-room rate? Free parking? Restaurant or theater vouchers? One or two little perks can add up to more than the 10 percent you might have gotten as a discount.

Join the club. If you travel often, whether for business or pleasure, pick a hotel group and try to stick with it. Many of them have programs such as the Hyatt Gold Passport or Starwood Preferred Guest that, when you reserve a room under your member number, will allow you to earn points or rewards for stays, and that can result in free stays, additional discounts, restaurant vouchers, and other perks down the road. Some will also let you redeem points for airline miles or other bonuses and incentives.

Scoring Deep Senior Discounts at Chain Hotels

Even if a hotel is part of a major international chain, there's a good chance that the hotel is independently owned and operated like a franchise; as a result, the discount you're able to get may vary from place to place. A 10 percent discount—be it a senior discount, a AAA discount, or an AARP discount—is pretty easy to get at just about any hotel chain. The particular benefit to the AARP discount is that the discount starts at 50 for the long list

Ka-Ching!
Major Travel Savings,
COURTESY OF THE AARP

Over 50? Here's something to celebrate: Get an AARP card and you will never have to pay full price again at a hotel. The following AARP partner hotels will offer you a senior discount of at least 10 percent off the standard rate (and often a lot more off the rate at luxury properties—sometimes as much as 50 percent). Always be sure to check for specials that may give you an even better rate.

If you're an AARP member, you should also look into the AARP Passport Program—it's a one-stop shopping site for a wealth of travel options. When you're looking for a travel discount, it's likely that AARP has been there ahead of you and already negotiated a rate for its members—and always with the added benefit that you can start getting the discount at 50, instead of waiting for 60 or 62, as many outlets require. Booking through the Passport Program ensures that you automatically get any AARP-negotiated discount with any travel operator or cruise line or hotel without having to ask. Visit www.travelocity.com/AARP/home for more information.

Baymont Inn & Suites	1-800-364-6072
Beaches Resorts	1-866-498-3218
Best Western	1-800-618-2277
Cambria Suites	1-877-424-6423
Clarion Hotels	1-800-424-6423
Comfort Inn	1-800-424-6423
Comfort Suites	1-800-424-6423
Days Inn	1-800-364-6072
Econo Lodge	1-800-424-6423
Four Points	1-877-778-2277
Hampton Inn & Suites	1-800-426-7866
Howard Johnson	1-800-364-6072
Knights Inn	1-800-364-6072
La Quinta Inns & Suites	1-866-573-6722
Luxury Collection	1-877-778-2277
MainStay Suites	1-800-424-6423
Quality Inn	1-800-424-6423
Ramada	1-800-364-6072
Rodeway Inn	1-800-424-6423
Sandals Resorts	1-866-498-3218
Sheraton	1-877-778-2277
Sleep Inn	1-800-424-6423
St. Regis Hotel	1-877-778-2277
Suburban Extended Stay Hotel	1-800-424-6423
Super 8 Motel	1-800-364-6072
Travelodge	1-800-364-6072
W Hotel	1-877-778-2277
Westin Hotels & Resorts	1-877-778-2277
Wingate by Wyndham	1-800-364-6072
Wyndham Hotels & Resorts	1-800-364-6072

of AARP partner hotels. At other hotels without an AARP agreement, the senior discount generally doesn't kick in until age 60, 62, or even 65. Getting an AARP discount at a hotel means you can get 10 to 15 years' worth of extra discounts!

Here's a rundown of the AARP savings that you can get at many of the major hotel and motel chains across the United States. Our information was correct at press time, but, as always, be sure to ask about the discount and confirm when you book.

You have a Choice. If you are an AARP member 60 or older, Choice Hotels offer a 10% off Senior Rate on advance reservations when you call their 800-424-6423 line. Sign up for their Choice Privileges membership, and save up to 20% on advance, prepaid bookings. Members earn points for free stays, travel on Amtrak, cruises, restaurant gift cards and gas cards and also qualify for Airline Rewards, frequent flyer mileage on domestic and international airlines. Get details and enroll at www.choicehotels.com or call 1-877-424-6423.

Get Marriott for less. If you're 62 or older, you can save 15 percent off a room at any of Marriott's more than 2,000 locations worldwide, including:

Fairfield Inn
Marriott Courtyard
Marriott Vacation Club International
Renaissance
Residence Inn
Springhill Suites
TownePlace Suites

You can book up to two rooms per visit at the special senior rate, but you must present valid proof of age when checking in. Visit www.marriott.com or call 1-888-236-2427.

Discounts at "The World's Hotel Company." The InterContinental Hotels Group offers travelers 62 and older a discount that varies somewhat depending on which of its family of hotels you're booking:

Candlewood Suites
Crowne Plaza Hotels and Resorts
Holiday Inn Express
Holiday Inn Hotels and Resorts
Hotel Indigo
InterContinental Hotels
Staybridge Suites

Be sure to ask for the discount, and join its Priority Rewards club to rack up points each time you stay at an IHG hotel. Visit www.ihg.com or call 1-877-424-2449.

Shine on at Starwood. The luxury properties owned by Starwood Hotels have an agreement with AARP that offers significant discounts. You can get 5 to 15 percent off with your AARP ID. Starwood also has a Preferred Guest Program that lets you accrue points to be exchanged for free stays later—and one of the benefits is that it requires far fewer points to do so than most luxury hotels, and there are no blackout days on using those freebies. The participating Starwood Hotels are:

Aloft Hotels
Ascend Collection
Element Hotels
Four Points by Sheraton
Le Méridien
Luxury Collection
Sheraton
St. Regis
W Hotels
Westin

Visit www.starwoodhotels.com for information. The individual hotel chains also have toll-free numbers.

Embassy Suites. With Embassy Suites, a part of the Hilton Hotels group, you can get a discount with your AARP card. While the Hilton group has discontinued its Senior HHonors program, it may be worthwhile noting that Embassy Suites offers a discount to government and military employees with ID. Visit www.embassysuites.com or call 1-800-EMBASSY.

High on the (Hyatt) hog. Because

the Hyatt corporation has an arm that specializes in luxury assisted-living residences for seniors, you might expect that it would offer senior discounts at Hyatt Hotels and, in fact, it does. Seniors can save up to 50 percent off the rack rate, although the actual percentage may vary depending on where you're staying. Some hotels do not participate so call 1-888-591-1234 to find out specific details for the hotel location of interest to you.

Early Bird Secret

Booking the Unknown Can Save Big Bucks

Like to gamble—with your hotel reservation? Go to www.hotwire.com or www.priceline.com, and book your hotel in your destination of choice. You can choose from a range of two-, three-, and four-star hotels in major cities across the United States at bargain basement prices. The deal at these "opaque" sites, as they're called, is that hotels with rooms unsold post them anonymously. The details are usually pretty specific, such as the general neighborhood, the star rating, the price, even the check-in and check-out days for which that price is valid. The catch is that you won't be told *which* hotel you'll be staying in or its address until you've already paid. So if you find you don't like it, it's too late—no refunds, buddy. But if you're flexible and don't mind taking a risk, you can save a whole lot of money and, with a bit of luck, enjoy a stay in a luxury hotel.

Getting "rad" at the Radisson. Even though we've been telling you over and over to check and compare rates, Radisson makes it easy for you in the Specials and Packages page of its site. Visit its Web site, and if you click on one of the changing roster of "Hot Deals" hotels, you have the option of searching for the lowest available rate, the AAA rate, the government rate, and the senior citizen rate. Take a moment to view them all and see what you find. And then don't hesitate to call its reservations line and see if there's anything you may have missed! Go to www.radisson.com (Click on Specials and Packages, then Hot Deals) or call 1-888-395-7046.

Bargains at Bed-and-Breakfasts...and Beyond

Because the vast majority of bed-and-breakfast inns are relatively small and private affairs, there is no consistent senior discount, but there is almost always someone capable of making decisions on the other end of the phone line. You're more likely to get a senior discount at a larger inn. If you ask at a small B&B, such as one with three to four bedrooms where your hostess may also be the owner, cook, dishwasher, and bed maker, you may be imposing more of a burden on her than you would be by asking at a larger establishment. Then again, it never hurts to ask! Meanwhile, there are lots of other exciting alternatives to traditional lodgings.

Join the Evergreen Club. A special and almost ridiculously inexpensive lodging option just for seniors comes from membership in the Evergreen Club. This organization is specifically for those 50 and over and consists of more than 2,000 members who open their homes to serve as B&Bs each for just one guest or couple. With your annual membership—$60 for singles or $75 for a couple—you get a catalog twice each year with the full listings and photos. You choose where you want to go, call the host, and plan your visit. The club asks that you pay your host a small amount, less than $25 per night, toward expenses. It's a way not only to travel without excessive costs but also to make real friends and connections around the country. Visit www.evergreenclub.com or call 1-815-456-3111.

Swap your space! Even before the Internet, savvy travelers around the globe were putting their names on house swap lists. Since the Internet, the trickle has become a deluge. The lists pair people who want to visit each other's cities or countries, and you go stay at their home or apartment while they come stay at yours—all for free. You get the comforts of home, an exciting place to visit, and no hotel bill. You can sign up for fee-based online organizations that give you access to other members and photos of their homes. The benefit to this is that you can go with a swap site that's specific to seniors (so you can be sure that you won't have college students on spring break in your Florida apartment!). If you're new to the world of house swapping, visit these sites for more information:

www.seniorshomeexchange.com
www.homeforswap.com
www.homeforexchange.com
www.craigslist.org (Choose a city and click on Home Swap under the heading Housing.)
www.sabbaticalhomes.com (This is mainly a swap site for academic professionals, but others are welcome to search it as well.)

Welcome Traveller. Similar to the Evergreen Club, but free to join, Welcome Traveller is unusual in that members can distinguish themselves by their interests. If you're a crafter or quilter, a runner, or an educator, for example, you can stay with like-minded hosts who welcome you into their

Ka-Ching!

Vegas Is Not Just for Gambling!

Okay, we have to be clear: The whole point of Las Vegas is to separate you from your money as pleasurably as possible. Don't go expecting to come home richer in much of anything other than experience. This hot city is an amazing destination for folks of all ages. Here's how to keep your cents and sense about you:

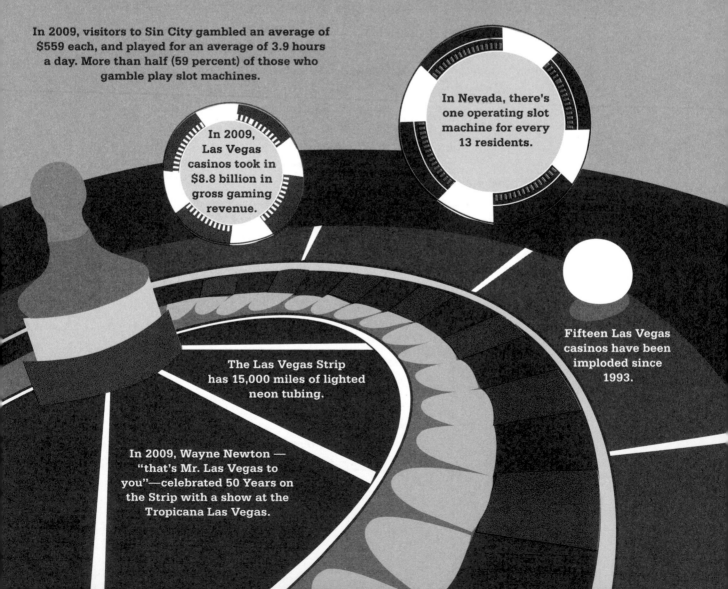

In 2009, visitors to Sin City gambled an average of $559 each, and played for an average of 3.9 hours a day. More than half (59 percent) of those who gamble play slot machines.

In 2009, Las Vegas casinos took in $8.8 billion in gross gaming revenue.

In Nevada, there's one operating slot machine for every 13 residents.

Fifteen Las Vegas casinos have been imploded since 1993.

The Las Vegas Strip has 15,000 miles of lighted neon tubing.

In 2009, Wayne Newton — "that's Mr. Las Vegas to you"—celebrated 50 Years on the Strip with a show at the Tropicana Las Vegas.

GET A PACKAGE.

Las Vegas makes its *real* money in the casinos, so they're interested in getting you there, and finding you somewhere to sleep, in a very reasonably priced way. Check out the packages on offer from hotels, airlines, and tour operators. This is one case where the super-low rate might, in fact, be the super-best deal, without a lot of hidden fees and surcharges.

STAY ON THE STRIP.

Don't assume that you have to avoid the biggest, brassiest, brightest places on the Strip to save money. Those hotels are also the ones that are likeliest to have super-low rates to keep the rooms full and thus keep the restaurants and casinos buzzing. Unless you're staying at the super high-end places, such as the Bellagio (where suites can be north of $1,000 a night!), you can probably stay at a three-star hotel in a very nice room for as little as $60 to $70 a night.

DON'T BOOK A SHOW IN ADVANCE.

Show tickets can be had on the day of the show for as much as 50 percent off. Unless you're absolutely determined to see one specific show, wait until you get there and see what kind of special offers await you at your hotel, in the casino, or at the box office. At the very least, you're sure to get $5 to $10 off unsold seats at the last minute.

NEVER RENT A CAR.

Whether you're staying right on the Strip or on a quieter street, all your travel can be done on foot or in a taxi for less than the cost—and hassle—of renting and parking a car. Be aware that the complimentary airport shuttle that came with your hotel booking may take a lot longer and be a bit hotter and more crowded than a taxi, but if you're prepared to expect that, it's certainly your least expensive option for getting to and from the airport.

The Rio and Wynn casinos don't have floors that begin with "4." The number is bad luck in Chinese culture.

TAKE THE BUS.

Traveling up and down the Strip and getting to your hotel and other attractions, hop on the Citizens Area Transit bus that runs up and down the Strip. A one-way trip is $1 for seniors 60 and older with ID. If you're doing a lot of moving around, you'll do better with the 24-Hr. General Market Pass—good for unlimited trips. It's $2 for seniors, instead of the regular price of $5.

homes simply to be hospitable, and to go visit others in their turn. There is also a category for travelers, either couples or singles, who are 50-plus and for women traveling alone. (You can simply register as General Interest traveler, too, if you prefer.) Visit www.welcometraveller.org for more information.

Wrangling Rock-Bottom Prices on Car Rentals

Senior discounts can be a tightrope walk when it comes to car rentals. Too young and you won't get a discount—too old and you won't get a car! Many, many companies provide a good discount and make special accommodations for their senior renters, and the tips here will help you get the best rate you can, wherever you're renting.

Check the AARP rate. As always, AARP has already negotiated discount rates for its card-carrying members with partner companies. For cars, there's a wide range of benefits, not only in terms of discounts off the weekly rate, but also other perks such as free upgrades. Here are some recent offers from partner rental companies at the AARP travel site, and new offers arise all the time.

Alamo: Free upgrade, last-minute weekend rental for $18 per day.
Avis: Rent for five days, pay for four.
Budget: Take $25 off a weekly rental.
Enterprise: Free upgrade, 5 percent off a rental.
Hertz: Get $50 off weekly rental, free day on weekend rental.

When in Rome... If you're going to Europe, reserve your car through Auto Europe. This organization has more than 4,000 car rental locations around the world, and it also rents specialty cars and RVs. Its excellent prices will be quoted in dollars, and you confirm and pay on your credit card at the time of booking, which can be a real benefit if the dollar takes another dramatic slide before your trip (or could end up losing you some money if the dollar suddenly rallies). It also has 24-hour customer support on its toll-free U.S. number, and the Web site lists toll-free numbers from every country in Europe so you can always call for support. Write down the number for the country you're visiting before you go. The base rate at Auto Europe is likely to be less expensive than the senior discount at a larger corporation, so be sure to compare it before you make your decision. Recent special deals included a free Portable GPS with minimum 5 day car rental, free upgrade with early booking, and 15% off a Mercedes-Benz or other luxury car rental. Visit www.autoeurope.com or call 1-888-223-5555 for information.

You May Be Too Old to Rent a Car

If you're planning to rent a car outside the United States, be aware that there are some countries that impose an upper age limit on rentals. In Ireland, for example, you may pay an extra fee if you're over 70, and in Ireland and Israel, you can't rent a car at all if you're over 75. Similarly, in the United Kingdom and Northern Ireland, 69 is the age limit for rental at many agencies, although some will allow rentals for drivers over 70 by adding a hefty fee. Greece, Turkey, Poland, Malta, Romania, and the Czech Republic limit rentals for those over 70, and many Denmark agencies don't rent cars to drivers over 80. If you're close to or over the limits, check and then check again when booking your car—even if the American branch of a large agency tells you it's okay. Its European counterpart may disagree, so check with the source to be sure you're not left without wheels at the end of a long flight.

Go National. To find the best car rental deals National has to offer, visit their Web site and click on Car Rental Specials to Go, where the latest local, regional and international rates plus e-coupon discounts can be found. These include daily, weekly, weekend and one-way rental car specials as well as their Last Minute travel discounts, available for a limited time only so check weekly. Reservations online at www.nationalcar.com or call 877-222-9058.

Enterprise, Dollar, and Thrifty. Enterprise offers weekend rates starting at $9.99 per day for Friday through Monday rentals and special discounts and rental coupons when you sign up for Email Extras. And they pick you up. Dollar and Thrifty give you a 10 percent discount when you pay with the American Express card. Check the Web sites for other specials and offers at www.enterprise,com, www.dollar.com and www.thrifty.com.

Don't rent at the airport. It's more of a hassle, but if you use the rental company that's *not* actually in the airport terminal, you'll nearly always get a lower rate. Look for the fine print when you're booking. It will say something like, "shuttle available from Terminal A" or "at 1234 Route 10," and that generally means you're going to have to go an extra mile to get there, so to speak. Hertz will never be outside the terminal. Enterprise might.

Rent for a week. The weekly rental rate is always better than the daily rate, so always inquire about it, even if you only need the car for a few days. Depending on the renter, it might be less expensive to return the car after four days of a weekly rental than to pay for four individual days—especially if there's a weekly special at the moment.

Big Savings on International Travel

The weak dollar means that there's been enough of a drop-off in European travel from the States that the industry is more eager than ever to lure Americans to the Old Country. Nonetheless, deals need to be very good to offset the dramatically higher costs, now that the euro is worth so much more than the dollar. Some Americans decide just to ignore it—if that café au lait costs $8, that's just the cost of seeing the City of Lights!—but savvy travelers want to squeeze every ounce of good out of their dollar when it doesn't stretch as far as it used to.

Go out of season. Getting to Europe in winter costs a lot less than going there in the height of summer, when you can hardly walk down the streets of perennially popular cities such as Florence or Venice. Book your travel for times when hotels aren't packed and tourist attractions have some breathing room. Go to the Caribbean in June or July rather than January—the temperatures on the islands tend to stay consistently warm, so chances are you won't find it much hotter than the place you left!

Globetrot on the cheap with Elderhostel. Elderhostel is the granddaddy of senior travel organizations, helping seniors travel the globe since 1975. Elderhostel runs more than 8,000 programs across all 50 United States, in 90 countries—and on all seven continents. Sail a Swedish icebreaker to Antarctica to see whales. Or ride a camel through the burning sands of Egypt. It's hard to conceive of a trip that Elderhostel doesn't already run in some form. Order a catalog or take a spin through its Web site for inspiration, whether you've always meant to visit Mount Rushmore, study art at a New York City museum, go bird-watching on the Georgia coast, or ride a horse through Shawnee National Forest. It's a not-for-profit organization so you can't beat the prices compared to the typical for-profit tour operator. The Web site features a long list of U.S. multi-day trips for under $600. It's also reassuring to go with the pros, who have been doing this so well for so long. Visit www.elderhostel.org or call 1-800-454-5768 for information.

Take a cruise. You're far more immune to the high costs of gas, lodging, and food for Americans on the ground in Europe if *you're not on the ground*! Take a cruise that hits major ports of call around Europe, so that your primary food and lodging expenses are already covered, on the ship, in dollars. This way, you're far more protected from currency fluctuations that could leave you gasping at the exchange rate of your hotel bill.

Early Bird Secret

Lock In the Price before You Go

As the euro, the British pound, and other currencies have strengthened against the dollar, tour operators have become keenly aware that the exchange rate can be a significant deterrent to travelers who might otherwise have been eager to hop a plane across the pond. Thus, a number have offers that lock in the dollar rate you pay for the accommodations and travel in Europe before you go. Of course it's a gamble: If the dollar keeps weakening, you can come out significantly more ahead than if you were paying in euros. But if the dollar suddenly rallies, you could end up paying significantly more. The key? Find out the exact rate at which the tour company proposes locking in your price, and then make a decision based on the best possible information available to you: Does the dollar seem to be trending up or down? How far away is your trip? (Six months away is riskier than two months away, for example.) And, not least, use the Internet to research the local price if you weren't buying a package through an agency. Too much padding on your hotel bill to make up the agency's profit might make it all a wash.

Take the train. If you are a European senior citizen, your train travel would be free. Many countries, such as Ireland, present citizens with a free rail-travel pass when they turn 65. The good news is that even Americans get to take advantage of Europe's generous senior travel discounts, when it comes to rail travel. If you're 60 and over, you can buy a Flexipass for 15 percent less than the standard cost of a first-class pass. First class can be quite luxurious on a British train, with large plushy seats and waiter service, but the second-class pass, for any age, is almost 30 percent cheaper than first class, so you may want to save that extra 15 percent and just go second class, which is perfectly comfortable. That's not necessarily so in France, where first class is *decidedly* nicer, and a first-class pass for seniors costs less than $300 for travel three days out of a one-month period. Additional days can be purchased at the discount price for about $40. For more information, contact www.britrail.com or www.raileurope.com.

Fly local. If you're headed to Europe and plan on flying between countries once you get there, don't book every leg of your trip through an airline based in the United States. Instead, go online and check out the local discount airlines, such as Ryan Air (www.ryanair.com), which flies all over Europe for a fraction of the price of other airlines, including specials where one leg of your

Want to Learn a New

Mais Oui!

Traveling to Spain and don't even know how to ask for a *cerveza* in the local tongue? Many specialized language courses are geared specifically toward older adults, and a bunch even have a study-abroad component. Check out these and you'll be able to *hablar español* and *parle francais* before you know it!

AMERISPAN STUDY ABROAD

This company offers opportunities to learn over 15 languages in more than 45 countries. Visit www.amerispan.com or call 1-800-879-6640.

THE CHAUTAUQUA INSTITUTION

Based on Lake Chautauqua in New York, this institute offers a "55-Plus Residential Week" with programming that presents lectures, discussions or films. The Exploritas Programs offer learning adventures for 55+ adults with domestic and interational travel. For information on their Encore Chorale Camp at Chautauqua for singers, visit EncoreCreativity.org. More information is available on the Institute's Web site at www.ciweb.org or call the Office of Group Sales and Senior Programming at 716-357-6262.

CLOSE UP WASHINGTON

Ever want to know more about how this country *really* works? Attend a week of seminars in the nation's capital and get an insider's perspective on politics. Visit www.closeup.org or call 1-800-256-7387.

ELDERHOSTEL EXPLORITAS ROAD SCHOLAR

This new program from Elderhostel offers domestic and international active experiential learning programs with small groups (no more than 24) of active Explorers. Features include hands-on presentations in the field, behind-the-scenes experiences that would be difficult

Language?

or impossible to arrange on your own, ideally located accommodations and independent time to explore topics of interest to you. Recent offerings included Cultural Heritage and Traditions of Japan, Turkey's Living Treasures and Switzerland by Rail. Closer to home trips included Essence of Hawaii, Ride Colorado's Historic Railroads and Northwest Currents: Seattle to Victoria, BC to San Juan Island. Details at roadscholar.org or call 1-800-454-5768.

EXPERIENCIA CENTRO DE INTERCAMBIO BILINGUE Y CULTURAL AC

Learn to speak Spanish quickly and easily at this school in Cuernavaca, Mexico, that caters to students of all ages. Visit www.mexicoamigos.com or call 866-477-2647.

NATIONAL REGISTRATION CENTER FOR STUDY ABROAD

This organization offers programs specifically for mature adults, with programs in many countries. Find out more at www.nrcsa.com or call 414-278-0631.

SMITHSONIAN RESIDENT ASSOCIATE PROGRAM

Established as a division of the Smithsonian Institution, this continuing education program offers seminars and study tours. Membership is $35 and offers you 25 to 40 percent off on trips and programs. Get details at www.residentassociates.org or call 202-633-3030.

trip might cost, for example, two euro. Be aware that discount airlines tend to fly into lesser known airports, often outside the major city you're flying to, but hop on a bus (at the senior discount) or pick up your rental car (again, don't forget that discount) and enjoy the savings. But how could you possibly know what all the little low-cost carriers are in Europe? Simple. You'll look them up at flycheapo.com, a Web site that gives you all the names and where they fly (although you'll have to go to each airline's own Web site to book your flight). The name may be a little silly, but it's what we're trying to do!

Family and Friends

A Good-Times Guide to Living It Up with Your Loved Ones

Good Grandparenting, the Early Bird Way

Congratulations! You now have the quality time to spend and wisdom to share with the little ones. But what kind of grandparent can you be? Well, there are as many kinds of grandparents as there are people. There is no one right way to be a good grandparent. Some grandparents are willing and able to spend ample time with their grandkids, while others may only see them on holidays. Grandchildren, especially when they're young, just want to know that you love them, and there are many, many ways to express that fruitfully, without spending boatloads of cash.

Give them your time. If you have already retired and live close to your grandkids, your time may be the most valuable gift you can give them and your own kids. Most children would rather have their kids in the care of a trusted family member than in the care of a babysitter or day-care center. So all three generations will benefit if you are able to spend time with your grandkids regularly.

Give them treats. Why not? It's a grandparent's prerogative, right? (Right!) If you are not able to see the grandkids as often as you'd like—if you are still working or if you live far away—you might plan a short vacation for them, with you as the destination. When you do see them, just make sure the time is as special as possible. Schedule outings that might be enjoyable or memorable. Just make sure that you are focusing on the little ones when you visit. It can be easy to get caught up in grown-up pursuits or just want to relax but undivided attention from Grandma or Grandpa is treat enough for most kids.

Give money. Okay, we admit, it's pretty transparent. But we're not talking about fives and tens here. If you have the means to do so, consider helping your kids save for their kids' educations. You can set up or contribute to a 529 college savings plan for your grandkids (see page 243). They will certainly appreciate it later.

Help out with child care. Not every parent can afford child care, and if you live close by, they may not have to. Moreover, lucky is the child who has grown up under the watchful eye of a doting grandparent. Just make sure that you take these precautions:

- Childproof your home. Store medications and cleaning products where kids can't reach them. Consider using gates to close off rooms in which there are fragile objects or dangerous stairs.

- Adjust to your limitations. You may not move as quickly as you used to, so if you are taking the children for walks around the neighborhood, the

11 Things

to Do with Your Grandchildren That Cost (Almost) Nothing

1. Plan a **picnic** at your local park or beach.

2. Take them to a **storytelling** session at your library.

3. Teach them how to **putt** into a plastic cup in your backyard.

4. Teach them how to make **pizza** (with store-bought dough, if you prefer), and let them add the toppings.

5. Have a picture drawing **contest** of each other.

6. Make **chalk drawings** in the driveway.

7. **Water plants** with a plastic mister bottle.

8. Go **fishing**.

9. Start a **scrapbook** of magazine clippings, mementos from their visit, or photos of their parents.

10. Visit the local **fire station** (make an appointment first).

11. Play **dress-up**.

museum, or the mall, make sure you can keep track of them, whether this means using a stroller, a walking harness, or training them well not to run off. Be sure that you are able to operate all car seats and gear properly.

- Refresh yourself on first aid. Do you remember how to do the Heimlich maneuver? Do you remember basic first aid? Freshen up before you take responsibility for small children.
- Prepare for their arrival. Make sure that your house is a welcoming place. You have nutritious food and snacks for the kids and a cozy, safe place for napping and relaxing.

Pass on your Early Bird wisdom! Children are most enthralled by the simplest pleasures. Learning to blow the fluff off of a dandelion with Grandma can easily become one of the most memorable moments of a person's childhood. Need some inspiration? Think back to your own grandparents and what they taught you. Usually the lessons related to everyday tasks, but they were precious nonetheless and stuck with you forever. This falls into "The Best Things in Life Are Free" category.

Show them where they came from. Kids absolutely love history, so take the little ones to visit the places of your past and, if possible, those of your parents and grandparents. Show them the school you went to, your childhood home, and so on. Tell them stories of your past—that your own grandfather rode to school on a horse because there were no cars back then; that your grandmother kept chickens in the backyard, and you were in charge of feeding them. Whatever the family stories are, no matter how small, they will help give your grandchildren a sense of their place in the world.

Get them cooking! Kids love to get their hands dirty, and there is no better place to do that than in a bowl of bread or biscuit dough. Or, make it a real learning experience and pass down simple family recipes. You can talk about where your family originated, who invented the recipes, and why they are so beloved. And then you eat the result!

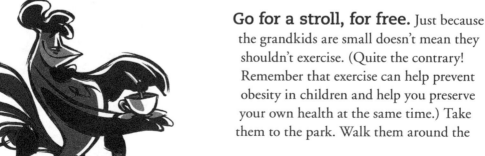

Go for a stroll, for free. Just because the grandkids are small doesn't mean they shouldn't exercise. (Quite the contrary! Remember that exercise can help prevent obesity in children and help you preserve your own health at the same time.) Take them to the park. Walk them around the block. Play catch. Rainy outside? No problem. Get thee to a bowling alley and exercise your senior discount!

Read to them. Go to the library together and rediscover the books of your youth. Share the story of *Mike Mulligan and His Steam Shovel* by Virginia Lee Burton with little boys. Read the girls the *Betsy-Tacy* by Maud Hart Lovelace. Share books on the topics you find meaningful with them. And help them find books on topics that they are excited about. Help them sign up for library cards—it's a thrill to have one of your very own! Most libraries have excellent outreach programs for kids. Visit the American Library Association site at www.ala.org to find links to libraries in your area, news, and reading suggestions.

Top 10 Must-Read Books for Kids and Their Grandparents

Granted, we all have our favorites, but our experts found that these books had major staying power when read to young children. Feel free to add to this list or start your own!

1. **Ramona the Pest** by Beverly Cleary

2. **From the Mixed-Up Files of Mrs. Basil E. Frankweiler** by E. L. Konigsburg

3. **Charlotte's Web** by E. B. White

4. **Stuart Little** by E. B. White

5. **The Adventures of Huckleberry Finn** by Mark Twain

6. **Where the Wild Things Are** by Maurice Sendak

7. **Harold and the Purple Crayon** by Crockett Johnson

8. **The Lorax** by Dr. Seuss

9. **Blueberries for Sal** by Robert McCloskey

10. **Rabbit Hill** by Robert Lawson

What are *your* favorites?

Get growing and plant some herbs or vegetables. Doesn't matter whether you live in the country, in a house, or in an apartment, all you need is a sunny spot or window, some dirt, a few small pots, and a package of seeds. Let the little ones scoop out the dirt with a small child's shovel (or better yet, their hands), and use their pinkies to poke holes for the seeds. If you're planting seedlings, show them how to transplant and pack the new soil around the "baby" plant. When the goods start to grow, let them do the harvesting!

Introduce them to the classics! Most kids just love movies, and this is your chance to get them interested in the classics that have entertained generations. You may think that middle schoolers wouldn't enjoy a Mickey Rooney–Judy Garland movie, but guess again! Here are our experts' favorites:

Musicals: *Singing in the Rain; The Court Jester; The Sound of Music.*
Comedy: Anything featuring the Marx Brothers or the Three Stooges; *It's a Mad, Mad, Mad, Mad World; The Absent-Minded Professor.*
Animals: *Black Beauty; The Yearling; Old Yeller* (have hankies handy for the kids and you).
Classics, old and new, for little kids and grown-up kids: *Mary Poppins; Lady and the Tramp; Cars; Beauty and the Beast; The Little Mermaid; Hans Christian Andersen.*

Listen to good music. Rainy out and nothing to do? Spend the day listening to music! Dust off that old record collection and show them what vinyl really sounds like! Then listen to their favorite songs. Make sure you give and take and don't get hooked on that expensive iPod. By the end of the day—who knows—you might be able to rap!

Visit a museum. Museums are amazing places for children, and you'll probably both get age-related entry fee discounts. Similar to the mall on a rainy day, they have wide open spaces for kids to explore, and you to get some exercise, but museums don't offer as many temptations for you to spend money on frivolous things. You can just wander around, of course, but why not create a treasure hunt for your grandchild? Count the princesses, knights, flowers, dogs, or whatever appeals that you see in the artwork. Talk about the different types of pieces you see—is it a sculpture, a painting, a tapestry? Even if you find museums crushingly boring, remember: There are museums for every kind of person, including ones dedicated to fire trucks, soup tureens, nuts, sports cars, tennis, rock and roll, and even bricks! (No kidding! Visit the Haverstraw Brick Museum in Haverstraw, New York.)

Make something. Break out the paints, the toothpicks, the glue, the construction paper, the crayons. If you have access to a computer, you're in luck. The Internet has a world of advice for fun projects. Just search on Google for "family crafts," and you'll come up with abundant listings, including sites like these:

http://familycrafts.about.com/
http://crafts.kaboose.com/
http://www.amazingmoms.com

Otherwise, a box made of Popsicle sticks is always a big hit, especially when decorated with some seashells!

Get them outside! Where they used to play outside until dark, many children now play in front of televisions and computers. What to do? Grab a birding book, lace on their tiny hiking boots or sneakers, and go for a nature walk, right in your own neighborhood. Look for different kinds of birds and wildlife, and see if the kids can remember the names of trees. It costs nothing to be outside, and the rewards are enormous—for everybody.

Teach them about spirituality. You can share your faith with your grandchildren for no money at all. It's a gift that will give them comfort and a connection to you throughout their lives. Take the kids to services or special events with you. Read them stories that explain your religion. Tell them family stories about your parents' and grandparents' faiths.

Forget Computer Games!

Strange but true: Most kids just love old-fashioned board and card games. If you don't have any, see if any of your neighbors do, or scope out local tag sales where they can be had for very little money. Our experts found that there were favorites among children polled, including:

Candyland

Monopoly

Connect Four

Checkers

Rummy

Old Maid

Dominoes

Older kids even took to card games like pinochle, contact bridge, and backgammon!

You be the student. Ask the grandkids to teach you something from their worlds. Together you can play Wii, make a video for YouTube, learn the lyrics to a hit song, or another activity that you would be unlikely to explore without a child's help and that will make you the coolest grandparent on the block.

Preserving and Sharing Memories

So many of us have our most precious photos and mementos in shoe boxes in the closet. Thankfully, today's technology can rescue even the most dog-eared pictures and enable you to restore them for next to nothing and share them with everyone in your family. Go ahead and haul them out and preserve your past for future generations.

It doesn't matter what you've got: old black and white Polaroids, Kodak Instamatic snapshots, SX-70 "instant" color photos from the 1970s—old photos of people near and dear to your heart are worth their weight in gold and are worth preserving, protecting, and sharing. If you are a real photo fan, think about contacting your friends and family from around the country and have them send you their images, too. You be the designated copier, and once you're done, everyone will have complete sets of images.

Storing Treasured Photographs

How many bags of photos do you have lurking around your house? If you're like us, you have them in every room of the house. This is definitely not the best or most efficient way to store what really are prized possessions. How to keep them safe? Read on.

Find a dry closet. If you're relegated to storing your old photos in a closet, make sure that it's a dry closet. Keeping your photos in the damp basement will hasten curling and disintegration.

Use protective papers and mattes. Make sure protective papers or mattes are acid-free and lignan-free and are intended specifically for photo preservation. Paper should be made from cotton or purified wood pulp. Plastic sleeves should be polyester or polyethylene, not PVC.

Store in albums or boxes. Photos can last for generations if you store them correctly in photo-specific boxes or albums, taking care to make sure that edges don't dent and the photos don't curl.

Sign them to remember. Label photos with a soft pencil on the reverse side in the margin. Never use a pen and never write on the surface of the photo or the rear surface of the photo.

Frame and clean! If you choose to display your photos for all to see, do so in a UV-protective glass frame, which will reduce fading. Clean the glass covering framed photos sparingly and with a soft rag; refrain from spraying glass cleaners directly on the glass itself because it can seep under the edges and damage the photo.

Early Bird Secret

Old Photos Make Great Christmas Gifts!

It's true! If you come across a stash of old photos long forgotten but much beloved, take them to a local photo lab—which may offer you a senior citizen's discount—and have them reproduced. Pop them into inexpensive frames, and surprise friends and family with one of the most heart-warming, thoughtful gifts they'll ever receive. One of our experts framed five long-forgotten family images from the 1930s for her older aunts; the result was sheer delight!

Making Copies of Your Favorite Images

Photos, like many other things in life, alas, fade. The only surefire way to protect old photos to guarantee that they will last for generations is to have them copied, reproduced, or digitally duplicated. You'll be glad you did, and so will your loved ones!

Make color photocopies. The most inexpensive way to reproduce photographs, it's also not ideal because of quality issues. Choose this route for second-tier photos and make sure to copy them onto good-quality, acid-free paper.

Have the photos shot. Ever wonder how museums make posters of famous paintings? They "shoot" them using a film camera, and get a negative produced that then can be reprinted at any size, on any sort of paper. You can have the same thing done for high-value photographs, and the result will be a quality reproduction along with a negative (so you can make more reproductions in the future). Check with your local university's photography department, and you may be able to have a student provide services at a steep discount.

Go digital. This is, by far, the soundest way of making sure your valuable images are both able to be copied, retained in tip-top shape, filed for easy sorting, shareable, and printable at any size. To do this, have your photos scanned—anyone from a teenager with a scanner to a photo shop can do this for you. Then, have the scanned images saved to a CD or a photo Web site, like snapfish.com or flickr.com, and you'll be able to print copies whenever you want them. File away the CDs by event, name, or year.

Reaching Out and Touching Someone—with Technology

One of the best ways to stay in touch with friends and family who live far away is to make audio or video messages with just a recorder or a camcorder. Although they are still referred to as videos, nowadays nearly all moving pictures of your family will be shot with a digital camera, making the results instantaneous. Here are some ideas to make your home videos original and fun.

DIY StoryCorps: *Family Interviews Are Worth Their Weight in Gold (and Won't Cost a Penny)*

Back in 2003, a national project called StoryCorps: The Conversation of a Lifetime, captured the country's attention and spread like wildfire. A recording booth was set up in New York's Grand Central Station, and folks like you and me stepped inside with a loved one, and one interviewed the other. Eventually, the project went national and the results—now into the hundreds of thousands—are archived at the Library of Congress. Why not be your own StoryCorps? Give an interview to one of your kids or grandkids, tape record or videotape it, and it will become a treasured gift to your family.

Move over Bruce Springsteen! Why not make your own music videos? Record a few songs that your grandparents taught you. Sing the kids that special song you danced to at your wedding. Have someone tape you while you bounce a grandchild on your knee and sing "The Itsy Bitsy Spider." If you don't like to sing, read your favorite poem and explain what you like about it.

Give a house or garden tour. Do you have a fabulous green thumb, resulting in spectacular summertime blooms that are the envy of your

7 Ways to Make Digital Photography Pay Off

Thinking about hiring a photographer to document a special event? Think again! Become your family and friends' photographer of record, and save yourself—and them—a bundle by going digital.

The highest cost you'll incur will be the price of the camera ($89 and up). You can download the results onto your computer, e-mail them to friends and family, and let them print whatever they want (or not). No developing costs, no mailing fees, instant results, and you get to delete any shots where you accidentally stuck your thumb in front of the lens.

With a digital camera, you can:

1 Photograph your grandchild's first day at school and have the entire family see the results (wherever they live) almost instantly.

2 Get snap-happy at your family reunion cookout.

3 Photograph your child's wedding.

4 Offer to take neighborhood prom pictures.

5 Be a home food photographer and show off your hubby's culinary creations.

6 Offer to be chief photographer on your next vacation.

7 Photograph your local Little League games.

friends? Do you grow your neighborhood's greatest tomatoes? Grab that digital video camera, take a walk around your garden or house, and give a grand tour. If it's spectacular enough, your local garden club may even put you on its list as a formal tour stop next season!

Transfer tapes to digital video. Do you have a bunch of old Betamax or VHS or even Super 8 family movies in your closet that your family hasn't seen in years? Digitize them by sending them to www.preserve-your-memories.com. For a nominal fee, they will send you a DVD with your selected movies, and they'll last for years.

Telling the Story of Your Life

What better treasure could you leave your family than your **memoirs**? Think about it: Your whole family will see you, your parents, your siblings, and your grandparents in a way that they never otherwise could. Sound daunting? It isn't! There are many resources to help you along, including a number of excellent books and Web sites that can boost your creativity and jog your memory.

You're not being graded. Rule number one when writing for yourself is: There are no grades! No one will check your grammar or grade you on how quickly you complete your project. All you need is a pen or pencil and some paper, or a computer. Sit down and tell your story.

Remember life's little pleasures. The smallest everyday occurrences are often the most interesting, so don't feel that you have to focus on life's landmark events: the weddings, graduations, and so on. How about when you learned how to drive a car? Or taught junior how to ride a bike or read? How about that spectacular cake your grandmother taught you how to make, that you now bake every holiday? Get creative!

Is it a memoir or a novel? Feel free to write your tale in whatever format suits you. Here are some ideas of quirky ways to pen those stories:

- Lists. You could easily fill a book with various lists: my favorite songs; what I wanted to be when I grew up; my favorite friends; my most memorable moments in the kitchen; most memorable moments with my husband; favorite vacations; and so on.

- Cookbook. Many memoirs and novels interweave the author's recipes. Yours can, too. If food is important to you, pass down your recipes and memories all in one place.

- Book of answers. What are the questions you wish you had asked your own mother or grandmother? Ask them of yourself and offer the answers. The book will be in question-and-answer format.

- Mixed media. Like a scrapbook, add photos and ephemera to your memoir. You can let the objects you paste in determine what you want to say in writing.

Scrapbooking on a Shoestring

What was once a matter of simply pasting photos into an album has become a multimillion dollar industry. It's never been easier to find high-quality scrapbooking materials than now, but why buy them when you can make them for virtually nothing? Scrapbooking lets you creatively catalog your past. And a huge benefit of the hobby's popularity is that it has a social component. You can find scrapbooking groups or take scrapbooking classes, which makes it even more pleasurable and makes it easier to meet new friends if you've moved. It creates an easy, seamless way to talk about your interests and your past.

Early Bird Secret

How to Be a Scrappy, Money-Saving Scrapbooker

Scrapbooking is a great way to pass the time, *and* you end up with a treasure that will delight family and friends. Unfortunately, supplies can really add up, so follow these tips to save money on the bells and whistles.

Put the scrap in scrapbook! Ask your local wallpaper store if there are sample rolls being thrown away, and graciously offer to take them. Visit the last day of your local annual library sale to see if design books are being tossed. Save gorgeous wrapping paper every time you open a gift. You'll harvest beautiful patterns for your albums this way.

Make your own stickers. Look through old magazines for images that can become your own signature stickers. If you see something you like and want more than one, make color copies. You'll save a fortune.

Print out the letters. Instead of buying them, print out alphabetical letters from your computer. Just cut the shape out and glue where you want them.

Second that notion! Forget about buying expensive gewgaws and doodads for your scrapbook. Raid your sewing kit, or visit a notions store, where you can get things like thread, lace edging, and more—for less.

Writing

Here are some questions to help spark your memory as you pen your autobiography.

Family and Friends

Which of your family members do you most resemble?

Who resembles you?

What is your favorite family story or legend?

Do you know anything about the day of your birth?

What is your earliest memory?

What was your childhood room like?

What were your parents like?

What did you like best about the neighborhood where you grew up?

Who were your childhood friends?

What games did you play?

School Days

What do you remember of elementary, middle, and high school?

Did you have favorite teachers?

Who was your best friend in each grade?

Were there special moments that you remember: pranks pulled, outings enjoyed, subjects you loved to study?

Were there outfits you liked to wear to school?

What was your best subject?

Did you play sports or join clubs?

Your Story

School Days

Did you go to the prom?

What did you do during summer vacations?

When did you get your driver's license?

Who taught you to drive?

Did you attend college? Where did you go and what did you study?

What was the most valuable thing you learned there?

What music did you listen to?

Work

When did you first leave home?

What was your first apartment or house like? Did you have roommates?

How did you decorate your house?

What did you wear to your first interview?

What was your first real job like? Describe an average day.

What was your first boss like?

Do you remember your first paycheck?

What were your special indulgences back then?

Of all the jobs you've had, is there one you really loved?

Did you have to travel for business? What were your best trips?

continues

Writing Your Story

Love and Relationships

When did you have your first date?

....

Your first kiss?

....

What are your three favorite love songs?

....

How did you and your true love meet?

....

What was your wedding like? Your honeymoon?

....

What were your best vacations?

....

What happened on the days your children were born?

....

What were they like as toddlers? As schoolchildren?

....

What made you most proud?

....

Finding a group. It's far easier to find a scrapbooking group than you might think. Check with your senior center or even a local gallery owner to see if someone is holding classes. One of our experts in Montana turned up a senior-specific class at the Paris Gibson Square Museum of Art in Great Falls—and better still, the class was free!

Starting a group. Can't find one? Start your own! Let all of your friends and neighbors know that Tuesday afternoon at your place is scrapbook day, and invite everyone over. Ask your friends to bring a shoebox filled with their materials and a scrapbook. You supply the tape, the soda pop, and the snacks!

The sky's the limit! Don't throw away that movie stub! Hang onto that postcard! The best bits of ephemera to save for your scrapbooks are newspaper clippings; report cards; party and wedding invitations; stubs from concerts, movies, and sporting events; stubs from airline or train tickets; cards and letters; favorite menus; play programs; announcement cards; and receipts from trips and vacations abroad (or at home!).

Getting to the Root of Your Family Tree

Genealogy research is booming along with us Boomers, who are all grown up and are now interested in finding out about our forebears. Thankfully, the Internet has made this much easier. It has given us the means to connect to faraway lands and old records almost instantly, and computer software has made mapping your family tree a piece of cake. What are the benefits to tracing the past? Read on to learn more!

Connecting with your family. The easiest place to begin your research is with your family. And it's one of the most pleasurable, too. This process will cause you to strengthen your bonds with your family and give you an excuse to see people. It may also cause you to reconnect with lost family members as well as discover new family that you never knew you had.

You'll get to travel. You may need to travel if you get serious about your research. There is a lot you can do over the phone and on the Internet, but in some cases, nothing can take the place of a personal visit.

You'll get to play Sherlock Holmes. Tracing family history often necessitates a lot of sleuthing. You'll find yourself turning over rocks and dusting off old papers to learn as much as you can about your family. Here are a few places to start:

- Old files. Many old files are not electronic and never will be. If you want to get a look at the real estate deed on your mom's birthplace, you will probably have to visit the local town hall and dig it up yourself. Make sure if you are planning a visit in which you want to access records or do local library research that you have checked the hours of operation of the town hall, library, historical society, and any place else you'd like to go.

- Conduct interviews. If you found out that your grandfather's best friend is still alive, you might want to see him in person. You will be more likely to see photos and other mementos if you can pay a visit yourself.

- Sightseeing. If your mother came from, say, Ireland, and you've never been, why not book a vacation there? You may be able to do some genealogy research while you are there. At the very least, planning a visit will cause you to focus on the place. You might want to read some books about it in advance. And while you are there, you may find family. Even if you don't, you'll have the chance to speak to the locals about what life was like in your mother's day.

You Don't Have to Leave Home to Get Started

Starting research on your family history is as simple as turning on the computer. There are many hundreds of excellent Web sites designed to aid you in your search for your past. Most of the sites are good for doing preliminary research, like determining what your father's hometown will have to offer as you delve into his past. Will there be a town library? A town hall? You might find other useful information on the Internet, like what your father's hometown used to look like or what the various historic buildings looked like. Here are some great places to start.

http://www.archives.com

http://www.cyndislist.com

http://www.accessgenealogy.com

http://www.refdesk.com/factgene.html

http://www.ellisisland.org

You'll grow a beautiful tree. If you're planning on putting the results of your research into tree form, you may wind up with something stunning. Some family trees are gorgeous works of art. They can be drawn on large papers, the lettering done with calligraphy. They can be cross-stitched into muslin alongside designs that represent the people. They can be made into a kind of scrapbook, with photos and clippings interwoven with the family tree. Your family tree can be as beautiful or as simple as you like.

You'll uncover valuable information. Your research may lead to important information about your family. It may put your mind at ease about strange choices in the past that were made or inheritances that were given. In these days of rapidly advancing science it may solve family medical mysteries. A look at the life spans of your forebears might give you crucial information about your history that your kids and grandkids could benefit from.

The 7 Keys to Solving Your Geneological Puzzle

It's an exciting challenge to try to complete the puzzle of where you came from, but figuring out where to begin can be overwhelming. Break the process into its individual parts and it's easier. These are the first places to start your quest:

1. People. What could be easier than just asking a simple question and receiving an answer from someone who remembers? The more information you can glean from your relatives and neighbors, the more smoothly the rest of the process will be.

- First step: Sketch out a rough family tree, and then ask each member of your family to help fill in the blanks. Does anyone remember the street on which grandma lived? Which church did the family attend? What was the name of the guy Aunt Sally married? Did Jean and David have four children or five? Isn't one of their kids living in the next town? Does anyone have his number?

- Next: Ask family for any documents they might have that you can borrow. This could be birth certificates, diaries, newspaper clippings. Be organized as you collect precious materials. Note what you received, when and from whom, and the date on which you returned it. Some things that you receive may appear to have no value, but they might be a crucial link that will lead you someplace else.

- Finally: Take notes as you speak to your loved ones. Little things they say like, "Oh, if only Charlie Farrell were alive—he'd remember!" might be useful. Charlie Farrell might have passed on, but his daughter may remember and like to speak to you. Follow up on everyone and every place mentioned. Find out as much as you can about who Charlie Farrell was and where he lived and if he had any family. Every piece of information you receive should ideally lead you to another piece of information. Don't worry if you feel the path is crooked. It may eventually lead you to where you want to go.

2. Town halls. Town halls keep information on property sales, marriages, births, deaths, taxes—all the big stuff in life. Researching your family will be much easier if you have something to go on—ideally, gleaned from family members or family papers: the street address of your family's house, your mother's birth and death dates, her parents' names. Before you plunge into public records, have as much material at your fingertips as possible.

3. Libraries. The library in your father's hometown probably keeps back issues, likely on microfiche, of the local paper. Find out how far back the records go. You might be able to find mention of your father's Little League team or Christmas pageant. Enlist the librarian in your search. She will probably be delighted by a challenge and have other ideas for you. There may be records besides newspapers that she can point you toward, including material from the local schools, like yearbooks.

Early Bird Secret

Check and Check Again

Our genealogy experts offer two key tips that may prove invaluable in doing family research.

Check your facts. There is a lot of bunk that gets passed down through the years. Just because Aunt Margaret said it's true doesn't make it so. And realize that sometimes mistakes were made in old records. Dates are transcribed with errors or false assumptions made. Don't let a clerical error throw you off. Make sure you dig for the truth.

Tinker with spelling. We've all heard the stories of immigrants whose long names were changed for simplicity at Ellis Island. Some families Americanized their own names to avoid discrimination. The Medvedevs became the Medveds. The Stramskis became the Strams. If your name is Griffin and you pull up a listing for a Griffen, take a look. Could be that a town clerk made a simple error. Don't overlook misspellings and variations, or you might be passing over a pot of gold.

4. Churches and synagogues. Houses of worship usually keep excellent records of their members. If you know where your family worshipped, you should be able to find records of marriages, baptisms, bat mitzvahs, and so on, depending on your faith.

5. Cemeteries. Cemeteries also keep good records and should be able to give you basic information on your family. You can simply read the grave marker, if you know where it is, to receive the fundamentals. Or you can ask for a more detailed record of the burial plot, who is there, their names, and birth and death dates. Many a family secret is discovered this way. Did you know that Aunt Hilda was Elmore's second wife?

6. Historical societies. These institutions act as your town's memory bank. They are filled with eager and helpful volunteers who will be delighted to aid you in your search for information about your past. Use this invaluable resource that many towns offer. Not only do most historical societies keep written records, they often have excellent photos of the town. Think of how meaningful it would be to find a photo of the snowy street where your father used to sled when the trolley couldn't run.

7. Immigrant resources. If your family came to this country within the last few generations, you may be able to get help at a resource center devoted to your country of origin. You can check the Internet, the phone book, and community newspapers to find out what may be available in your area. One of the biggest immigrant resources in the country is the museum at Ellis Island. More than 12 million immigrants to America claim New York's Ellis Island as their gateway to a new life. Ellis Island was open from 1892 to 1954. If you think that a relative of yours might have entered the country this way, check the Web site at www.ellisisland.org. You may be able to see the manifest entry and even a photo of the ship they arrived on. Incredible stuff! Every genealogist can use the free forms that the site offers as well as the advice on tracing your family. It's definitely worth a visit.

Reconnecting with Pals from the Past

Make new friends but keep the old. One is silver and the other gold. Remember that little ditty? It's easy to fall out of touch with old friends. Our middle years are dominated by working and bringing up babies so it's easy to let relationships slide. Your retirement years mark the perfect time to reconnect with old friends. They are likely in the same boat. The kids are grown, the job is winding down. Suddenly there is time for socializing again. Try these methods of getting back in touch with old buddies.

Staying in touch. What is true of genealogy research is true of finding old friends: Asking people is the easiest and most pleasurable first step. Call up the people you are still in touch with and ask if they have been in touch with other friends. Get contact information from them. Even if the old friends they are talking to are not the same as the ones you are looking for, they might be useful because the friends-of-friends might be in contact with the people you want to reach. This friends-of-friends strategy works well of school networks and old neighborhood networks, where there may have been large and overlapping rings of friends.

Remember your alma mater! Get back in touch with any schools you attended—high school, college, or any professional programs. Most colleges have active Web sites with a section dedicated to alumni affairs and many high schools do, too. You can sign up for the site, and you'll have access to the alumni directory and the alumni notes. Reunions usually take place every five years, with the "0" reunions—10, 20, 30, and so on—being considered the big ones. If you decide to go to a reunion, make your plans clear to your classmates. Sign up early when the paperwork comes around because the more people that are signed up, the more likely others will be to follow.

Did You Know?

Your Alumni Gift Matters If you get involved in your old school's affairs, consider giving money. Even if it is a modest sum, your contribution will matter. If you are still working and you work for a large firm, your employer may have a matching gift program where it will give the same amount you do, essentially doubling your contribution. If it doesn't, no matter. Your participation is what counts. When your school goes to solicit money from foundations, it is more likely to get help when the rate of alumni participation is high. So your $25 or $50 or more will go a longer way than you realize. And remember the tax deduction!

Your Fuzzy, Furry, and Feathered Friends

They make your blood pressure and cholesterol drop. They can ease depression and loneliness and increase your security. They force you to get out and get some sunlight and exercise. Three cheers for our pets! Our four-legged family members are the very essence of easy companionship and unconditional love. Many retirees find that they spend more time with their pets than anyone else upon leaving the workplace. In fact, they dote on them. And why shouldn't they? The kids are grown up. The grandkids are away or in school. We should all have someone to spoil.

Your Dog Is Good for Your Health

The link between pets and good health is no joke. If you do not have a pet but are thinking of getting one, consider these benefits. Pets have been proven to:

• Lower cholesterol, triglycerides, blood pressure, and stress;

• Raise energy and exercise levels (especially dogs);

• Restore a sense of usefulness and meaning;

• Offer companionship;

• Connect you to the world (especially dogs—you meet people as you walk them);

• Offer security (especially dogs); and

• Occupy your time with care and play.

Finding the Right Pet for You

If you are in the market for a pet, first talk to pet owners about their experiences. Go to the local dog park if you are thinking about a dog, or if you think you'd like a cat, visit the pet store and chat up the lady buying kitty litter. You need to make sure that you will choose the pet that best suits your lifestyle and personality.

Man's best friend. Dogs are goofy, loving, and responsive to you. They can also be messy, energetic, and time consuming. If you think you'd like a dog, realize that you'll have to walk it three or four times a day (or hire someone to help you). And you'll need to make sure you are home enough to be a good companion. If you are interested in bringing a pooch into your life, ask yourself the following questions:

- Do I want a puppy or an adult dog?
- Will I buy one from a breeder or rescue one from a shelter?
- Have I puppy-proofed my home?
- How much do I know about the breed I'm interested in?

Make sure you have the answers to these questions firmly in place before you do something on impulse. Dogs are a long-term commitment. But they'll repay every ounce of love you give them with double that amount.

What's new, pussycat? Ever hear the expression "It's like herding cats?" There's a reason for it: While they may be elegant and charming, they are also more aloof and resistant to training. They may scratch things—you or the furniture. And they may not cuddle on your schedule, only theirs. But they don't need to go outside. They are small and portable. And they don't mind being home without you. So if you have a demanding schedule for work or play, they might be just the thing for you.

Birds of a feather. Birds are not as cuddly as dogs and cats, but they are certainly affectionate and love their people. They are easier to take care of than dogs because they don't go outside. Some birds live a very long time. Parrots can live 40 to 80 years. Even parakeets are long lived at an average of 18 years. If you plan to get a bird, realize you may be in for a lifelong commitment, and make arrangements for the animal in your will.

Fishing for compliments? Fish, like cats, are elegant. Their graceful turns around the aquarium are positively hypnotic and calming. They don't require too much maintenance, but you do need to clean the aquarium, and you might need help with that. Depending on the size of your aquarium, you may need to hire someone to come to your home to care for the fish when you take a vacation.

Other creatures to love. There are other choices out there—rabbits, gerbils, lizards, snakes, and more. Make sure you fully investigate the pros and cons of an animal before you commit to it. Many of these pets are small and quick and untrainable, which can make them challenging for people who are slowing down or have conditions like arthritis or back pain.

Seniors Get Free Pets!

If you are longing for the companionship of an animal but just can't see spending a hefty fee to adopt one, ask the shelter to waive its fee. Some shelters and rescue groups get grants from corporations and the government to pair seniors with pets. Examples of programs include Purrfect Pals, which matches senior cats with senior folks (http://www.purrfectpals.org/About/SeniorsProgram.asp) and Purina Pets for Seniors (www.purinapetsforseniors.com), which offers pet adoption assistance.

How Much Is That Doggy in the Window?

If you plan to buy a gerbil or a fish or another offbeat animal, a store is fine. But for dogs and cats, it's the worst place you can go. Dogs that end up at pet stores are often born in "puppy mills," terrible farms where canine mothers do nothing but breed, and animals are not carefully bred, which can lead to congenital defects. Puppy mills also churn out animals that are not in tip-top health. You don't need the heartbreak of bringing a dog home and bonding with it, only to have it die a week or a month later. So if not to a store, where to go?

Going to a shelter. Think of the dogs and cats—and sometimes birds and other animals—you find at shelters as "certified preowned." These are animals that for one reason or another have lost their homes and need new ones. You'll find all kinds of breeds and ages and conditions at a shelter, and you should look to the shelter staff to help match you up with the right animal for you. Adoption fees are usually minimal so this is the humane and economical choice. The best place to start browsing is on Petfinder (www.petfinder.com). You'll get a sense of the range of animals looking for homes, and you'll be connected to shelters in your area. Other places to look include The Pooka (www.thepooka.com/rescue.html), the American Society for the Prevention of Cruelty to Animals (www.aspca.org), and humane societies (www.americanhumane.org and www.hsus.org).

Going to a breeder. If you know what breed of dog you'd like and you don't mind paying top dollar for it, then go to a reputable breeder. The American Kennel Club (www.akc.org) can recommend breeders in your area.

Going to breeder rescue organizations. Something of a cross between shelters and breeders, these are organizations that are dedicated to taking care of homeless dogs of a specific breed. So if you'd like, say, a corgi, you can research if there is a corgi rescue group in your area and see if there are any dogs that need homes.

Fetching Ways to Have Fun with Your Pets

Beyond offering love, companionship, and tons of health benefits, pets also offer a wonderful chance to meet new people and pursue new activities. Some of our favorites include the following.

Volunteer opportunities. The connection between good health and animals is so strong that many hospitals and nursing homes invite people and their pets to visit patients. The best way to pursue this is through a service organization like the Delta Society (www.deltasociety.org). The Delta Society registers you and your pet and teams you with people who will benefit from a visit. It operates in all 50 states and 11 countries. The training to be a "Pet Partner" is minimal, and many kinds of animals can participate, from dogs and cats to goats and pigs!

Dog shows. If you have a purebred dog that is "intact"—not spayed or neutered—you can show your animal at dog shows. Most people have seen the Westminster Kennel Club Dog Show, the New York City-based dog show that is broadcast every year on TV. What you may not realize is that there are many smaller, regional shows that happen throughout the year. Check with your breeder about getting started or contact the American Kennel Club (www.akc.org) for more information about showing and other dog events.

Agility training. Agility training is a rapidly rising sport that is getting dog lovers together in the fresh air with their pooches for some fun and exercise. If your dog loves you so much you think he'd jump through hoops for you, take him outside and see if that's true. There is a lot of information on the Web about this at sites like www.agilityability.com.

Did You Know?

Keeping a Pet Can Get Costly Pet care costs can add up, but ask a pet owner if she has any regrets and the answer is bound to be "Absolutely not!" This chart will give you a sense of how much your pet will cost you each year. These numbers do not including start-up costs like buying a crate or having a dog or cat neutered. Nor do they include grooming, which will be a big expense for some dogs, very little for others.

Dog: $400 to $750, depending on its size.

Cat: $500

Rabbit or guinea pig: $700

Parakeet: $100

Fish: $50

In the Dog House, Not the Poor House

It's absolutely true what they say: Take care of your pets, and they'll give you years of love and affection, not to mention pennies in your pocket instead of a veterinarian's. Here's how to keep the expenses down.

Spay or neuter. You will have fewer health problems down the road. Contact the ASPCA to see if you can get a discount on this. Find details at www.aspca.org.

Keep them trim and fit. Just because Ralphie wants a biscuit doesn't mean you have to give it to him. Obesity in pets has very similar effects as it does in humans. It can exacerbate or cause heart disease, joint pain, and diabetes, all of which are expensive to treat. So make sure to feed them high-quality food, and get them outside for some exercise (if you have a pooch).

Find a great pet clinic. Pet superstores like Petco often offer basic health care on site, so make sure to check with your local branch. You can also check with your animal shelter to see if it can recommend affordable services. Your local pet store might even offer a senior pet health day in which just seniors get free basic pet care.

Shop around for pet medications. If your vet's prices are too high, comparison shop to get the best deal. Ask the vet for a prescription, not the actual pills. You may be able to get the drugs for less elsewhere. Try www.kvsupply.com, www.discountpetmedicines.com, www.discountpet-drugs.com, and www.1800petmeds.com.

Ask your vet for a discount. Your vet may be happy to give you a senior discount, so make sure you ask. If he isn't able to, he may refer you to someone who will.

Coping with the Loss of a Beloved Companion

The death of a beloved pet can be just as devastating as the loss of a person. Pets are members of the family, and you may never be closer to yours than when you are a child or a retiree, spending lots of time playing, snuggling, and bonding. Follow these tips to ease the pain.

Allow yourself to grieve. You have the right to feel sad. Your pet was a beloved companion, friend, and family member. Don't hesitate for a moment to let yourself grieve this loss as completely as you would any other.

Get support. If you are feeling despair, consider getting help from a professional. Your church, your hospital, even your vet may be able to point you to inexpensive, often free resources that will help you get through this difficult time.

Honor the memory of your pet. Will you buy a burial plot for the cat or will you bury him in the backyard? Do you want the doctor to handle his remains and just have your memory? Are you considering cremation, which is surprisingly inexpensive? Your vet should be able to help you make a decision.

Hold off on getting a new pet. It can be tempting to try to replace your beloved friend right away. Dealing with a new animal, especially a kitten or a puppy, seems like it would offer delightful and consuming distraction. Give yourself time to grieve for your late pet and only start thinking about a new one when you believe you will not be looking at the animal as a replacement. Experts suggest that you not give your new pet the same name as the old one and that you try to create a visual distinction between the two, as well to remind yourself that this new pet is its own beast.

Early Bird Secret

You Can Provide for Fido after You're Gone

The Humane Society of the United States offers a free kit to help you plan for your pet's care after you are gone. "Providing for Your Pet's Future Without You" contains a six-page fact sheet, wallet alert cards, emergency decals for windows and doors, and caregiver information forms. Send an e-mail to petsinwills@hsus.org and check the Humane Society's Web site (www.hsus.org) for other information and goodies.

Taking Care of Business

Figure Out Your Finances
Once and for All

Collecting the Social Security You're Entitled To

President Franklin Roosevelt initiated Social Security in 1935 as a way of supporting older Americans. The program was to ensure that those who were no longer in the workforce, or who couldn't find a job, would still have a safety net. In an ideal world, retirees use a combination of private savings including IRAs and 401(k)s, pensions, and a part-time (or full-time!) job to provide income in their golden years. Most of us don't do that. It is estimated that 20 percent of married couples and 41 percent of unmarried people rely on Social Security benefits for 90 percent or more of their retirement income.

Know when you're eligible and when to start collecting.
We all think of retirement as starting at 65. But does it? Not anymore. The government has adjusted the age at which you are eligible for full retirement benefits. How to figure out what is coming to you and exactly when? If you were born in or before 1943, you are eligible for full retirement benefits now. If you were born between 1943 and 1954, you are eligible at the age of 66. If you were born between 1955 and 1959 you will be eligible sometime in your 66th year. If you were born in 1960 or later, you will be eligible at 67. When you actually begin to collect benefits is one of the most important decisions of your retirement, and there is no right answer. To determine what timing is right for you consider these points:

- Your life expectancy. Are you in terrific health? Does longevity run in your family? The average American lifespan today is 77.6 years old. If you (and your doctor) believe that you have a good chance of living a long time based on family history and your great health now, you may want to delay receiving benefits for as long as possible to ensure that you will receive higher payouts when you are older and need them more.

- Your other liquid assets and income. Do you have a pension? A 401(k)? If you have other assets from which you can draw, again, it might be best to delay receiving Social Security and treat it like the safety net it was intended to be.

Did You Know?

You Can Be a Really Early Bird! You may be able to start receiving retirement benefits as early as age 62. Your benefits will be reduced because you will be starting earlier than most Early Birds. Your draw will probably be about 75 percent of what you would receive if you waited for full retirement age.

- Your work life. Do you still work? Do you enjoy it? If you find your work—and your paycheck—enjoyable, then why not keep at it? Work keeps you connected to your friends and your community and may give you a sense of purpose. As long as you are still working, there is likely little point to collecting a Social Security payment. You probably want to sit on that Early Bird nest egg a little bit longer.

- Your spouse. If your spouse did not work outside the home, then he or she is entitled to 50 percent of your benefit while you are alive and receiving benefits. This makes the case for receiving your benefits early.

- The economy. Take the recent economic downturn into account when making your decision. You might be better off taking Social Security sooner rather than later if you have other investment assets like a 401(k). The longer you delay tapping into your investment portfolio, the more likelihood the stock market will continue to rally, and you may recover some of your losses.

Always check your statements. Each year, you receive an estimate of your Social Security benefits. Open it, read it closely, and make sure it's correct! If something is wrong, contact the Social Security Administration immediately to have it corrected.

Know that you may be entitled to more than your own benefit. If you and your spouse worked, you are entitled to the greater of 50 percent of your spouse's benefit or your own benefit.

Early Bird Secret

Waiting for Payments Pays Off

Are you able to wait until you turn 70 to receive your Social Security benefits? If so, you will receive an additional monthly benefit, which may be as much as 8 percent for each year beyond your full retirement age that you waited to receive your checks.

Take advantage of direct deposit. Did you know that you can have your check deposited directly into your bank account, be it checking or savings? This way you avoid having checks get lost or delayed in the mail.

Don't forget the ex! If you were married for at least 10 years, you can collect benefits based on your ex-spouse's earnings. Your benefits will stop if you remarry.

See your accountant. If your income is more than roughly $34,000 as a single filer or $44,000 as a married joint filer, you may have to pay tax on 85 percent of your benefit. Each year, these income limits are adjusted for inflation; your accountant can help clarify your Social Security tax liability.

Collect your benefits overseas. You are eligible to receive your benefits even if you move abroad. (There are a few exceptions—Cuba and North Korea among them—but these are unlikely to be your retirement destinations.)

Free Retirement Help Is a Click Away

If you are computer savvy, you'll be pleased to know that there are many free calculators available to help you run the numbers of your retirement. Here are some of the best: http://www.ssa.gov/retire2/index.htm and http://money.cnn.com/retirement and http://bulletin.aarp.org/yourmoney.

Learning the ABCs of Medicare

Medicare is the federal health insurance program for American senior citizens, and generally speaking, it works very well. If you are turning 65 soon, you need to start planning your transition from private insurance to Medicare so that you don't miss any deadlines and can get the preventive care that you need. If you are 65 and already collecting Social Security benefits, you do not need to sign up for Medicare; you will receive your Medicare card automatically in the mail. If you are *not* planning to receive Social Security benefits when you turn 65, then you need to sign up for Medicare three months before your 65th birthday (just call 1-800-772-1213 or visit www.medicare.gov online). You should sign up for Medicare parts A, B, and D.

Familiarizing yourself with the labyrinthine maze that can be the Medicare system is the key to getting all of the benefits you deserve. Recently passed legislation means that there may be some adjustments to the coverage, but we asked our Medicare experts to walk us through the basics to help you find your footing. Armed with this knowledge, you'll be the savviest Early Bird around:

Medicare Part A. This is the part of Medicare coverage that relates to hospital treatment. It covers:

- Inpatient hospital services (up to 90 days per "spell of illness")
- Skilled nursing facility services (up to 100 days per spell of illness after a hospital stay of three or more days)

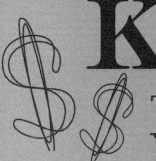

Ka-Ching!

The Fine Print Is Money in Your Pocket

Medicare scams abound and often involve some very familiar names in the insurance industry. Several of our experts uncovered shady practices, including more than a few companies that promised beneficiaries they'd receive better coverage with private insurance than they would on Medicare Part C. When it came time to cover the beneficiary for procedures as ordinary as a broken hip or cataract surgery, their claims were denied. Keep your money in your pocket, and always read the fine print. If your plan sounds too good to be true, it definitely is. Here are some basic ways to avoid scams:

Never open the door

to insurance salespeople. If they call you on the phone, hang up.

Never, ever give your personal information

to anyone claiming to be a representative of Medicare or a private insurance carrier. This goes for your birth date, your Social Security number, your Medicare number, or your address.

Read the fine print.

If you decide to buy additional coverage, make absolutely sure it is from a company that really works with Medicare. This information is easy to find on the Medicare Web site: www.Medicare.gov.

- Home health care (up to 100 visits per spell of illness after a hospital stay of three or more days)
- Hospice care
- Inpatient psychiatric care (up to 190 days during your lifetime)
- Blood (you pay for the first three pints per year)

Medicare Part B. This part of Medicare coverage relates to ordinary, daily medical care. It covers:

- Physicians' services, including office visits and a one-time physical examination for new beneficiaries.
- Medical equipment (for example, wheelchairs and oxygen) and supplies
- Outpatient hospital services
- Outpatient mental health services
- Lab and diagnostic tests
- Outpatient occupational, physical, and speech therapy
- Home health care not preceded by a hospital stay and visits over the 100-day Part A limit
- Some preventive services (for example, mammograms and diabetes screening)

Medicare Part C. Medicare Part C is also known as the Medicare Advantage plan. It basically bundles Parts A and B and has services provided by a private insurer, which include HMOs.

Medicare Part D. This part of the plan is the prescription drug program.

Sure Ways to Lower Your Insurance Premiums

The best way to be a savvy Early Bird and to save save *save* everywhere from health insurance premiums to prescription costs is…you guessed it: don't get sick! The truth is, maintaining good health goes a long way to preserving your happiness as well as your nest egg. Make sure that you are doing what your doctors agree will keep you younger longer. Bad habits may be challenging to break, but they may also result in better health not only for you, but for your bank account, too! Replace them with great habits, and you'll have more than savings to bank on.

Stop smoking! It's smelly, smoky (of course), and your grandkids probably yell at you when they see you light up. But beyond that, smoking aggravates high blood pressure and diabetes, is a documented cause of heart disease, and can lead to emphysema and lung cancer. If those weren't reasons enough to quit, consider the cost: the price of cigarettes is increasing all the time, from $5-7 per pack—and much more in some places. For someone who smokes a pack a day, that's $1,800 a year. Experts estimate that tobacco use costs the United States about $167 billion a year in direct medical costs and lost productivity. Furthermore, if you are in the market for life insurance or disability insurance, your rates will skyrocket if you are a smoker; in fact, most smokers pay double the amount that nonsmokers pay for their health insurance. The good news? Most insurers consider you a nonsmoker if you haven't had a cigarette in a year. Quit today!

Protect your bones. If you're a woman who has gone through menopause, you have likely started to lose bone mass already, and you will continue to unless you do something to stop it. The first thing to do is to have your bone mass measured by your doctor so you know where you stand. And then get to work!

Work on your balance. Exercises that increase your ability to balance well, like yoga and tai chi, are widely praised. The better your balance, the more you protect yourself against falls. The fringe benefit? Both activities are low-impact, increase flexibility, and are weight-bearing.

Enjoy red wine on occasion. If you do drink wine, make it red, which contains a key component called resveratrol. Studies have shown that a glass with dinner may benefit your heart, blood sugar, and overall health.

Stop and smell the roses. Retirement doesn't guarantee stress-free living: studies have shown that many American retirees are still as overextended and overstressed as they were when they were in the work force. This stress can put unnecessary strain on your general health, specifically, your heart, your immune system, and your metabolism. What to do? Take a slow, mindful walk; look at the trees; go to a museum. In other words, get quiet. Your body and mind will thank you.

Be a pear, not an apple! Doctors believe that your waist-to-hip ratio is a very strong measure of cardiac health. In other words, aim to be a pear, not an apple shape, and try to keep belly weight to a minimum. Check in with your physician, and once they okay it, do some light cardio exercise at least three times a week, and get involved in your community. People who have close ties to their communities and who are active and social with family and friends have been shown to live longer than loners. Life is a party—join in!

6 Pill-Free Ways to Get Your Calcium

You may have to take a supplement prescribed by your doctor, but if you don't (and even if you do), increase your calcium intake by:

1. **Eating leafy greens.** A serving of collard greens contains the same amount of calcium as an 8-ounce glass of milk.

2. **Opening up a can of sardines.** Three ounces of sardines is a delicious way to get more calcium and omega-3 fatty acids into your diet. Mash up a can with half a cup of low-fat cottage cheese, and enjoy on whole grain toast, for added benefit.

3. **Drinking your orange juice.** An 8-ounce glass of orange juice contains 25 percent of the recommended daily calcium intake for folks 51 years and older.

4. **Going a little nutty...**For nuts, that is! Roasted, unsalted almonds are a boon to calcium, so grab a small handful (some experts recommend 12 almonds) once a day.

5. **Saying cheese!** Eaten in moderation (like everything), cheese includes among its health benefits hefty doses of calcium. Look for lower fat varieties, like goat cheese and mozzarella, to enjoy as a snack.

6. **Doing light weight-bearing exercises.** Studies have repeatedly shown that lifting light dumbbells regularly can actually build bone mass—not just stave off bone loss.

Follow doctor's orders. Although pills are more expensive than ever, they are cheaper (and less traumatic) than a major health crisis, so take your medications as directed; you are spending money to save money. Other ways to save? Get regular checkups. Women should have regular mammograms and pelvic and breast exams. Men should have regular prostate exams. Everyone should have a colonoscopy at age 50 (or earlier if suggested by your physician) and once every 10 years afterward if their first screening is normal. See the dentist every six months, and always remember to floss your teeth (a strong connection between gum health and heart health has been established—that little waxy string may save your life!).

Maximizing Retirement and Rainy-Day Savings

Just as your body needs quality care and attention (and hopefully, you already take our expert advice to give it everything it needs to stay healthy), so too does your financial life. Savvy Early Birds know the ins and outs of the system—how to reap the benefits of long-term savings, how to make the most of short-term investments, and how to come out smelling like a rose. Some of the most familiar investment tools for Early Birds are pensions, IRAs, 401(k) plans, and annuities.

Pensions and Annuities: What's the Difference?

Pensions: the Packards of retirement plans. These are big, comfortable financial vehicles that have all but disappeared. For most of our parents and grandparents, pensions were a major part of their retirements. Back then, you worked at the same company for 40 years, got your gold watch and retirement party, and then started collecting your pension, which supported you for the rest of your life. Nowadays, most companies offer contribution plans, like 401(k)s, rather than traditional pension plans.

If you do expect to receive a pension from a reliable employer, you will receive compensation in the form of a percentage of your former salary. Here are the few things you may need to think about:

- Are you going to take the maximum contribution, spread it out over your lifetime, and gallop off into the sunset?
- Do you prefer to take a reduced contribution, but one that will continue to compensate your spouse after you die? If your spouse is much younger than you are, this might be the right bet.
- Are you entitled to Social Security? Some people who receive a pension, like some state employees for example, may not be eligible for Social Security. Make sure you know what you are entitled to as you plan your retirement so you don't come up short.

Understanding annuities. Annuities act as a safety net to guarantee you an income for the rest of your life. They are a conservative tool meant to give you peace of mind and guarantees. You hand an insurance company a wad of cash, and they guarantee you an income on that money, the amount of which depends upon how much you contributed. Annuities can get complicated so if you like to keep things simple, look for fixed annuities from a reliable seller.

Early Bird Secrets

How to Shop for Annuities

You wouldn't buy a carton of milk without looking at the price and making sure you were getting the best deal, right? Same goes for buying an annuity. The most important thing to do when considering one is to comparison shop. There are a huge range of annuities out there, and some of the exact same investment tools can have very different prices. Here's how to do it.

Make a note of all of the features you are looking for, and then compare the plans of several companies.

Make sure you are comparing the exact same terms so that you get an apples-to-apples comparison that is accurate.

Insist upon knowing *all* of the fees or commissions of each plan up front. Companies don't like to disclose these so you may have to push. You don't want hidden or unnecessary costs to pick away at your valuable nest egg.

Is an annuity right for you? If you receive a pension that you can live on from a reliable source—an example would be a teacher who is receiving a pension from the state—then you may not need an annuity, which is afixed income similar to a pension. On the other hand, if you are living on a small Social Security check and a small nest egg that you feel you are dipping into too much or that has eroded in a soft economy, an annuity may be right for you.

How much risk can you stand? Do you want to turn over most of your savings to an annuity? Or do you just want your annuity to be a part of you retirement strategy? The answer will depend on how risk-averse you are: If you want to play it safe and you are sure that the annuity will pay you enough to survive for the rest of your life, then it may be for you. If you don't mind some risk, then maybe only a part of your savings should be converted to an annuity. Another issue to consider: Do you want to leave any money to your children and grandchildren? In most cases, once you buy an annuity, your money is gone, no matter if you die a year later or if you live another 30 years. No money from that annuity will be left for your heirs.

Do you need an annuity? Investment advisers suggest an easy back-of-the-napkin calculation to help you decide if you need an annuity and, if so, how much money you need that annuity to yield. They call it the Income

Gap Calculation. First, tally all your sources of income: pension, Social Security, investments, and anything else. Second, tally all of your expenses: your rent or mortgage, food, travel, entertainment, and most importantly, health care. Third, subtract your expense money from your income money. If there is a negative balance, then that is your income gap—the amount of money that you need to maintain your lifestyle. An annuity might be the perfect thing to fill it in.

When is the right time to buy an annuity? The answer depends on whether you need a long-term income stream or a short-term one. Should you wait until later in your retirement when your savings may have shrunk and your lifestyle may have become quieter (and less expensive) to buy an annuity? Or do you want to use an annuity as a way of delaying dipping into your other investments or starting to collect Social Security? There are annuities for both of these scenarios.

Did You Know?

Understanding the Drawdown Rule The 4 percent drawdown rule is something that may give you peace of mind. It used to be thought that a retiree could comfortably pull 6 percent or so from savings annually and not be at risk for outliving his or her money. But studies have changed the prevailing wisdom. Nowadays, conservative advisers believe that if you stick to 4 percent a year, you will always have enough money to live on (but voices on the horizon are suggesting that other factors, such as the psychology of the individual, must be taken into account). To start, look at your savings, calculate 4 percent, and add it to your fixed income—things like pensions and Social Security. Try again with a number like 6 or 8 percent. Are these number something you can live on—even if you live to 100? Great! If not, it's time to see an investment adviser to make a new plan.

Building Up Your Retirement-Cash Coffers

Know the nuts and bolts of 401(k)s. For most investors, this program will make up the bulk of their retirement savings. Whereas once the company you worked for might have offered you a pension, now most companies offer a savings plan in the form of the 401(k). These plans enable you to put away a portion of your own earnings before taxes are taken out, which reduces the amount of your take-home pay, which in turn reduces your taxes. The earnings are taxed when you start making withdrawals in retirement, but, presumably, you'll be in a lower tax bracket when you retire so you'll save again.

The secret to making the most of your retirement savings. Simply contribute the maximum possible to your plan. If you are not able to contribute the maximum amount, make sure you at least contribute enough to get the full benefits of any matching contributions your company offers. If you are over 50, take advantage of the "catch-up" provision.

Invest sensibly. Invest your money for the long term, and understand the offerings of your plan. Diversify your portfolio, choosing a selection of stocks and bonds. Traditionally, if the stock market drops, the bond market increases. Make sure you keep an eye on how your funds are doing, and reshuffle accordingly, as the market changes.

Leave your money alone. You are able to withdraw from your 401(k) for hardship or to buy your first home. Resist the urge to do so! You must repay the money you borrow, which means that you must stay at the company until you've done so. And you are not maximizing the effects of tax-advantaged compound interest if your money is not in the account.

Play catch-up if you're a late starter. Not all of us start saving when we should; thankfully it is possible to play catch-up by making, literally, "catch-up" contributions. Start putting the maximum into your retirement plan (if you aren't already), and if you are over 50, take advantage of the catch-up contributions, which enable you to add much more. You can add an additional $1,000 a year to an IRA and an additional $5,000 a year to a 401(k).

Postpone your retirement if you can. Every year you don't retire is another year that you are saving for retirement and not breaking open your nest egg. You can look into cutting back your hours, going freelance, becoming a consultant in your field, or finding a new part-time job. For many people, not going straight from full-time work to retirement is the best option as it eases the transition in addition to creating a financial buffer.

Cut your spending! You are already a savvy spender and saver but maybe your belt needs to be tightened even more. Are there areas in which you can do even better? Can you cut back from two vacations a year to one? Do you really need two cars when one would do? Is there still some waste in your food budget? Take a good look at your budget, and whatever you can trim out should be saved for retirement.

Consider relocating. Is it cheaper to live in New Hampshire than New York? You bet! Not only is the cost of living more favorable, but there is no income or sales tax in New Hampshire. Relocating is not for everyone, but the time to start thinking about it is well before retirement. For instance, if you are going to sell your New York-based business and move to New Hampshire, the time to sell is *after* you have established residency in New Hampshire. Then you'll really take advantage of the fact that the granite state does not tax residents on their income.

Get Free Retirement Information

There are terrific resources on the Internet to help you plan your retirement. They range from simple to very complex and can run all kinds of scenarios, from when you can retire to how long it will take you to earn a target amount of money. Here are a few:

http://www.smartmoney.com/personal-finance/retirement
http://individual.troweprice.com/public/Retail/Planning-&-
   Research/Tools-&-Resources/Retirement-Planning
http://www.fool.com/calcs/calculators.htm.

Are You Financially Fit?

You take good care of yourself, knowing that your body won't hold up if you don't treat it right. Guess what? Neither will your money. What to do? Give yourself an annual checkup to make sure that your finances are in the best of health. The ideal time of year to do this is in the fall so that you still have a couple of months left in the year if you've forgotten to do something.

Make sure you contributed to your plans. Did you contribute the maximum that either you can afford or the government allows to your IRA, 401(k), and 529 college savings plan? If not, make sure you do by the proper deadlines.

Check your investments. Do your accounts need to be rebalanced? If some funds are doing very well and others are underperforming, you may find that your allocations are no longer balanced. Make sure that the distributions align with your wishes and your risk tolerance. If you are not sure how to balance your portfolio, consider an age-based (also called life cycle) fund. These funds adjust the risk every year, becoming more conservative the closer you get to retirement.

Watch the taxes. You can reduce your tax exposure by making sure that traditional IRAs, which grow tax-deferred, hold your assets that pay high dividends. Transfer high-growth but low-dividend stocks to your taxable accounts.

Check your beneficiaries. Make sure that if you don't live to enjoy your savings, your loved ones will. Be certain you have named the beneficiary of your choice and that your wishes haven't changed in the wake of a big event like a birth, death, or divorce. Many funds send you a beneficiary review form every few years; if you have never received one, be sure to ask.

Consolidate your funds. Hardly any of us spend our whole lives working at one company anymore, which can mean that by the time we hit retirement, we have accounts scattered around at a number of companies. Decide whether to keep the funds where they are or to roll them over into an IRA. If you choose the former, keep track of your money in its various accounts; if you choose the latter, make sure you do a direct rollover so that you don't take a tax hit.

Did You Know?

Understanding the Sandwich Generation Two out of five families in which the parents are in their 50s include a child who is still a minor. Welcome to the sandwich generation in which seniors struggle with helping their own aging parents, preparing children for life on their own, and planning for retirement. This begs the question: retirement or college savings? If you can't save for both, which is more important?

The answer is retirement. Why? Because you can finance your child's college tuition. You cannot finance retirement. There are loans, student work programs, scholarships, and other tools available to pay for college. No such luck for retirement. So if you are in your 50s, move retirement savings to the front burner and turn up the heat!

Giving to Family, Giving to Charity

You've saved for years, you've pinched every penny, and now it's time to enjoy your golden years. One of the great rewards of hard work and careful spending is being able to help your family. While you may have carefully planned where your money will go after you die by making sure that your will is in order and maybe even setting up trusts for your heirs, you may not have considered giving money away during your lifetime. Living gifts can be one of the true joys of your golden years. It's nice to know that your family will be taken care of after you're gone, but it can't compare to the pleasure you'll receive by seeing with your own eyes how much your money can make a difference to your children, grandchildren, and even charitable organizations. Here are some of the ways in which your dollars can help.

Helping with tuition. Tuitions have skyrocketed over the last decades, and it is not at all uncommon for colleges to charge over $30,000 a year—not including room, board, and supplies! That can be a heavy burden on parents who are trying to fund their own nest eggs while they worry about how to finance their kids' educations. Consider opening 529 college savings accounts for your grandkids. These plans are:

- Run by most states. Make sure that your plan allows students to attend college out of state. Many do. Visit www.savingforcollege.com for more details.

- Tax-advantaged. You may be able to deduct your contributions from your taxes, and the interest on the money you save grows tax-free. Best of all? The contribution limits are high! Most plans have around a $60,000 limit per year and a $200,000 lifetime limit.

- In your control. You decide what funds to invest in. And your grandchildren cannot access the money themselves. There won't be any worries that the money will go toward anything other than legitimate school fees.

- Sometimes helpful in getting discounted tuition. More and more colleges and universities are encouraging families to use 529s by offering tuition discounts to those who do.

- Easy to transfer back. If your grandchild decides not to go to college, you can change your beneficiary, or you may get your money back after you pay tax and a small penalty on the earnings.

Giving gifts of cash. You are free to give as much money as you like to anyone at any time. But be careful! You—the donor—will have to pay a "gift tax" if that amount is more than $12,000 a year. The recipient does not pay tax on gifts. Your lifetime tax-free limit on gifts to one person is a whopping one million dollars. And gifts are deducted from your estate tax exclusion, which is even more: in 2009, the amount was three million five hundred thousand dollars! This means that if you give your child $100,000 during your lifetime, the amount of money that can flow from your estate tax free would be $3,400,000 (these numbers undergo occasional adjustment, so check with your accountant for the most up-to-date information before making a gift).

Taking advantage of the Uniform Gifts to Minors Act.

If you'd like to give to your grandkids but you don't want to contribute to the 529 and you don't want to give them cash, take advantage of this nifty way to give. You can fill out a set of papers with your banker that will enable your child to receive money into an account (the $12,000 a year limit applies), but the child will not be able to access the money until he turns 18 (or whatever age you choose). Here are two caveats to be aware of:

- Don't name yourself as the custodian. You will have to name a custodian who will manage the money until your grandchild comes of age. If you are the custodian, when you die, the account will be included in your estate and subject to taxes and delays.

- Consider how this will affect financial aid for college. The money in your grandchild's account will be considered when it comes to financial aid. It might reduce scholarship possibilities.

Early Bird Secret

Use Your Noodle for Tax Savings

If you've come into some extra money and want to pass it on to your children, you can avoid taxes and maximize your gift. Say you and your spouse have come into $50,000 unexpectedly and would like to pass it on to your son. Will it take you four years to give him the money because of the $12,000-a-year limit? Heck, no! You and your spouse can each give him and his wife $12,000. That's $48,000 in one year with no tax implications. You can enlarge your gifts even more by each giving money to his children!

Gifts that have multiple benefits.

Your family will certainly appreciate gifts of cash or college savings money. They may also appreciate gifts that aim to do greater good in the world. Gifts that enrich charities may also enrich your soul and pass on valuable lessons about your values to your heirs. Consider these ways of giving:

- Sponsor a child. You can sponsor a child through any number of organizations including www.savethechildren.org; www.sos-usa.org; and many others.

- Sponsor an animal. You can sponsor an endangered animal through www.worldwildlife.org. Check your local animal shelter for opportunities to help with abandoned pets.

- Give a gift to a family in need. You can give an African family a goat. Go to www.oxfamamerica.org for ideas. Or give a childless American a toy for Christmas through your local newspaper or other organization.

Charitable remainder trusts.

One living gift that will keep on giving in a very real way is a contribution made to a charitable remainder trust. You donate your money to charity and then you receive income from the gift for the rest of your life, much like an annuity. The upshot?

- Tax benefits. You do not pay capital gains tax on the assets you donate, and you get a tax deduction. In addition, your estate taxes are lowered because your gift is no longer a part of your estate.

- You have little control. Your gift is irrevocable. You cannot change your mind years later and get the money back. But you can have some say in how the assets are invested.

- Pleasure. You get the benefit of seeing your money appreciated and used. You may get invited to organizational benefit dinners or have a plaque dedicated in your honor. This is not something you would experience if you left the gift in your estate.

- Risk. There is some risk attached to a charitable trust. You must do your homework to make sure that the institution you give to is solvent so that your gift will not be wasted and so that you will continue to receive your annuity. Some states are highly regulated; others less so. Once you have chosen a charity to contribute to, call your state's insurance department and make sure that the institution is worthy of your attention.

Did You Know?

There Are Three Kinds of Charitable Remainder Trusts

Charitable remainder annuity trusts: These pay a fixed amount each year—very similar to classic annuities backed by insurance companies.

Charitable remainder unitrusts: These pay a fixed percentage of the trust's value every year. The trust's value may fluctuate according to how it is invested and how the stock market is doing.

Charitable pooled income funds: These are set up by the charity and enable many donors to contribute to the same fund. Think mutual fund meets annuity.

Tax Tips That You Can Bank On

There is a world of financial advice out there for seniors, much of which is discounted or free. Even if you end up paying top dollar for tax and planning advice, a good certified financial planner and CPA will earn back what you pay them in no time. Here are some great places to start.

Free advice. Free tax and financial advice is something most people either don't know about or are wary of. The Volunteer Income Tax Assistance program (or VITA) is run by the Internal Revenue Service (IRS). It pairs people of moderate income (usually $40,000 and less) with tax experts who offer free advice and is worth its weight in gold (almost).

Senior-specific free tax advice. The Tax Counseling for the Elderly (TCE) program is similar to VITA. Also run by the IRS, it is staffed by trained volunteers and caters to people 60 years old and above. Tax-Aide is part of the TCE program, which is sponsored by AARP. During peak tax preparation season, before April 15, there are 7,000 locations around the country where seniors can receive free advice.

The IRS itself has a help line that is open 24/7: 1-800-829-1040. Ask about the VITA, TCE, and Tax-Aide programs there. You can get more information on Tax-Aide (and taxes in general) at the AARP site: www.aarp.org.

CPAs and CFPs. Sometimes, the best advice must be paid for, and this is where a good certified public accountant (CPA) or certified financial planner (CFP) comes in. Our experts agree that these two kinds of advisers, at best, can save you a ton, both on your taxes and in your investments. But there are some things to do before you hire one:

- Check the person's credentials. You want to make sure that an accountant is a CPA (certified public accountant) or that your financial planner is in fact a CFP. If you are not sure, ask for the person's license number and check credentials through your state's licensing office.

- Pay by the hour. It might sound expensive to pay by the hour, but it will be a savings in the long run. If you are not using a fee-based planner, you are paying a percentage of your portfolio or commissions.

- Retain control. Never sign over control of your accounts to your financial planner, and if you are pressured to do so, find a new adviser. Remember movies in which the accountant ran away with all the money? You won't have that problem if you don't let anyone else access your assets.

Reel in Big Refunds with These Write-offs

We all know people who have tried to deduct some crazy things from their taxes: doggy day care, consulting fees for the arsonist who accidentally torched a fizzling business concern, cable TV (it's research, right?); the list goes on and on. But there *are* some excellent, off-the-beaten-track tax deductions out there that will help fund your lifestyle—if you take a little time to uncover and pursue them. As always, remember that tax law changes from year to year, so check with your accountant or financial adviser on the current regulations and specifics regarding any write-offs you're hoping to take. However, many deductions continue to exist each year, and only the details might change a bit, such as how much per mile you can deduct for transportation costs to and from medical treatment. Then check out the following unusual and surprising deductions, and ask your financial adviser about others—they can really add up.

Yes or No?

I've just installed a chairlift for my husband. Can I deduct it?

Chairlifts added to a home are tax-deductible; elevators are not. A lift to help you up and down the stairs is considered a legitimate expense to help a handicapped person with mobility, whereas an elevator is considered a capital improvement that increases the value of your home and thus is not deductible.

What about medical costs? Even with health insurance, out-of-pocket medical expenses can amount to a lot in this day and age, but the IRS generally won't let you deduct them from your federal income tax unless they total more than 7.5 percent of your adjusted gross income. However, in addition to insurance premiums, there are a lot of other ways to count medical expenses. Taken all together, they may well push your costs toward that magic threshold. When calculating your costs, don't forget:

- Insurance payments taken from after-tax dollars. If your monthly premiums are not automatically deducted from your pretax income, as they generally are if your insurance plan is through your employer, then you're likely paying for them out of income that has already been taxed—and thus they become a deduction. If you have long-term care insurance, this is usually taken from after-tax money and can be deducted.

- Uninsured medical treatments and accessories. False teeth, extra glasses, hearing aids, contact lenses—if you're wearing or buying these things on the advice or prescription of a medical practitioner, they count toward your total medical deductions.

- Travel to and from medical treatment. This allowance generally runs in the range of 20 cents per mile. If you drive 10 miles each way to the doctor, that's a $2 deduction per visit—and don't forget the trips you take with dependents.

- Medical conferences. Even if you're not a medical practitioner, you could attend a conference concerning a malady suffered by you or your dependents and deduct the costs of travel and admission (though not the cost of food and board, so don't treat it like a vacation!).

- Specialty treatments. Costs of alcohol- and drug-abuse treatment can be deducted, as well as laser vision treatment (check on that first with your medical practitioner or financial adviser if you're planning to take a write-off).

- Medical hardware. If you have to buy crutches or a wheelchair or have to install handrails in your home, these items may be deductible. Structural work on your house to assist in medical conditions, such as widening doorways or adding ramps, can also be a write-off, with a doctor's advice and IRS approval. Also, if your doctor recommends that you add a special filter to your home heating system, for example, to help with your allergies or asthma, you may be able to deduct part of that cost on your income tax.

Yes or No?

My husband does a little handyman work as a hobby, but everything else in our tax life is very straightforward. Can I deduct the costs of his tools on our joint return?

Probably not.

Nearly all these specialized deductions are only for people who itemize on their tax returns, not for people who fill out a 1040EZ and take the standard deduction. The exceptions tend to be for educational deductions, which are considered an "above the line" deduction by the IRS and can usually be taken on the EZ form.

Should I itemize?

Only if you're deducting more than these standardized amounts (but always be sure to double-check this year's amounts):

Single or married filing separately: $5,700

Heads of household: $8,350

Married couple, joint return: $11,400

If your total deductions (including mortgage interest, medical expenses, and charitable contributions) are higher than these thresholds, you should itemize. If less, you're better off taking the standard deduction.

Mortgage points. If you took out a mortgage in the tax year, whether for your first or second home, the fees you paid the lender, also known as mortgage points, can come off your taxes *even if you didn't pay them.* In many cases, a motivated seller will cover the points of the mortgage (that is, pay those fees for you) but for federal tax purposes, the buyer taking out the mortgage—not the seller—gets to deduct them.

Traveling for good. If you traveled to do charitable work, your travel costs may be deductible, whether it's the standard mileage rate for driving your car around for the local branch of Meals on Wheels, traveling to a different state to build houses for a charitable organization, or ferrying your Girl Scout troop to an event. You can also deduct fees for parking and tolls paid.

Deduct good works. In addition to your travel, you can deduct any materials or supplies you purchase specifically for a charitable group, such as office supplies for the group's use. You can also write off the costs of a uniform, such as the outfits that some hospital volunteers wear or those of a Boy Scout troop leader; it also means any upkeep on that uniform, whether it's a dry-cleaning bill or paying a tailor to hem it.

Educational costs. Go back to school yourself and earn tax credits toward the cost of your tuition. Up to $4,000 of tuition and fees can be deducted *even if you don't itemize*. Note that the coursework must be for credit, not sport or hobby classes (unless they are required as part of a degree program), and the $4,000 ceiling is for your entire household, so you can't deduct $4,000 for your own continuing education and another for your dependent child who's a full-time student. However, recent adjustments have made this credit accessible to a broader range of taxpayers, so be sure to check if anyone in your family qualifies.

Deduct your savings. If you're a moderate- or low-income household, the IRS allows you to deduct half of the first $2,000 you put away for retirement in your traditional or Roth IRA. Because it's an IRA, you get to deduct the $2,000 from your overall income, and then you get an additional $1,000 credit on your taxes—it's quite an encouragement to save!

Taking a loss. It's cold comfort if you've been the victim of vandalism to your property or outright theft, but these are losses that can often be deducted on your tax return. If the amount of the loss is more than 10 percent of your adjusted gross income, subtract $100 off the total amount of loss and deduct the rest. You can also deduct damage from an automobile accident—unless the accident was due to your negligence as a driver.

Random receipts. Deducted everything you could think of and still have lots of receipts in your desk drawer? There might still be room for some "miscellaneous" deductions, as long as they total more than 2 percent of your adjusted gross income. This category can include subscriptions to professional journals, fees for membership in professional organizations, certain costs for hobbies, and other expenses. The advice of a professional tax preparer can be a real benefit when you get into this hazier side of deductions, but that's okay: That person's fees are deductible as well!

Yes or No?

Are there any charitable donations that are not tax-deductible?

Yes.

1. The value of your time given in volunteer work, or the value of the income you might have forfeited while volunteering.

2. Money given to any group that was formed to lobby for changes in the law.

3. Money given to an individual, no matter how much the person needed the aid.

4. Personal expenses while volunteering, such as the cost of gas, lodging, or meals (although transportation can be deducted at about 14 cents per mile).

5. Money given to civic leagues, homeowner associations, chambers of commerce, and sport or social clubs, unless these clubs specifically meet IRS guidelines for charitable institutions.

6. Fees to appraise the value of property you are donating (although the value of the property may well be deductible).

Public debt. Any money you contribute to the U.S. Treasury to help relieve public debt is directly deductible from your personal tax bill. Public debt is the money that the government "borrows," through selling savings bonds and securities, to keep itself running. You can help lower this debt by sending a check made out to the Bureau of Public Debt along with your tax return, and you can deduct the exact amount as a charitable contribution.

Asset appreciation. If you bought $100 worth of stock in Google when it was just starting out and that stock is now worth $1 million (or whatever Google is worth these days), you could donate that stock to a charity and deduct the full $1 million, not the original price that you paid. This assumes that the charity is set up to receive appreciated property, and also that you're willing to give up your Google stock! The benefit to an appreciated-asset donation is that you pay no capital-gains tax and take as a deduction the full value of the property.

Choosing Insurance That's Right for You

You should have life insurance if you think your dependents will suffer hardship in the event of your demise. If you have enough money saved that your spouse and children will be able to live off of your savings and retirement plans, you probably don't need life insurance anymore. But if your spouse and children rely upon your income, then you need to calculate how much money they would need to survive without it. Consider these points as you make your decision:

Do you have life insurance through your employer?
Many employers offer automatic coverage, so if you are retiring and had been relying on your company's life insurance, you need to make new plans.

If you have a plan, is it current? If you bought life insurance many years ago when your family was young, the plan, which may have lasted for 20 years or so, might expire soon. It's a good time to review your coverage, see when it ends, and decide whether or not you need to extend it.

Choose between term or whole life insurance. If you decide that you do need insurance, keep it simple! Look for term life insurance. Most people don't need permanent or whole life, which is more of an investment vehicle and is very complicated.

Long-Term Care Insurance

Americans are living longer than ever, which is great news. But the dark side of longevity is that more of us may need health care that goes above and beyond the basics. At some point, we may need home care, or we may need to be cared for in a long-term care facility. And these are expensive! More and more people are buying long-term care insurance, which is designed to protect your assets, minimize the financial burden on your family, and give you some control over the quality of care you'll receive.

Ka-Ching!

The Secrets to Keeping Life Insurance Costs Down

Before you have a physical to obtain life insurance, there are a few things you can do to try to make your premium lower.

Lose weight	That spare tire will cost you, so try to unload it.
Quit smoking	You are considered a nonsmoker if you haven't smoked for a year.
Eat well for a week	Cut way back on sugar, salt, and fatty foods.
No alcohol	Don't drink any alcohol for at least three days before the exam to make sure your liver enzymes aren't elevated.
No caffeine	Cut out the caffeine the day before and day of the exam. Caffeine elevates blood pressure.
Reduce medication	Don't take any medication that you don't have to—ibuprofen, aspirin, decongestants, and so on. Do continue to take doctor-prescribed meds for serious conditions.
No exercise	Don't do anything strenuous the day before the exam.
Fast	For 10 hours before your exam, consume only water, but only if your health permits.
Sleep	Get a good night's sleep the night before your exam. The more relaxed you are, the better chance you have of doing well.

If you are shopping for long-term care insurance, consider these points carefully:

When should you buy coverage? Do you want to buy coverage now or wait until you are older? The older you are the higher the premiums will be, and there is no guarantee you'll get coverage if you develop a costly condition. On the other hand, the younger you are, the more time you'll spend paying the premiums.

What kind of coverage will you need? You can choose coverage that will only pay for home care or only pay for a nursing home. Or you can do a mixture of care styles.

What is the daily or monthly benefit? This is the amount of money the insurer will pay for each day or month of coverage. If your care costs more than your benefit allows, you need to pay the difference.

What benefit period will you choose? Do you need a fixed benefit period of several years or do you need the care to last the rest of your life?

Is there an elimination period? If the coverage makes you wait for a while, sometimes as long as three months, you'll pay for your care during that time. The longer the elimination period, the lower the premium.

Do you need inflation protection? Most experts we spoke with said yes; with inflation on the rise, it pays to be protected.

Setting Up Sound Wills and Trusts

Everybody should have a will, especially people who have others relying on them: parents with young children and couples who rely on one another's income and assets. If you die without a will, as two out of three Americans do, the government is left to decide what happens to your estate—not a desirable option. Making a will is relatively simple and straightforward.

Hire a lawyer. While do-it-yourself forms have proliferated on the Internet and much software is available for the most straightforward wills, you may find that it's nonetheless preferable to use a lawyer. An attorney drafted will is far less likely to be found invalid, and your heirs will be less likely to be able to overturn it.

Choose an executor. Make sure you choose someone reliable, close to you, and best, someone who does not stand to gain from your demise. If you choose a beneficiary as an executor, you can run into trouble with conflicts of interest. If you ever have a falling out with your executor or he or she dies, make sure you update your will and name a new executor.

Choose a guardian. If you have minor children, you must name the person who is to care for the children. Make sure that you have asked permission of the guardian you choose. The point of a will is to protect your heirs; you don't want any surprises.

Include specific instructions. Most will boilerplates do not include this but it's a nice addition. A letter of instruction outlines who gets which of your possessions. If you do not explain your wishes, then your executor will have to make difficult choices, and your family may find itself bickering over Aunt Mary's knickknacks.

Keep the will someplace accessible. Make sure that your will and other important documents are kept someplace where your family will be able to find them easily. It's nice to have a safety deposit box for important documents, but in the turmoil of a family's loss, your children will be more likely to find your papers if they are in a filing cabinet in the house. An original copy should be kept elsewhere, too, in case of burglary or fire—at your lawyer's office certainly and in a safety deposit box, as well, if you like.

Living Wills

Just as you have a will that dictates what will happen to your property after you die, you should have a living will that dictates what you want to happen to your body should you require medical treatment and not be able to tell doctors what you want. Here are some things to consider when writing your living will:

Have it drawn up by a lawyer and notarized. If you decide to use a form that you find on the Internet or use legal software, make sure that it will be recognized by your state and that you have the final result notarized.

Be specific. Do you want to be kept alive no matter what? Do you want heroic measures taken to save you? Would you approve being kept on a respirator? For how long? Under what circumstances? Are you planning to be an organ donor? There may be many things to think about at the end of your life. The more you can plan in advance, the happier you will be with the management of your care.

Include a health-care proxy. If you are a not able to make your health-care decisions for yourself, who will make them for you?

Give a copy to your physicians and executor. If you are being treated for a condition, make sure all of your doctors have a copy of your wishes. If you end up needing care unexpectedly, make sure that your friends and family know where you keep your important papers so they'll be able to find your living will.

Living Trusts

A living trust, or a "revocable trust" as it is also called, allows your heirs access to your estate without a messy and public trip to probate court. A living trust is also useful in case you become incapacitated. For instance, if you need to check with a trustee to access a large sum of money, you will be less likely to be scammed by a caregiver. Your trustee will review the reason for the withdrawal, and if the money is not going directly to your care—say, instead, into the pocket of an unscrupulous employee—your trustee will realize what's going on and be able to protect you. Here are some key reasons why a living trust might be right for you:

It allows you to pass your assets on in an orderly way. If you die leaving a minor child, for example, a trust enables the child to not inherit a lump sum, but puts the money into the control of a designated trustee until the child is of a reasonable age to handle the money.

It protects you in case you become incapacitated. You will be less likely to be swindled—by anyone—if your money is in a trust. A designated trustee has to approve large withdrawals, which effectively creates a checks-and-balances system.

Early Bird Secret

Make Haste with Your Trust

If you decide that a living trust is right for you, don't procrastinate setting it up. There are good reasons not to wait. The most important may be the Medicare "look back." If you make a claim that you are unable to afford services and want Medicare to cover them, Medicare may insist upon looking back into your financial records to make sure that you have not transferred your assets recently. If you have moved money around in the last five years, you may not get the benefits you'd hoped for from Medicare.

Safe and Sound

The Necessity of a Safety Deposit Box

If you are worried about the security of your valuables, you might be in the market for a safety deposit box. This can be a strong box or safe that you keep somewhere in your home or it can be a box that you rent at your bank. The bank's box is less likely to be subject to burglary, fire, or water damage. But it is less easy to access, though only slightly. Some insurance companies will lower their premiums for items stored at the bank.

ITEMS THAT SHOULD BE STORED IN A SAFE DEPOSIT BOX:

Original documents including insurance policies; birth, marriage, divorce, and death certificates; deeds, titles, mortgages, leases; contracts; stocks; bonds; certificates of deposit; valuable, durable objects like jewelry, medals, rare stamps, coins, and other collectibles; photos of your home and its contents for insurance purposes; and anything else that is irreplaceable to you.

ITEMS THAT SHOULD <u>NOT</u> BE STORED IN A SAFE DEPOSIT BOX:

Anything that you might need at the last minute: Original documents including powers of attorney, living wills, medical directives, passports, funeral and burial wishes, and your will. You can put a copy of your will in a safe deposit box but keep the original elsewhere, because some states require a court order to open the safe-deposit box of a deceased person, and that can take time. The originals are better off at your home and with your lawyer.

It reduces taxes paid by your estate. You'll still pay estate taxes with a living trust but couples may be able to effectively raise their unified credit tax exemption with a trust.

You'll avoid probate. You'll save money, hassle, time, and publicity by avoiding probate.

You'll avoid a will contest. Wills are relatively easy to challenge. Trusts, however, are not. If you are concerned about this matter, a living trust may be ideal for you.

It may provide a Medicare cushion. Many seniors complain that the government seems to want them to be dirt poor before it will step up to the plate and pay for things that should be covered by Medicare. Families, naturally, worry about letting Mom drain her coffers to pay for medical treatments. A trust might offer a way around this dilemma. If Mom transfers nearly all her assets to a trust, then she may become eligible for Medicare treatments she otherwise wouldn't have been.

Making Major Changes

The Dreamer's Guide to Life-Altering Lifestyle Makeovers

Starting a Second Career

It's true what they say: 60 is the new 40. So, for many seniors these days, retirement is simply the wrong word. Rebirth is more like it! Now is the time when you have the luxury to reinvent yourself. Try new things, travel to new places. Return to those activities you used to love that were almost forgotten in the swirl of raising children and pursuing your career. For many of us, it means considering significant changes in the way we live and support ourselves. And these changes can be exhilarating. This is your second act, and you are the star. And if you do want to slow down a little, now is a wonderful time when you can smell the roses and enjoy the grandkids. Whatever the next years have in store for you, you'll find our expert tips and suggestions in the coming pages to be worth their weight in gold!

Search your soul. Some people already know that they want to open that bait shop or become a nature photographer. Others aren't quite sure. The first step to deciding on a second act is figuring out exactly what you like and don't like. Assess your skills and your passions. Figure out what will translate to other jobs. One of the best aids in soul- and career-searching is the classic book *What Color Is Your Parachute?* by Richard Nelson Bolles, which will walk you through the process of figuring out what you really love and are suited for. There are also many Web sites that offer quizzes to help you in your search, including www.monster.com, which has one in its advice section, as does www.careerpath.com.

Stay put. The easiest way to have a second career might be to do so at the company where you already are, assuming you're still working. Is there a way for you to reduce your hours? Is there a different department you can work in that would excite you more? Could you work from home all the time or part of the time? Could you become a freelancer and sell your services to the company? There is a huge safety net associated with staying where you are known and appreciated. Consider simply tweaking your current job. There's lots of good advice and helpful tips for this at http://seniorliving.about.com.

Network. It's true what they say: it's all who you know. Think of the number of times you have made a sale or gotten a job or performed another transaction in your life thanks to a connection. Your second act job search will work the same way. Start talking to friends, clients, and acquaintances about what you are thinking of doing. See if anyone has any ideas for you or knows of any positions available or knows of anyone else you should be talking to.

Do your homework. If you *are* thinking of making a big change, do your homework first. Pick the brains of people who know more than you do. Read the trade papers of the field you are considering entering. Take a part-time job in the business if you can to make sure it really will suit you and that you'll acquire some of the skills needed before you make the leap. Consider companies that are friendly toward the over-50 crowd. You can find a list of these on the career section of the AARP Web site (www.aarp.org).

Review your finances. Make sure that any move you make will be advantageous to you. Can you take a pay cut? Or will a pay raise bump you into a higher tax bracket? Are you able to take out a loan to start your own business? How will this job change affect your Social Security benefits? Can you afford any training you may need to pursue your dream? Do you need to (and are you willing to) make a radical change like selling your home to finance your dream?

Early Bird Secret

Begin Your Job Search on the Web

There are loads of Web sites that can help you in your job search. Here is a handful of some of the best:

http://www.retirementjobs.com

http://www.civicventures.org/nextchapter/overview.cfm

http://www.retiredbrains.com

http://www.seniorjobbank.org

http://www.thingamajob.com

http://www.aarp.org/money/careers/employerresourcecenter/bestemployers

http://www.doleta.gov/seniors

http://careeronestop.org

Upgrade your skills. If you are looking to start over in a new field, do you need to go back to school to earn a degree? Apply for certification? Learn a new computer program? If so, now is the time to think about it. Ideally, you can take classes for your new career before you've quit your old one. Your current employer might even have a tuition reimbursement program you can use to pay for it. (If so, make sure that you don't have to stay for some length of time after taking classes.)

Qualities That Make You a Great Hire

The over-50 set deserves its props—we've earned them! Make sure that you stick up for yourself and your peers as you hunt for a job in your new field. There can occasionally be subtle (and not-so-subtle) resistance to hiring an older person, especially someone who is making a big change. If you encounter any, you might want to confront it head on. Seniors are well known to trump younger workers in many ways including:

Experience. You've been around the block and are not ruffled by workplace dramas, business cycles, and regime changes. You've already been there, done that. You are unflappable in the face of stormy weather. And your savvy means the company won't worry that you'll waste time on petty matters.

Work ethic. You have spent a lifetime getting up in the morning and getting things done. You are not a kid who came of age during the Internet bubble and expected things to be handed to you. You are dependable, perseverant, and focused. You are always appropriately dressed and behaved, and you project a good image, both internally and to clients.

Did You Know?

 **Size Does Matter!** If you are sensing any age resistance to your plans to change careers, consider companies at both ends of the size spectrum. You may find that small companies are more creative, open-minded, and flexible. On the flip side, many large firms are good about maintaining programs and jobs that are geared toward seniors. The Wal-Mart greeter position is an example of this.

Customer service. You are mature and can relate to customers who are upset. After all, you've been impatient with shoddy service yourself. Your verbal skills are top-notch, meaning that you can communicate well and show empathy—just what customers need.

Loyalty. Younger employees have grown up believing that they have to jump from one job to another to get higher pay. Seniors are much less likely to agree. Retention saves companies a lot of money on training.

Time. Your kids are older now and maybe even out of the house. You are no longer juggling the demands of a young family with your job. You can devote more time and attention to your job than a younger person at a different stage of his or her life.

Motivation. Studies show that older workers are more highly motivated to succeed than younger ones. They have been shown to have a positive effect on product quality, cost control, and customer satisfaction. Take that, Junior!

Great Gigs for Seniors

What's next for you in the job market? If you are thinking about making a change, think seriously about these fields, which are magnets for seniors.

Consulting. You've got a lifetime's worth of knowledge in your field. It would be a shame to waste it. Why not hang out your shingle as a consultant? The job is flexible—you work whatever hours suit you, you take on only projects you like, and you set the pay rate. And you have all the contacts you need to get started—the clients and colleagues you already know.

Temp. You want to work part-time? Have flexible hours? Temping is all about flexibility. You are basically acting as a substitute worker. Many temp jobs pay well, from $10 to $20 an hour. And you can be a temp anywhere in the country and even the world. The largest temp service is Manpower, Inc. (www.manpower.com).

Government work. The U.S. government is very serious about non-discrimination. So if you are, say, a CPA and are looking for a new position, check the IRS for openings. If you are a teacher, look for a position at the board of education.

Eldercare. This subset of health care is growing steadily as longevity increases. You may be asked to offer companionship, personal care, and basic services like cooking and shopping to the elderly. Care may be in-home or in a facility.

Education. Teachers are badly needed, and if you have a bachelor's degree, it takes about a year to become certified to teach. Start with the U.S. Department of Education to learn more: http://www.ed.gov/admins/tchrqual/recruit/altroutes/index.html. This concerns public schools. Certification requirements may be different—and easier—for some private schools.

Hospitality. If you are a people person, then hospitality careers might be right for you. If your first career was in a finance field or if you have an outgoing personality, then working in a casino might be the perfect fit. More seniors are finding work they love at these resorts. Those who find the fit ideal praise the sense of constant action and meeting new people.

Launching a New Business

Seniors today are younger at heart and in better health than ever before. So what's a vigorous, young 65-year-old to do in retirement? For many, the answer is to start your own business. The benefits of starting a business in retirement are many.

It will keep you active. Running a business keeps you on your toes. You've got to stay on top of news and trends, keep up your contacts, and generally be engaged in the world. You'll never worry about sitting around twiddling your thumbs. There is always work to be done if you have your own business.

You'll learn new skills. You will very likely have to learn new things as you launch your enterprise. You'll certainly learn something about accounting (whether you want to or not!), and you'll have to educate yourself on how businesses are run and the tools and technology of your new field— not to mention sales, merchandising, and customer service. All this helps to keep your brain in tip-top shape.

You'll earn extra income. You may have started your business for fun, and you may be running it for fun, but, hey, a little income is still welcome, right? And who's to say your little venture won't take off? Besides the financial rewards, when people pay you for your goods or services, it means that they like what you are offering. That's a great feeling.

Did You Know?

It's Never Too Late! Colonel Sanders was 65 years old when he set about franchising his little fried chicken restaurant. He ended up with a lot more than play money.

You'll reap tax benefits. There are wonderful tax benefits to running your own firm. If you set yourself up as a nature photographer, then your trip to the national park becomes a business trip. You should keep all your receipts and track your mileage because these are deductions if you itemize. If you and your wife are in business together and you have a monthly partners meeting in a nice restaurant, save that receipt! It's a write-off.

You'll be able to save even *more* for retirement. If your business takes off, you may be able to feather your nest a bit more. It might be worth your while to set up a retirement account like a Keogh or a simplified employee pension (SEP) plan. For instance, the law allows you to contribute 20 percent of net earnings to a SEP account each year.

Your Interview Skills

Refresh your interviewing skills before you look for a new job. Here are some of the best questions you might be asked in an interview:

Tell me about yourself.

Why are you interested in this industry? This company?

Tell me about your education.

How does what you've been doing apply to this job?

What do you like most about your current job/field? Why do you want to leave it?

What is your greatest strength?

What is your greatest weakness?

How do you work with others?

What experiences have you had in managing others?

How do you see yourself fitting in here?

Where do you see yourself in three years?

Do you have any questions for me?

When it comes time for you to ask questions, be prepared with the following:

What is the history of this position? Is it new? Are you replacing someone?

Which aspects of this job would you like to see performed better?

What do you see as the key challenges of the job?

Where can I go from this job, assuming that I succeed in it?

How would you describe your ideal candidate?

What are the company's short- and long-term objectives?

In what ways does the company excel? What are its limitations?

When and how will I be evaluated?

Who will I report to? Will anyone report to me?

What is the environment of the company or department?

When will you make the hiring decision? When may I call to follow up?

Enterprising Ideas for Entrepreneurs

Let's say that you know you want to run your own show. What kind of business should you start? There are a number of things to keep in mind when deciding to hang out your own shingle.

Stay in your current field. This is the path of least resistance and can mean an easy segue into entrepreneurship. You use all your current contacts, all the skills you've built up, all the same equipment. What could be easier? You can simply go freelance and take jobs as they come up, or you can become a consultant, which is a more formal way of being a freelancer. Many seniors find that their old firms are eager to hire them for outsourced work; most firms love to work with known quantities and former employees are just that. Staying in a familiar field will give you a baseline level of comfort.

Turn a hobby into a business. Have you been an avid calligrapher throughout the years and just haven't had time to devote to your passion? Now's the time! Seniors around the country are taking their crafting, sporting, and other leisure activities to the next level by milking them for cash. And they are delighted when it works! You would be quilting anyway, so it makes sense to get a little something extra for your efforts. You'll experience the thrill of knowing that other people are enjoying your talent and hard work.

Buy a business. You might consider stepping up to the plate and buying a business from someone who is retiring. The advantage is that the company usually has a built-in customer base, and you'll be inheriting all the tools, equipment, and leases you need to start right up. Think of this as being a hermit crab—you can move right into a fully furnished new shell. Unlike other options, this one requires some capital to get started. Have your lawyer carefully review the books and other documents before you sign on.

Do what you love. Your first career may have been filled with obligations. Let your next one be filled with pleasure. Choose a field that has always interested you, and you will be more likely to succeed. If work is fun, you are going to be eager to go to your place of business and willing to put in the hours it takes to give your new enterprise its best shot.

Reduce your risk. Having your own business means taking on some risk. Most entrepreneurs can tell you stories of the failed businesses they started before their successful ones took off. If you are in your 20s, you can afford to make mistakes because you have time to recover from them. If you are in your 60s, it's better to get things right on the first go. It's important, then, to make sure that you are conservative with your finances and that you are insured for anything that might expose you to undue risk.

Review your finances. Do whatever you can to keep the costs in check. Where are you going to get your start-up money if you need any? Experts advise you not to raid your retirement accounts. You would be better off borrowing money from a line of credit or home equity loan. Build your cash reserves well in advance of starting your business if you can. If you know that in five years you'll want to retire and try your hand at something new, now's the time to start socking away capital. Experts advise you to save double the amount you think you'll need to get started. Better safe than sorry.

Open a business checking and savings account. Make sure that your business has its own accounts for banking and credit. This way you'll be able to keep track of how it's doing and keep its finances separate from your personal ones.

NO KIDDING? Seniors Make Great Entrepreneurs!

Many retirees fall into entrepreneurship. They happen to see a need that is not being met and decide to address it themselves. And oftentimes the businesses set up relate to the senior community. Just as new moms start baby gear companies and new dog owners start fashion leash companies, many seniors discover opportunities that make sense for their peers.

Realize time is on your side. While retirees don't have the benefit of recovering from losses as easily as younger people do, they have the luxury of concentrating on their work as little or as much as they'd like. This lifestyle change works especially well for seasonal businesses. The retiree who opens a clam shack can pour his whole summer into the work, knowing he'll have the rest of the year to recover from all that hard work. A younger worker would be worried about how to make a living during the other months.

Consider your lifestyle. Are you brimming with energy or are you more low-key? Do you want a job that is going to let you really sink your teeth in, or are you looking for a distraction for a few hours a day? Do you want to take lots of vacations while you keep your business running? These lifestyle factors should be taken into account when you decide what kind of business to run. If you decide to open a bakery, you'd better be a really early riser (like 4 a.m.!) who is game for lots of physical labor. If you are going to do some bookkeeping, you can be on your porch in your bathrobe with your feet up. Make sure you know what your health and lifestyle is best suited for before you jump in.

Moving Down in House

After the kids move out, you may find that you have more house than you need. Many retirees decide to downsize their homes as they approach retirement for a number of good reasons.

Homes take work to maintain. Do you notice that by the time you are done dusting the last room in the house that the first one looks like it needs attention again? Do you find that the more space you have, the more clutter seems to accumulate, even if it's just you and your spouse living there? Does the expanse of lawn that used to represent games of catch and barbecues now just represent a lawn-mowing headache? A smaller home can mean a lot less headache and backache when it comes to maintenance.

Homes take money to maintain. The gutters need replacing. The burst pipe in the spare bathroom means a check to the plumber and the contractor. The high property taxes that were once well worth the money for the good school district no longer make sense because the kids are grown. A smaller home in a different neighborhood would require less money to maintain and the taxes would be lower. And what about heat? With the cost of oil going through the roof, wouldn't it be nice to have a cozy little ranch house instead of your drafty big Victorian?

Early Bird Secret

Make Your House Pay You!

Isn't it time your house paid you back? If you have paid off your mortgage or have a lot of equity in it, consider getting a reverse mortgage, and the bank will pay you to live in the house. You don't need to worry that you'll be thrown out at some point if you arrange for a mortgage that enables you to stay for as long as you are alive. The caveat: your heirs will not inherit the house. And it means that you will lose your equity in the house so that if you need to go to a care facility in 20 years, you can't sell the house to pay for it.

Your house is incompatible with your health. Those three flights of stairs used to be nothing to you. But if you have certain health issues—knee troubles, hip problems, or you get winded easily—do they really make sense?

It's good to make new memories. Out with the old; in with the new! Sometimes it's a good thing to have a fresh start, a clean slate. You are embarking on an exciting new phase of your life so think about if it might make sense to clear out the clutter and start again in a new space. Do you really need those life jackets you've kept in the basement since you sold your boat 20 years ago? We didn't think so.

You want to cash out. Property values go up and down, but if you've been in your home a long time, you have almost certainly seen yours go up. Maybe it's time to hang out the For Sale sign and listen to the sound of the cash register ring.

Selling Your Home—and Finding a New One

When the time comes for you to actually put the pedal to the metal and plan your move, take time to do it as painlessly as possible. Here are a few keys to a smooth move:

Consult a real estate agent. A real estate agent will give you a realistic sense of what you can expect to get from the house in the current market. The market has undergone some serious fluctuations in recent years, and an agent will be able to give you tips on things you can do to get the best possible price for your most important asset.

Declutter. Now is the time to unburden yourself of the many things you don't need. It also may be the time to make some money on a garage sale (see box on page 270), donate old things to charity (get a receipt in case you decide to take a tax deduction), divvy up mementos among the kids and friends, and keep only what you believe to be useful and beautiful. Decluttering is worth doing, even if you decide not to sell. It will clear your mind as well as your cellar.

Run the numbers. Determine how much you'll get for the house and how much it will cost to buy and maintain a new place. Consider the taxes, the maintenance, moving costs, and other things that might affect you.

Ka-Ching!

No More Pink Foam Hair Rollers

(And 46 Other Items You Own and Never Use That Add Up to a Great Yard Sale)

If you're considering downsizing, why not have a garage or yard sale to declutter and make some money in the process? Our experts gathered up 46 items that most frequently sit unused or are duplicated by newer models you have purchased.

1 Exercise equipment and sporting goods

2 Blenders

3 Bread machines

4 Microwave oven

5 Sewing machine

6 Small televisions

7 **Stemware and flatware**
Mismatched pieces get the toss

8 Kids books, toys, and clothes

9 Stereo components

10 Typewriters

11 DVDs and CDs

12 Books

13 Old magazines

14 Curling irons

15 **Hotel soaps**
Unused, unopened soaps and shampoos (you know you have a shoebox full!)

16 Occasional tables

17 Mismatched chairs

18 Old computer components—keyboards, monitors

19 Miscellaneous appliances and electronics—toasters, radios, toaster ovens, hair dryers

20 Costume jewelry (When exactly was the last time you wore the rhinestone ball earrings and matching three-inch flower pin?)

21 Odd pieces of dinnerware and serving platters

23 Fabric

24 Notions

25 Dress patterns

26 Art—real and otherwise

27 Lawn mower

28 Garden hoses

29 Tools, especially duplicates of items like hammers, saws, and screwdrivers

30 Muffin tins and other bakeware

32 Old purses

33 Canvas tote bags

34 Draperies

35 Shot glasses, barware, coffee mugs

36 Luggage

37 Dining room table

38 Buffet and china cabinet

40 Rugs

41 Bottles: little bottles, Jim Beam, Avon, Kara Brooks, old medicine, Mrs. Butterworth, miniatures, fruit jars, baby food, and insulators

42 Camping gear

43 Needlework and other handmade items

44 Yarn, knitting needles, crochet hooks, and sweater and afghan pattern pamphlets

45 Comic books

46 Dolls and their clothing

22 **Records**
If you haven't listened in one year, they're good to go

31 **Mini blinds**
Broken, tangled, unnecessary

39 **Ceramic figurines**
How many Hummels do you need?

Like, in your new place, do you still need a car? Think forward to the resale value of your new property as well. Will it be as easy to sell as you hope, if you need to move to a facility sometime in the future?

Make repairs. As your real estate agent will tell you, you should spiff up your home before you sell it because you'll get more money and sell it quicker this way.

Don't look for a gorgeous old property. Think new. Newer homes are easier to care for and usually easier to sell than older ones when the time comes.

Keep maintenance in mind. Your new home should be easy to care for. If you are moving to an apartment, you'll eliminate yard work and other property hassles. If you are moving to a house, make sure that the lawn is not expansive and the house is of a size that is manageable for you to handle and has fixtures that are up to date.

Think of your lifestyle. Look for a home that suits your lifestyle and that you can age into. If you love to walk, make sure the sidewalks in your neighborhood are well maintained and that the streets seem safe. If you just had a hip replaced, maybe stairs are not a good idea. If you have knee problems, make sure you can take a shower without having to climb over a high tub edge and that handles can be installed easily if you need them.

Remember taxes. If you moved to your current home in part because of the good schools, you may be paying more taxes than you need to be. Take a close look at the tax burden of homes while you shop. School districts make a big difference but so do streets. There may be a highly desirable street in your town where taxes are astronomical, whereas on a little cul-de-sac right off of that street the houses are just as nice, but taxes are much lower.

Relocating to a Retirement Community

Do these two words get you excited? They should. Once upon a time, your immediate response might have been "Ho hum" or "Not me" or even "Yikes!" By the time you are finished with this section, you will be more inclined to think *Love Boat*. Retirement communities these days are some of the most happening, social, and quickly growing spots in America.

Active/independent communities. These are residential spots with no medical or graduated support for seniors. It's an especially good option for couples with a wide age difference, where one is retired and the other still working. Many active communities may not be that different from the neighborhood you just left—you have your own home or apartment, you are surrounded by nice people, and you remain quite independent. There may be a clubhouse to belong to or perhaps a golf course. Your member fees mean that you may not need to deal with headaches like lawn mowing or snow removal, and the community may be gated or have a guard posted at the entrance. On the other hand, there may be some restrictions. These communities are for seniors so the policy toward children might limit the grandkids' visits.

Understanding the Facility's Fees

There are some variations, but most communities require an entrance fee, which must be paid in cash. (It is not something you can finance and is comparable to the cost of a house—from $40,000 all the way up to the millions for luxury properties.) Then residents pay a monthly maintenance fee, which may range from $800 to $5,000 (the high end, again, is the luxury option). The fee includes certain things like some meals and activities. When residents need more help with daily life, staffers attend to them in their own apartments. When their care needs to be stepped up, they move to the assisted-living wing of the residence. When they leave the community, either by choice or death, a portion of their entrance fee is returned to them or to their estate.

Continuing care retirement communities (CCRC). These communities offer the best of both worlds: independence *and* care when you need it. They create an even stronger sense of community than their active/ independent counterparts because they usually have more common areas, more activities, and are generally more social. They are like cruise ships or college campuses—you can feel like you are in your own little universe within the grounds. And this can be a great thing. As you age and your care needs change, you won't need to uproot yourself. You will be able to get the care you need either in the same apartment or room or a new one within the same facility. This makes for an easy transition from independence to assisted care during a time of your life that might otherwise be difficult. Entrance levels vary at a CCRC. You usually have the choice to join with an extensive, modified, or fee-for-service contract. The extensive is the most

Checklist

Before you visit retirement communities to which you're considering moving, make sure to have this list of questions in hand.

Financial

What's the entry fee? Is it refundable?

What is the daily or monthly rate?

Are there charges for additional services you may want or need?

Are utilities, phone, cable, and Internet services included?

Will there be many extras you'll pay for separately?

What type of notice period is required should you need or want to move?

How often are rates for accommodation and/or services increased?

What is the average annual rate of increase over the last few years?

What kinds of opportunities are available for a resident to receive further care as a condition or problem requires?

Is the facility connected with a nursing home or other kind of facility?

What are all the types of housing available (private versus shared, apartment, suite)?

Is the housing furnished? If so, what is included?

Is there a kitchen in your unit?

Are there restrictions on the types and amounts of personal belongings you may bring?

What happens if you are unable to pay for services?

What are the payment, billing, and credit policies?

Lifestyle

What are the admission requirements?

How close is the nearest hospital?

Is the community affiliated with any religious or cultural group?

How close are the churches, parks, and shopping centers?

How accessible is public transportation? Does the community offer it?

Do the residents stay year round? (You don't want to move to Vermont only to discover that the place clears out in the winter, leaving you nearly alone.)

How big is the facility? (Larger facilities may offer more activities, get-togethers, and transportation. Smaller communities may be more intimate and low-key.)

Are pets allowed?

What are your dining options? What kinds of meals are offered?

Can residents bring their own cars?

What are the facility's visiting hours? What types of accommodations are available for visitors? Are there any restrictions on having guests?

Do many residents take part in activities and outings?

How often are each resident's needs reassessed?

Things to Observe on Your Own

How clean is the facility? Does it look good? Does it smell?

How do the residents look? Friendly? Happy?

How do the staff look? Is the staff friendly? Are they courteous?

expensive, as it will cover unlimited long-term nursing care at an agreed-upon price, but if you live a long time, it might be the most economical in the long run. Modified care contracts cover a specific amount of long-term nursing care. Fee-for-service does not include long-term nursing care. It's inexpensive now, but it may not be in the future.

Assisted living. CCRCs include assisted-living accommodations and services, but facilities specifically for assisted living are strictly for people who absolutely do need assistance. Assisted living centers, just like the assisted living programs in CCRCs, offer residents some care with necessities like eating, bathing, dressing, doing chores, and taking medication. Other than these kinds of tasks, residents support themselves. Some medical care will be offered, but it won't be as intensive as what you'd find at a nursing home or hospital. One key difference between CCRCs and assisted living facilities is that in a CCRC you can plan ahead for the level of care you'll get and fix a price. When you enter an assisted living center, you pay for the services you need upon arrival. Deciding which one is right for you depends on your budget, risk tolerance, lifestyle, and health. If you think you'll be just fine on your own for a long time, it might pay to wait until you need an assisted living center. If you like the idea of establishing community ties in advance of your elder years and want to be sure that you'll get coverage however soon you'll need it, then a CCRC sounds like a better match.

Choosing the Right Locale

It may be time-consuming to visit every place you are considering, yet choosing a community is one of the biggest and most expensive decisions you might ever make.

Talk to the residents. It's a good idea to talk to a variety of people at the community. How long have they lived there? Are they happy? Would they change anything if they could? Were they surprised by anything about the place or the lifestyle? Do they have any advice for you?

Sleep over. Ask if you can spend the night. Nothing will give you a better sense of the place than an overnight visit. Make sure you take advantage of everything you can. Join or watch an activity. Try several dining options if possible. Soak up the atmosphere and see as much of the place as you can.

Make a return visit. Visit more than once. See the community in the morning and in the evening. And if you can see it in two different seasons, so much the better.

Make your tour comprehensive. Don't just see the rooms and common areas. Ask to see the treatment rooms, the kitchen, stairwells—as much as you can. Definitely visit the assisted-living accommodations in case you end up needing them.

Get the paperwork. This includes menus, activities lists, calendars, and other paperwork that will give you a sense of the lifestyle, as well as contracts and admission paperwork.

Hire a consultant. There are firms that will help you make this important decision. You will pay a fee for their services, of course, but considering the investment you'll be making, it may be well worth it.

Setting Up Residence in Another State

Moving is one of the most exciting adventures you can have at any age. And many seniors, when they start to think about downsizing, decide to not only move to a new home, but to a new state. And we're not just talking about snowbirds moving from the Northeast to Florida. Seniors these days are moving to some surprising places (Asheville, North Carolina, and Madison, Wisconsin, come to mind)—and loving it. Before you consider a move,

make sure you figure out what you are looking for and determine which locations will best meet your changing needs. Here are some guidelines.

Job market. If you are planning to work in retirement, you need to keep an eye on the job market in your field. Is the economy where you are considering moving vibrant or sluggish? Is there a need for your skills in that market? Is there something else you'd like to do that will be supported by the local economy better?

Cost of living. What will it cost to live in a new state? Hawaii sounds great, but what do homes cost? The national median price of a home is about $215,000. How do the homes in your dream city compare? What does food cost? How are the taxes? And what is the price of a plane ticket to Georgia, where the grandkids are living? Make sure you do your homework and consider lifestyle factors. For instance, if you think you want to live on a farm someplace, figure out how long it will take you get to the grocery store. If you are moving from a city, you might be surprised by the amount of gas and automotive wear-and-tear from simple shopping tasks.

Taxes. Do you want to move to a state that has low taxes? Try Alaska, Florida, Nevada, South Dakota, Texas, Washington, and Wyoming. These states have no personal income tax. Consider New Hampshire and Tennessee, too; these tax only income from investments, not wages. If you love to shop, realize that five states don't have sales tax: Alaska, Montana, Delaware, New Hampshire, and Oregon. If you like the South and you don't like to pay property tax, then consider Alabama and Arkansas, which have some of the lowest property taxes in the country.

Early Bird Secret

Move within Shouting Distance

If the idea of making a big move is unappealing, then what about a small one? For example, if your primary residence is in New York City, you could be paying state and city taxes equal to 11 percent of your income, and that's not including federal taxes. Moving just 70 miles northeast to Pennsylvania could cut that state tax bill to less than 5 percent. You'd be just a pleasant day trip away from your old neighborhood and would save a bundle in the process.

Family. Most seniors say that they don't want to live more than three hours away from family. How close you want to stay to your family might be a big factor for you. Do you like flying to visit family and have the means for it? Do you prefer to drive? Will the family be more likely to want to visit you in one location versus another? Can you afford an extra guest room for visiting family and friends in one location over another?

Safety. How safe is the place you want to move to? Is there crime? What kind is it? Crime against people? Property? The housing bust has left many once-affluent neighborhoods abandoned. You may be able to get a good deal on a house, but is it really a good deal if you are worried about getting mugged when you walk to the mailbox?

Your lifestyle. Do you long to live someplace warm? Do you never want to use a windshield ice scraper again or shovel a walkway? The most popular sunshine states for seniors have consistently been Florida, California, Arizona, North Carolina, and Texas. You might be longing for rugged outdoorsy pursuits instead. Many people are drawn to states like Colorado, Washington, Idaho, Utah, Wyoming, West Virginia, and Tennessee. They cite the skiing, hiking, clean air, and absence of crowds as major attractions. Are you a city mouse or a country mouse? It used to be that retirees fled to the country. Now they are as likely to choose a city to settle down in. Cities are filled with places to go and people to see, and most have excellent public transit systems, which can make all the difference between a social butterfly and a hermit crab.

Entertainment and culture. Are there museums? Theaters? Golf courses? Public parks? How's the shopping? Is there a university nearby? Make sure you have a sense of what you'll do in your free time and that your hobbies dovetail nicely with what your home has to offer.

Medical care. As you age, you will likely need increased medical care. Can your new town offer what you might need? Make sure it will, especially if you already have health conditions that require care.

Is Moving Out of State a Good Idea for You?

The excitement of moving is undeniable. Before you move far away from where you are now, ask yourself these questions to make sure it really is the right choice for you.

Are you happy where you are now? If you are perfectly happy where you are now, what is the point of moving? If it's to save money, then perhaps there are other steps you can take that will ensure you can stay in your familiar stomping grounds. Make sure that you are not thinking of moving just because "everyone is doing it" or it seems like that's what you're supposed to do when you retire. Now is the time to do exactly what *you* want.

Are you active in and attached to your community? If you are one of the regulars at your coffee shop, if you founded the local model airplane association, if you play senior softball twice a week, then maybe you are a joiner and would find similar events and ties wherever you move. Or maybe you have lived in your town for so long that you know everyone and feel really comfortable there. Some social butterflies thrive anywhere they go; others need the familiarity of their own garden. Which are you?

Have your friends moved away? Sometimes there seems to be a mass exodus from the neighborhood as friends retire and move away after their kids grow up. If this has happened to you, maybe you would be happier elsewhere. Sometimes neighbors retire together. If it doesn't matter where you live as long as you are among friends, then it might make sense to move with everyone else to the same area in Florida. If you find that you are making new friends in your old town, then it might be worth staying and just visiting your old friends a few times a year.

Is there someplace you've always wanted to live? If you have been deferring your dream of a bungalow in Los Angeles or a Cape Cod on, well, Cape Cod, then maybe now is the perfect time to indulge yourself. Search your heart and see if there is a tug pulling toward something you have always leaned toward. Then make sure you do the research before you take the leap.

11

Extraordinary Savings

A *to* **Z**

In today's

challenging economic climate, there are thousands of ways that seniors can save money besides simply getting a discount from merchants or big corporations. Use our A to Z guide to find innovative Early Bird ideas that will help put money back *in* your pocket. You'll discover ways to save every day, every week, every month, and every year. What type of baking dish should you use for maximum energy savings? How can you save big on a bag of potatoes at the grocery store? What does your television have to do with cooling costs? Can you make your newspaper subscription pay you back? Try any combination of these endlessly savvy tips, and you'll be amazed by the amount of money you've easily and painlessly put back in the bank.

A

Air conditioner

Don't work alone. Team up your air conditioner with a ceiling fan to spread cool air throughout the room. Using both at the same time lets you raise the air conditioner temperature by five degrees, which in turn lowers your cooling costs.

Stick with the program. Install a programmable thermostat for your air conditioner and cut down on your utility bill. Set it for several degrees warmer at night or when no one is home; you can save up to 10 percent on your cooling costs for every degree above 78 you raise the thermostat.

Don't light up your thermostat. Keep heat-generating appliances like lamps, computers, and televisions away from your air-conditioning thermostat. Their heat will trick the air conditioner into running longer.

Keep it clear. Make sure your air-conditioning vents are not blocked by furniture or other obstructions. (You don't want to pay to cool the back of your couch!)

Seal the leaks. Save on cooling costs by keeping the cool air you've paid for in your house. Seal or caulk dryer vents, pipes entering the house, and electrical outlets as well as drafty windows and doors. You'll keep warm air inside in the winter, too.

Shoot for the sky. Aim the vents of your room air conditioner at the ceiling, and let the cool air float down to you. You'll get more bang for your cooling buck (by cooling the room from top to bottom, rather than in just one spot), plus you'll have better air circulation as the cold air drifts down.

Airfare

Fly on Tuesdays, Wednesdays, and Saturdays. You'll generally find cheaper fares on these days. And be flexible about departure times and alternative airports, too—you'll save even more if you can accommodate the airlines' quirky schedules.

Take a companion. Look for special offers that allow you to bring a companion for half price. If it's a friend (and not your spouse, say), offer to split the savings you can get by booking two tickets together.

Wait until the last minute. This isn't normally sage advice for travelers, but it can work well for those with flexible schedules looking to save money on airfare (as well as hotels and cruises). Check out Travelzoo.com, SmarterTravel.com, 11thHourVacations.com, and LastMinuteTravel.com for good deals for procrastinators.

> ## Night owls save on flights.
>
> Book the best airfare just after midnight, East Coast time, when airlines cut prices on flights that are less than full. Calling your airline late at night can save you from $50 to $400.

Air freshener

Use a towel, not a spray can. Don't spend money on chemical scents that make you sneeze! You can eliminate odors in your house by soaking a hand towel in white vinegar, wringing it out completely, and swinging it over your head like a lasso a few times. You'll save the cost of air freshener and get a little exercise, too.

Alternative medicine

Make alternate arrangements. Surprisingly enough, alternative medicine—including acupuncture and massage therapy—may be less expensive than traditional treatments for some chronic health problems (depending on your insurance plan). Check your insurance policy for details.

Antacid

Don't be sour. Forget about spending money on antacid at the pharmacy next time you have heartburn, acid indigestion, sour stomach, or an upset stomach. Simply mix 1/2 teaspoon of baking soda into 1/2 cup of water (4 fluid ounces) until the baking soda dissolves completely. Then drink up for more settled times.

Appliances

The price will floor you. Ask your appliance retailer if you can buy the floor model of the appliance you want for a reduced price.

Don't be a fan. Shop for major purchases like appliances during sporting events like the Super Bowl or the World Series. Stores will be empty, and the salespeople will be ready and willing to negotiate so they can rack up some sales. You may easily knock at least 2 percent off the original purchase price of whatever you want to buy.

Art

Book it. Frame pictures from art books or magazines (that you own, of course) to spruce up your walls. Look for nice inexpensive frames to highlight your masterpieces.

> ### Be faithful—to your bank.
>
> Take money out of only your bank's ATM machine. You can be charged up to $3 by your bank for taking money out of another bank's machine, and then be charged again by the other bank. Don't pay another bank for access to *your* money.

ATM machine

Take only what you need. On average, consumers withdraw $60 per week from an ATM machine. And most consumers have no idea where that money goes. Figure out how much cash you really need each week, and take *only* that amount out of the ATM. You won't overspend because you won't have extra money in your wallet.

Bath

Just say no. Test the amount of water you use in a shower and compare it to the amount you use in a bath. Next time you shower, plug the bathtub and see how much water fills the tub. If there's less water than in your normal bath, you'll save money by taking a shower. Remember: an average bath uses 30 to 50 gallons of water, while a four-minute shower with a low-flow shower head uses only 10 gallons. Take short showers and save.

Battery

Baking soda for your car battery. Your car battery needs to be clean to keep working. You can remove corrosion and keep the battery clean with a mixture of 1 tablespoon baking soda and 1 cup of water. Use the solution to wash the outside of the battery (being careful not to let it get into the battery). Rinse it off with clean water and wipe to dry.

Belt

Cut it down to size. Don't toss a belt that no longer fits or doesn't work with your clothes. Size it to fit your pet as a collar.

Birdbath

Give the birds a bath (without taking one). Ignore fancy and expensive birdbaths at your garden or birding store. Just fashion an equally useful birdbath from an old pan on top of a flowerpot. Fill it with water and watch the birds flock to it.

Blinds

Be neutral. Buy blinds in a neutral color. You'll still be able to use them later if you change the color scheme of the room you're decorating now.

Books

Round up reading material. There's no need to buy books when you want to read something new. Organize an ongoing book swap with your church or a social or community group. Everyone brings in their latest and greatest reads and swaps them for others. Keep the books on an accessible shelf; you may need several shelves if your collection is a success!

Buy the latest bestselling books for half off.

Split the cost of one book with a friend (preferably at a discount), and give it to her to read when you've finished it. Then buy another one with the same friend, and let her read it first. It's like having your own private book club!

Boots and Shoes

Protect your sole. Make your boots and all your shoes last 10 times longer by going from the shoe store to the shoe repair and having sole protectors or heel and toe taps put on your new footwear. The protectors cost less than $20 and potentially save you hundreds since it's usually the soles that wear out first.

Let your footwear breathe. Don't store any shoes or boots in the attic or the basement during the off-season. The shifts in temperature will prematurely age them.

Place them in a closet that allows air to circulate and they'll last longer, saving you money and (yet another) a trip to the store.

Bottles as boot trees. Prolong the life of your boots by storing them with unusual boot trees. Put a clean, empty 1-liter soda bottle in each boot to help it retain its shape. You won't have to pay for boot trees or new boots.

Buttons

Old buttons, new look. Keep nice, fancy, or unusual buttons when you recycle or toss worn-out clothing. You can use them to change the look of a garment that's starting to bore you or to enliven a plain shirt that needs a little pizzazz.

Calendar

Save $15 by getting a calendar for free. Where? Try banks, insurance agencies, card stores, and your mail—you may find calendars from charities you support as well as from businesses you've used.

Candles

Keep your candles cold. Store your candles in the freezer for a longer burn life.

Car

Don't waste by waiting. If you plan to wait for someone in your idling car for more than one minute, turn the car off to save gas. You'll use less fuel starting up the car than leaving it on for even this short a time.

C

Warm your heart, not your car.

Today's cars do not need to be warmed up for more than 30 seconds. You car will warm up as you drive. If you warm it up in the driveway, you're just wasting gas.

Be an oily bird. Always ask your local lube center if it offers a senior discount or a multicar deal on oil changes. If it doesn't, keep asking until you find one that does.

Car wash

Fill up and wash up. Some gas stations offer free or cut-rate car washes when you stop to get gas.

Carpet

Go to pieces. Next time you need to replace your carpet, think about using carpet tiles for busy areas such as hallways and entryways. If a piece of the carpet gets stained or worn, you can simply replace the tile, rather than the whole carpet.

Pay more to pay less. Invest in a good-quality pad for under your carpet. It will protect the carpet from wear and tear, and let you buy a less expensive carpet.

Carpet cleaner

Salt it away. Don't use an expensive carpet cleaner next time you experience a nasty red wine spill on your carpet. Save that $5 to $10 and simply pour a pile of good old table salt on the spill. Leave the salt on until it dries, and then vacuum it up. The stain is gone!

Sprinkle on seltzer.

As soon as food hits your rug, wipe up the excess and then sprinkle it liberally with seltzer or club soda. Scrub with a brush, sprinkling on more seltzer or soda as needed. Blot dry with a towel.

Share it and save. Rent a carpet-cleaning machine for you and a neighbor, and split the cost. You can save big on a one-day rental.

Cash

Stash the cash. Cutting impulse spending can save big bucks, so if this is your personal bugaboo, try keeping only $20 to $40 in your wallet. The less you have in cash, the less you're likely to spend on impulse purchases. That $4 latte at the coffee shop will look a lot less appealing if it leaves you with only $16 for the rest of the day!

Cash register

Watch it like a hawk. Cash registers, as well as humans, make errors, so watch the register carefully to make sure it rings up the right price for the right item. You might get overcharged if the register mistakes your cream cheese for brie or if it hasn't been programmed with the current sale prices. Many grocery stores will give the item for free or at a sharp discount if the register (whether operated by a cashier or you on a self-checkout line) charges you the wrong amount.

Get the senior plan.

Verizon and AT&T both advertise a relatively inexpensive national senior cell-phone plan, but if you're buying your phone and setting up service with a regional carrier, be sure to ask about senior offers. If they say no, remind them that two of the majors have senior plans—one may be forthcoming for you.

Cat

It's the cat's meow. Save on vet bills by adding 1/8 to 1/4 teaspoon of olive oil to your cat's food. It will help prevent hairballs and keep your cat's digestive system purring along.

Cell phone

Talk isn't cheap. The average cell phone user faces a $60 bill each month, including taxes and miscellaneous fees. If you talk less than 200 minutes a month, you may be better off using a pay-as-you-go plan (as long as it charges 25 cents a minute or less). You can easily save $45 a month with a prepaid plan.

Extend your battery life. Try to run your battery out before recharging, at least every other time, for the longest battery life. Avoid buying a new cell phone battery and give your electric bill a break in the process by shutting your cell phone off before you go to sleep. Just remember to turn it back on in the morning!

Checks

Check it off your list. Is your bank charging a lot for printing your checks? If so, check out independent printers: most of them charge about half what your bank does for the same service. Try Checks Unlimited (800-210-0468 or www.checksunlimited.com) or Checks in the Mail (800-733-4443 or www.checksinthemail.com) or do an Internet search for "personal check printers," which will turn you up an additional range of printers such as www.checkswithstyle.com or www.checkworks.com. If you've ever wanted checks with John Deere tractors on them, an independent printer is the way to go!

Chicken

Buy it whole. Never buy chicken parts when you can buy the whole thing and make more meals from it, for pennies on the pound. Forget about fancy butchering: using strong kitchen shears, cut the chicken up the breast bone, up the back bone, and then cut those halves in half again. Cut off wings and legs, and you now have the kind of pieces that you'd pay hefty bucks for. Never again!

Coffee

Treat yourself—to a gift card. Buying a premium coffee regularly is the bugaboo of personal finance advisers, who see it as the ultimate waste of money, but it *is* okay to get one now and then. (Let's face it, they can be pretty tasty!) If you're inclined to overdo, buy a gift card for yourself for a budgeted amount each month, and enjoy every frothy, flavored cupful until the card runs out.

Cut the cost of home-brewed gourmet coffee. Even coffee made at home can be expensive, if you have expensive coffee tastes in fancy beans and roast. But you can mix the pleasure with savings if you combine one part of your favorite gourmet coffee with one part of a much less expensive store brand, and enjoy your high-end coffee tastes at a fraction of the cost.

Turn off the pot.

Nothing's better than a leisurely morning and a bottomless cup of coffee, but warming the coffee pot all morning isn't good for your electric bill—or your coffee, which will take on a flat, bitter flavor as all the essential oils evaporate. Brew directly into a thermal pot or pour your fresh-brewed coffee into a thermos, then turn off the coffee maker, and treasure your savings.

Pretend it's a day at the office. Even if you're drinking your coffee at home, think about buying it at an office supply superstore, such as Staples or Office Depot. You may find substantial savings on hot chocolate, tea, coffee, creamer, and sugar at the same place you get a good deal on your pencils and printer ink.

Coins

Hoard loose change. Dump your loose change into a jar at the end of every day, and once every six months or so (or while you can still lift the jar!), bring your change to a local bank that has a coin-counting machine. It's important to take them to a bank, which likely won't charge you a fee for the counting, rather than to one of the commercial coin-counting machines you see in grocery stores, which will deduct 10 percent of your hard-earned change. Ka-ching!

Computer

Think small to save big. Buy a laptop computer: it uses less energy than an Energy Star-rated desktop computer and monitor. A typical laptop draws from 15 to 25 watts when being used, while a conventional PC and monitor draw 150 watts. You'll be pleased with the evidence on your utility bill.

Go to sleep. Your computer continues to use energy even when you're not using it. In fact, you can cut its power demand by up to 90 percent if you make it automatically "sleep" after 20 or 30 minutes of non-use. (See your manual for programming instructions—it's usually a simple adjustment.) And when you finish a session of Internet surfing or e-mailing, turn it off altogether.

Confetti

Celebrate the savings. There's nothing more festive than a handful of confetti at a party, but don't spend money buying little bits of paper. Save leftover wrapping paper—even small pieces will work—and let your grandchildren use a hole punch or little scissors to create lots of circles or squares of colorful confetti. Use your homegrown confetti to celebrate family birthdays, News Year's Eve, or any happy occasion. (You can even vacuum it up into a clean hand vac to use again!)

Consignment shop

Pick your target carefully. One obvious way to cut back on clothing costs is to check out consignments shops. But don't choose just *any* consignment shop: find one close to a wealthy neighborhood, where you may be surprised at finding stacks of hardly or never-worn clothes, many from top designers and some items with the tags still on. You'll get amazing bargains on extraordinary clothes you won't find elsewhere.

Contact lenses

See your way through the mail. Save up to 50 percent on contact lenses and more on the necessary accessories (fluid and cleaning apparatus) by ordering through the mail.

You can order the exact type of lenses you currently wear—not a lesser brand—at a substantial discount by phone at 1-800-Contacts or online at www.1800contacts.com

Container gardening

Skimp on the soil. Save money on potting soil by using only as much as your plant needs—not what the deep container dictates. Put broken-up polystyrene chunks or packing "peanuts" at the bottom of the pot (making sure to keep the drainage hole clear), then add enough potting soil for your plant. You'll benefit from a lighter pot as well as a heavier wallet, and you'll find your pot drains better when it's not heavily packed with soil down to the bottom.

Create your own container.

You don't need to be restricted by traditional containers when choosing pots for your container gardening. Think about apple boxes, tin or colorful plastic buckets, bushel baskets, funky Italian tomato cans, an old trunk—any container that can have drainage holes drilled in the bottom.

Cottage cheese

Turn it on its head. Store your container of cottage cheese upside down in the refrigerator. It will last twice as long as if stored right side up.

Credit card

Edit your credit. Lose the temptation to spend by locking away your credit cards. Don't cancel them (it can hurt your credit score); instead, put them in a drawer, keeping only one in your wallet.

Dentist

Find a tooth trainee. If there's a local dental school near you, you may be able to get free or almost-free dental checkups and work done by supervised students (assuming your teeth are in good condition). Call to ask about the school's policy and go in for a cleaning to assess the school and see if you're comfortable. Chances are you can get excellent care for a fraction of the usual price.

Have a plan. Consider getting a dental plan rather than dental insurance. You pay an annual fee, ranging from $100 to $150, and get a 20 to 60 percent discount from participating dentists. Visit www.discount-dental.net or www.dentalplans.com to get more information and sign up.

Dentures

Do it yourself. Don't spend money over and over on expensive denture cleaning products. You can clean dentures easily and inexpensively at home with a soft toothbrush and a teaspoon of baking soda. Scrub gently and rinse in clear water. Then place the dentures in a small, microwave-proof container just big enough to hold them (a coffee mug, for example) and cover them with water. Add a tablespoon of white vinegar and microwave on high for two minutes. Allow to cool in the solution overnight, then in the morning rinse and wear. You can only do this if your dentures have *no metal parts*, but the microwave will kill bacteria far more effectively than anything you can buy.

Deodorant

Smell the savings. Save a fast few bucks by dusting baking soda under your arms instead of using commercial deodorant.

Detangler

Tame your hair for the price of conditioning it. Make your conditioner work overtime as a detangler. Simply mix 1 part conditioner with 5 parts water and spray the mixture on your wet hair, then comb. You'll be impressed by the versatility of your conditioner!

Directory assistance

411 for free. If you don't mind listening to a few ads, dial 1-800-373-3411 for free directory assistance. You'll save up to $2.50 per call.

Google it. Don't listen to a single ad. Dial 1-800-GOOG-411 (1-800-466-4411), say the place and number you're looking for, and Google can either give you the number or connect you directly—for free!

Try toll-free. Stop spending any money on phone calls that should be free. If you're calling any sort of national corporation and you don't have a toll-free number, call 1-800-555-1212 for free 800 directory assistance.

Discount store

Give it a hug. Discount stores tempt you not only with their excellent bargains, but also with their "I don't know what I was thinking when I bought this" impulse buys. How can you avoid these temptations? Avoid the shopping cart. Buy only what you can carry in your arms. You'll end up buying only what you really need and want.

Dishes

Pile it on. When you're stacking your dishes, use flattened coffee filters or paper towels between them (you can use the same ones over and over). You'll help prevent scratches and chips, which will make your dishes last longer, and you won't have to pay for overpriced "plate protectors."

Dishwasher

Laziness can pay off. Let your dishwasher do all the work. Wait until the machine is full to run it. Then happily note that if you had washed the dishes by hand, you would have used about two-thirds more water.

Let the disposal help the dishwasher. Prevent clogs in your dishwasher—and a plumber's bill—by running cold water through your disposal for 30 seconds before you use your dishwasher. The water will flush out any garbage caught in the disposal, which otherwise could get drawn into the dishwasher's drain line and possibly block it.

Disposal

Vinegar ice is nice for your disposal. Now and then, feed your garbage disposal a few frozen cubes of white vinegar and then flush with cold water after grinding. You'll help keep the disposal free of clogs and slow drains—and expensive repairs. The vinegar will also keep odors at bay.

Doctor

No longer the doctor's "office." You don't have to go to the doctor's office to get good medical help these days. Try going to CVS, Target, and Wal-Mart, many of which have opened in-store clinics, often run by nurse-practitioners. You don't need an appointment, and you'll get a diagnosis for about $25 to $60 (plus a prescription if you need one)—far less than a typical doctor's office visit.

Dollar bill

Go the paper route. Stop spending coins; they make you think you're not spending much. Instead, use only paper currency to buy everything, and put the change from all your daily purchases into a change bucket. You'll be likely to spend less and can save at least $20 a month with this trick.

Dry cleaning

Don't get taken to the cleaners. In fact, you can make out well with dry cleaners if you know when to go. Take in your drapes and bed linens in January, July, or August, when business is slow. Your local cleaner may offer a discount of around 15 percent on large items (or you can always ask for your senior discount if one isn't advertised); since drapes and bed linens can cost several hundred dollars to clean, you'll come out smelling like a rose.

Dryer

Keep it light. Dry lightweight fabrics with lightweight fabrics; save heavier fabrics for another load. The lightweight fabrics will dry faster when they're alone, so they'll spend less time in the dryer. You'll save time, energy, and money.

Keep it clean. A dirty lint filter forces your dryer to use 30 percent more energy to dry clothes. Clean the lint filter after every load and save a bundle.

Let it all hang out.

Try to use your dryer as infrequently as possible. Instead, hang your clothes on a clothes rack or clothesline to dry. Grandmother's ways were best! You'll save money on electricity, and your clothes (particularly those that contain elastic) will last longer, too.

Not the time for the timer. Stop using the timer when you dry your clothes. You can cut down on energy use by about 15 percent by using the moisture sensor instead. Besides, drying already dry clothes—which happens when you use the timer—can stress your clothes and reduce their lifespan.

Dryer sheet

Cut your softener in half. Half a dyer sheet works just as well as a whole one, so cut the sheet in half, and soften two loads for the price of one.

Don't just soften: clean! Put your used dryer sheets to work: dust your TV and computer screens, clean Venetian blinds, polish your bathroom taps, and wipe dry tile surfaces. You can even put them in shoes, wastebaskets, and laundry hampers for a fresh smell. You'll save money on all kinds of cleaning supplies.

DVD

A quart of milk, a burger, and...a movie? Looking to rent a recently released film? Free-standing video and DVD rental stores are falling by the wayside of new media and new ways to get films to customers. Check out your local grocery store or fast-food restaurant, where you can rent a new release from a Redbox kiosk for $1. If you typically rent one DVD a week, you can save up to $20 per month at a kiosk. Check out redbox.com to find a location near you.

Get it online and in the mail. Netflix has revolutionized movie rentals by mailing DVDs (with no shipping fee) to customers, who mail them back in a prepaid envelope when they're done. For a flat fee of $8.99 a month, you can get one DVD at a time, as many as you want in a month (they send the next one out when the first one is returned, typically in one business day), as well as unlimited viewing of online movies directly through your computer, dispensing with the DVD and the mail altogether. Go to www.netflix.com and check out the movie rental of the future!

Check it out. Most large libraries now have a DVD section that offers an excellent selection of up-to-date and classic movies that can be checked out on your regular library card (although you may not find the very latest releases). The rules vary depending on your branch, but generally you can check out as many DVDs as you want for one week, with steep-for-a-library fines, such as $1 per day, beginning on the eighth day. So get those DVDs returned on time and take out a fresh batch!

Education

Study with the experts. Book groups are always a good way to learn about many topics, and the book groups at Barnes & Noble Book Clubs offer you an opportunity to learn from authors and experts—for free! Here you'll find a history book club, a mystery book club, a book club devoted to literature by women, and more. See what interests you at www.barnesandnoble.com/bookclubs.

E

Electrician

Save on service calls. Unless you have an electrical emergency, don't call the electrician every time you need something fixed. Since you pay a set (and often high) price for each service call, you'll save by having several tasks done at once.

Electronics

Keep the vampires at bay. Electronics and appliances that sport clocks or work by a remote use electricity, even when you're not using them. Chargers do, too. In fact, 40 percent of the energy used to run home electronics is devoured when these energy vampires aren't turned off! So literally pull the plug and pull down your energy costs.

'Tis the season to scoop up returns...and savings. Shop the clearance section of electronics stores after the holidays. It's a good time to find open-box merchandise or other returned items that can't be sold for full price. You may just find a very merry bargain!

Do some due diligence. A little research can pay you back in spades when it comes to buying new electronics. Whether you're ready for a new TV or you want to buy the grandkids the cutting-edge toy of the moment, go to www.google.com and click on "Shopping" at the top of the page. Type in the name of the item you want in the resulting search box, and Google will instantly pull up a list of all the prices for that item that can be found on the Internet, making comparison shopping a breeze!

Entertainment

The more the merrier. Find friends, colleagues, neighbors, and relatives who like the kinds of entertainment you like, and attend concerts, sporting events, and exhibitions for less. Just buy your tickets in bulk, and you'll score a 10 percent (or higher) discount.

Look up savings at the library. You know you can borrow books, CDs, DVDs, magazines, and even more at your library for free, but the library is also the place to find free or discounted passes to local zoos, museums, aquariums, and gardens. Stop by to see how entertaining your library can be.

Save in different seasons. Check out free concerts sponsored by your local community during the summer. During the holidays, look for free concerts at churches and colleges.

Usher in the arts.

Save up to $300 on season tickets to the symphony, opera, ballet, or theater by working as an usher at your local performance hall. Simply call the hall and ask if you can usher, or search the Internet with the words "volunteer," "usher," and the name of your town.

Practice, practice, practice. Many orchestras and other performing arts groups open their rehearsals to the public, free of charge. Find out what's available in your community, and pocket the cost of the performance.

Try out the tunes. Why spend money on an album when you don't know which tracks you'll like? Instead, tune in to Pandora.com and listen to hours of music you know you'll enjoy for free. Simply enter the name of the singer or the song you like, and Pandora will provide you with similar songs. You'll hear music you want, and the price is right.

Sign up for the season. If you plan to attend many symphony concerts, you should probably buy season tickets at senior rates—you'll pay less per ticket and get better seating. But because season tickets can get expensive, consider splitting the cost (and the number of concerts) with a friend. The same idea applies to theater and sporting events.

Exercise

Go back to school. Enroll in an academic class at a nearby community college, then use your college ID to exercise at the college gym. Even if your class costs $60, you'll save hundreds on your annual gym membership.

Wear Silver Sneakers. Check out www.silversneakers.com to find the nearest health club that participates in the Silver Sneakers program, which is covered by most Medicare health plans. If your plan covers it,

all you have to do is enroll at the health club. Most participating gyms and clubs also offer a senior adviser to help you get started and keep you on track.

A school with a pool. Does your local high school or middle school have a nice pool or gym? Your school district may offer memberships to use one or the other at off-hours, and some may let neighbors use the gym for free. Even if the school district imposes a fee, it's probably less for residents than non-residents—and be sure to ask if there's a senior discount!

Ride those (membership) cycles. If there's no Silver Sneakers gym that's convenient, watch the ads to get the best rates. Some gyms discount memberships at certain times each year. Some offer anniversary sales, while others cut their enrollment fees at the end of certain months to meet monthly quotes. Still others offer free enrollment to tie in to special times during the year, like Breast Cancer Awareness Month.

Clean or garden your way to health. You may never have thought of vacuuming or raking as good exercise, but you should. Depending on your weight (and your physical ability—don't overdo it!) one hour of serious housework can burn 172 calories, while washing and vacuuming your car for 40 minutes can consume 177 calories. Spend 20 minutes raking and you've burned 78 calories. Best of all, garden for one hour and you can burn 320 calories. Now, that's a savings on health club fees!

Pay up front. If you're trying to get serious about exercise (and equally serious about savings), sign up for a series of group classes or a number of sessions with a personal trainer. With or without a senior discount, you should be able to get at least 10 percent off the cost of individual classes or sessions.

Try out your workout. Many gyms offer a free pass, good for a week or two, that lets you try out their facilities before you sign up for membership. The pass works well on two levels: you get to see if the exercise club offers what you want, and you learn quickly if you're the type of person who will actually use a gym once you buy a membership. If the gym doesn't live up to your standards or you think you won't frequent the gym, pass on the membership and keep your money.

Get in on the ground floor. Keep your eyes open for new health clubs. You may be able to sign up for a heavily discounted membership if you're one of the first members.

Eyeglasses

Nail polish for your eyes. Next time you tighten the screw on your glasses (to avoid even bigger trouble), add a spot of clear nail polish across the top of the screw. Your fix will last longer—and your glasses will, too.

Buy two, pay less. Ask for a discount from your eyeglass provider if you plan to buy two pairs of frames at a time. You may even get a higher percentage off than the senior discount already provides.

Think inside the (big) box.

Check out warehouse clubs when you're checking out glasses. You'll be amazed by the selection, quality, and—above all—price. You can easily find a complete pair of glasses (frames and lenses) for under $150, about half what it would cost elsewhere. Be sure to ask if a senior discount can shave even more off the price.

Fan

Use your fan to keep you warm. Ceiling fans are energy-efficient lifesavers in the summer, but did you know that they're equally helpful in the winter? Use the reverse setting on your fan to push the warm air at the ceiling level back down to you.

Let it rest. Your bathroom fan may be doing more harm than good in the winter, if you let it run too long. According to the Department of Energy, a bathroom fan can suck all the nicely warmed air out of your house in just one hour. So give your fan and your furnace and your wallet a break.

Farmers' market

Shop often—and late. Farmers' markets have the freshest produce and good deals—but you can get even better deals if you shop late in the day. Sellers don't want to bring unsold produce back home, so they often sell their inventory at reduced prices before the market closes. You may find sweet savings of up to 80 percent.

Flowers

Send flowers long-distance, but save by going local. Bypass excessive shipping and processing charges from national floral services and order flowers from a florist in the recipient's town. Find the names and phone numbers of local florists by visiting locateaflowershop.com or try 1-800-GOOG-411, the free phone information service, and say the name of the town and "florist."

Chill your flowers. If you're spending money on cut flowers, you want them to brighten your home for as long as possible. Trim the stems, change the water daily, and put them in the refrigerator when you're asleep or at work. They'll last longer.

Preserve the beauty. Some fresh-cut flowers come with a little packet of preservative to add to the water, but if yours didn't, make your own by putting 2 teaspoons of sugar and 1 teaspoon of bleach in a quart of lukewarm water. The flowers will last for many days longer.

Freezer

Keep it full. Stock your freezer with water-filled plastic jugs if it isn't full. The frozen jugs will make your freezer more efficient (and your energy money well spent). Plus, you'll always have fresh water in a power outage.

Frosting

Bag it, freeze it, squeeze it. Don't toss leftover frosting. Put it into a small, strong plastic bag and throw it in the freezer. Next time you need to decorate baked goods, defrost the bag, mix a little water with the frosting, cut a small opening in a corner of the bag, and use it like a professional cake decorator!

Frozen food

Flash-freeze some savings. Yes, frozen food can be more expensive than dishes you make yourself, but it's a bargain compared to takeout or restaurant meals. If you eat out once or twice a week, skipping the restaurant meals and eating a fancy frozen meal instead can easily save you $20.

Buy frozen blueberries in season.

When fresh blueberries are in season, that's the time to also consider buying the frozen variety. Grocers often mark down frozen blueberries—and frozen versions of other fruits and vegetables—when they're in peak season.

Funeral

Think it through. Write down exactly what you want done for your funeral, memorial service, or burial arrangement. You'll save your family or estate money—they won't purchase what you didn't want—as well as additional grief by planning ahead.

Go yellow to save green. Do you know what your options are when planning your funeral? Most people don't. Look in the Yellow Pages of your phone book under "Funeral Services" for a local funeral consumer association, which will give you information about the least expensive options—options that could save you several thousand dollars. If you can't find it in your phone book, search online for "Funeral Consumers Alliance."

Get the information now. Don't choose a funeral home until you've either called several to compare prices of similar services or visited some to get an itemized price list. According to the government, you are entitled to this information by law.

Go to a discount price club for a casket. Yes, it's true: you can buy your casket online through a warehouse club, the same place you buy your paper towels in bulk. And you'll save money on it, too. Not all warehouse stores offer this service, but check online and you may turn up some significant savings.

Furnace

Stay in tune and save 10 percent. Get your furnace tuned up every two years. You can save about 10 percent on your heating bills if you maintain it correctly.

Filter out inefficiency. Keep your furnace running at maximum efficiency by changing the filter every two months, not once a season. Filters are cheap and easy to change—slip the old one out, slip the new one in. You can usually get a better deal if you buy them in multipacks at your local big-box store.

Furniture

Design your price. When buying big items like furniture, a senior discount may be harder to find. So find your own discount: You may not be a professional designer, but you can still ask for the designer's discount—usually 10 to 15 percent off. If the answer is no, request free delivery or a free trial period for the piece you've selected.

Try two for one. If you're shopping for a couch but could use a chair too, ask the salesperson what kind of deal you can get if you buy both. You may be able to score a worthwhile price break.

Garden gloves

Clean, not green. Buy an inexpensive pair of gardening gloves to cut down on cleaning costs. Use them to wipe dust and dirt from window blinds and shutters. Unlike expensive cleaning wipes, you can toss them in the laundry and use them again and again.

Gas

Join the online traffic. Visit GasBuddy. com, a Web site that monitors gas prices. Simply type in your zip code or city and state, and GasBuddy.com will tell you where you will find the least expensive gas near you. If you're able to save 20 cents a gallon, you'll pocket up to $12 per month.

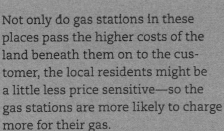

Avoid wealthy neighborhood gas stations.

Not only do gas stations in these places pass the higher costs of the land beneath them on to the customer, the local residents might be a little less price sensitive—so the gas stations are more likely to charge more for their gas.

Follow the crowd. Avoid lonely gas stations in general and lonely gas stations off the highway in particular. They'll charge you more than gas stations at busy intersections or in bustling areas, where several are fighting to fill up your car.

Think ahead and save. Try to anticipate traffic flow and avoid quickly accelerating or braking. Steady driving can increase your fuel economy by as much as 20 percent.

Take the pedal *off* the metal. Drive 55 mph rather than 65 mph, and you'll burn 15 percent less gas per mile. And with today's gas prices, that 10 mph can easily translate into a savings of $200 or more per year.

Cruise to savings. Use cruise control and let the steady rate help improve your mileage by 7 percent (unless you're driving through lots of hills).

Pump it up. Make sure your tires are properly inflated. Check your owner's manual or the door jamb of your car for the correct PSI (pounds per square inch). Even one tire under-inflated by 2 PSI will increase your fuel consumption by 1 percent.

Get extra credit for filling up. Sign up for a credit card that gives you cash back for spending your hard-earned money at the gas pump. There are still a few cards out there that give you up to 5 percent back on gas and car maintenance costs.

Take the junk out of the trunk. Try to carry as light a load as possible in your car. Take out the shovel, the bags of salt, and any other heavy objects in your trunk. You'll increase your fuel economy by decreasing your load.

Spend on maintenance, save on gas. Have your mechanic check for old spark plugs, dirty air filters, low fluid levels, and any other problems that may put a drag on your fuel economy. According to the Department of Energy, a well-maintained car can increase fuel efficiency by as much as 17 percent.

Be cool about your air-conditioning. Use your air-conditioning only when you really need it. You may use up to 20 percent more fuel when you turn it on.

Wait for Wednesday. Buy your gas on Wednesdays. Prices may have settled back down by a few cents after rising for the weekend.

Made in the shade. Park your car in the shade or garage to save on fuel. Gas can evaporate when the car is sitting in the sun, particularly if the gas tank cap isn't screwed on as tightly as it should be.

Rise and shine and fill the tank. Two important facts: one, gas becomes denser at the coolest time of day. Two, you're charged by volume of gas, not density. You'll get more for your money if you buy your gas in the morning, when gas is most dense.

Gas cap

Does your cap fit? Almost 150 gallons of gas are vaporized every year because nearly 20 percent of cars on the road have damaged, loose, or missing gas caps. Is your gas cap in perfect condition? Ask your mechanic to check.

Gifts

Become a fan to get a fan. A great inexpensive gift for a grandchild who's also a sports fan: a fan mail package from his or her favorite sports team. Some packages are free, some cost up to $15 (depending on the team), and most contain a crowd-pleasing assortment of items such as bumper stickers, magnets, team photos, and more. Check out the Web site of your favorite team for ordering info.

Keep it in the family. Here's a gift idea that will thrill all your relatives, as well as your wallet. Gather favorite recipes, copy them, and create a family cookbook for everyone in your family.

Give a gift certificate—from you. Give a friend or family member a gift of your time. Whether the recipient needs babysitting, cooking, snow shoveling, or gardening, use your talents and your time to give a welcome (and inexpensive) present.

Celebrate Christmas all year. Buy half-price gifts after Christmas, and give them at birthdays, anniversaries, and so on. You can also buy holiday gift sets at bargain prices, take them apart, and either give the gifts separately or repackage them for the appropriate occasion.

The perfect photo-op.

Give grandchildren inexpensively framed photos of their parents at the recipient's current age—the goofier, the better. You'll provide laughs and memories for everyone at a picture-perfect price.

The gift of practicality. If you're on a budget and don't know what to give as a gift, choose an inexpensive practical gift that anyone would appreciate. Stamps, stationery, pens, cookies, coffee, and other simple, useful, and expendable gifts are particularly welcomed by those who don't have a lot of space.

Don't go empty-handed (or with an empty wallet). Holiday parties are great fun, but they can get expensive if you take a gift to each one. Save on hostess gifts by buying thoughtful presents in bulk: cocktail napkins, bars of scented soap, pretty candles, and so on.

Greeting cards

Send sentiments for less. Forget about buying traditional greeting cards at the stationery store. Instead, buy packages of greeting cards (either all-occasion or blank) at your warehouse club, craft store, discount store, or mass-merchandiser. At $2.29 per individual card, you can save around $10 by buying a multi-card package. You'll also save on gas by not running out to get a card every time you need one.

Make sentiments for nothing. Collect bits of scrap paper, fabric, clipped-out pictures from magazines—the sky's the limit—and make your own greeting cards. The effort will not only be appreciated, it might be framed!

It's like printing money. If you have a color printer, design and print your own gift cards, either with a simple word-processing program, or with a special paper and software package that offers you hundreds of designs

and styles to make each card your own, available at stationery stores.

Groceries

Save hundreds with a pen and paper. How? Make a list of what you need before you head out to the grocery store, and stick to it. That way you won't be tempted by bite-sized marinated mozzarella balls or other unnecessary items. If you spent $5 on two frivolous items per shopping trip (that you may not use anyway), you'd waste at least $20 per month. Wouldn't you rather have that in your wallet?

Bag it. Save money and the environment by bringing your own bags to the grocery store. More and more stores are giving you money back for every bag you reuse.

Weigh in on savings. Whenever you buy potatoes or onions or any other produce by the bag rather than by the pound, weigh several bags and buy the heaviest one. You may get a 10 1/2-pound bag for the price of the 10-pound bag.

When old is new again. Don't fall for food described as "featured" in the aisles of your grocery store. The manager may just be promoting a commonly found food at its regular price.

Don't fall for limits. Keep your money in your purse when you see signs like "Limit six per customer." Stores know that customers will buy more of an item if they think there's a shortage—and there generally isn't.

Shop around (the store). You'll find necessities like meat, milk, and produce in the perimeter of the store. Less important prepackaged and preprocessed—and more expensive—items are generally in the center aisles. Stick to the perimeter.

> ## Bigger isn't always better.
>
> Grocery stores know that shoppers think the biggest box (of cereal or cookies or anything else) is the best deal—and often make the bigger package *more* expensive per portion than the smaller one! Always compare unit prices when shopping. You may be surprised where you'll find savings.

Be a latecomer. Visit your grocery store late in the day, when you may get unadvertised items on sale. Ask the butcher and the produce manager if they are cutting prices because of the late hour; smile sweetly and tell them you're looking for a senior discount. You may just get a great deal!

Double up. Try to stretch out the time between grocery-shopping trips. Instead of going once a week, go once every two weeks. You'll be forced to make your current food last longer and use up the food sitting patiently in the pantry and freezer.

Hair color

Lengthen the color of your locks. Stretch out appointments for hair colorings or touch-ups by using a shampoo designed for color-treated hair. The color-enhancing shampoo won't cost much more than your regular shampoo, and it can easily save you $100 per year on colorings.

Don't stray too far. Be sure to stay within two shades of your natural hair color when you visit the salon. Your roots will blend into the colored hair better when it grows out, allowing more time between colorings.

Haircut

Return to school. Head to the nearest beauty school or salon training facility to get a salon-style haircut (and color) at a barbershop price. A supervised stylist-in-training will cut your hair; you'll cut the cost of an ongoing expense. Visit www.beautyschoolsdirectory.com to find a school near you.

Alternate and save. Can't give up your pricey haircuts? Consider alternating appointments at your usual salon with visits to a less expensive one, where you can get maintenance cuts for a fraction of what you normally pay—and be sure to inquire about senior discounts for cuts.

Cut down on your cuts. If you can't give up your expensive stylist, try stretching out the time between trips to the salon. Instead of getting a cut every four weeks, aim for every five and save the cost of three visits per year.

Trim your costs. If all you need is an easy trim, head over to a barbershop instead of your usual salon. You shouldn't have trouble finding a cut for under $20.

Try something new. Or at least try a new salon. Many salons just starting out need new customers, and they often offer deals for haircuts. You can save up to 50 percent on a haircut in a brand-new salon.

Save up to $20 by saying no. Whether you're getting your hair cut or colored, skip the blow-dry. Salons often charge big-time for drying your hair, so tell them not to. Keep the $20 in your pocket.

Hanger

Hang on to your hangers. Don't toss out a good hanger just because it has rough edges. Dab a little clear nail polish on the rough spot, and it's ready to go back to work.

Double up for savings.

Is your coat falling off its flimsy hanger? Don't spend money on fancy hangers. Simply tape two or three wire hangers together and hang your coat back up.

Holiday cards

Cut back on paper and postage. Send postcards rather than traditional greeting cards during the holidays. If you normally send 50 cards, you'll save almost $10 on postage alone.

Christmas times two. Cut the decorative front part off the Christmas cards you received last year and use them as Christmas postcards this year.

Hospital

Pack a bag. Try to bring toothpaste, aspirin, tissues, and other necessities from home next time you head to the hospital. You will be amazed by how much the hospital will charge you for such ordinary items.

Check your bill. Hospitals have been known to charge patients for procedures they never received, rooms never used, and medicine never administered. Check your hospital bill carefully, and question anything that doesn't look right.

Wait for your surgery. Ask to be admitted to the hospital on the day of your surgery, not before—you'll pay dearly for that extra day. Early admission generally benefits the staff, not you or your hospital bill.

Don't take the same test twice. Make sure your doctor sends all test results to the hospital so you won't be subjected to the same procedures again. You'll save money—and a lot of aggravation.

Free health care. Hospitals frequently offer skin cancer screenings, cholesterol tests, wellness seminars, and other services as a way to connect with their local community. Call your nearby hospital to find out what kinds of services they offer for free.

Hotel

Make it like home. Hotels can be expensive, and eating out only adds to the cost of your vacation. The next time you book a hotel, ask for a room that includes a kitchen. This may mean spending more on a suite, but once you factor in the cost of three meals a day at restaurants, it will also mean big savings—probably more than $50 a day. Try an extended-stay hotel for a good deal on a suite.

Call the hotel directly. You may save money on a phone call by dialing a hotel's toll-free number, but you may save a lot more on your hotel room by calling the hotel directly. Staffers at the hotel generally have more flexibility in giving discounts on room rates than those at the central reservations number, and they may be able to give you a better price than the official senior discount that the main reservation line offers.

Choose a business hotel for a leisure stay. Many fancy chain hotels that cater to business travelers find themselves with empty rooms on the weekends. They often drop their rates to entice customers. Call one of them for a good weekend deal.

Look beyond the room for savings. Just because you got a great deal on a hotel room doesn't mean you got the *best* deal. You need to look for the hotel's additional money-saving features. Does your room have a small refrigerator? Does the rate include free breakfast? Does the hotel offer free parking? A free Wi-Fi connection? Factor in these freebies when you choose your hotel, and your good deal will look great.

Visit off-season for big savings.

Summertime visits to popular ski areas often result in local hotels and resorts offering substantially reduced rates. Hiking, swimming, fishing, and golfing are popular activities at these places, so they're just as much of a blast in the summer as in the winter.

House

Time it right. If you're thinking of downsizing, shop for a house in the dead of winter when other home buyers are staying home. (If you live in the Sunbelt, shop in the heat of the summer for the same reason.) Even in a buyer's market, the time of year can make a big difference. Your off-season timing may just knock a hefty percentage off the in-season price.

Housekeeping

It bears repeating. Never spend money again on expensive household cleaners. Save yourself money over and over by substituting a simple 1-to-1 solution of white vinegar and water in a spray bottle for commercial cleaning products. You'll never buy the other stuff again. You'll be green, and your home will be clean as a whistle.

Ice cream

Free ice cream. One day, once a year, most Ben & Jerry's stores worldwide give away free ice cream cones. All free, all day, no limit. Check out benandjerrys.com to find out the specific day and the location of a store near you. If it's your birthday (and you can prove it), Baskin-Robbins will give you a free 2.5-ounce scoop, no matter what your age.

Ice pack

Freeze your costs. Do you need an ice pack for muscle aches and pains? Don't bother spending your money on the drugstore kind. Instead, make a reusable ice pack by mixing one part rubbing alcohol and two parts water in a sealable plastic bag, and freeze. Because it doesn't freeze solid, it's particularly handy to have for sore knees or elbows. It may help the pain to know you're saving at least $5 every time you pull it out of the freezer!

Use food for sore spots. Try putting a bag of frozen peas on an aching shoulder, or freeze a small ketchup packet from a fast-food restaurant to tuck onto a small, hard-to-reach sore spot. You have them in your house already—why not use them to save on ice packs from the pharmacy?

Insurance (car)

Buy in bulk. Buy your car and home insurance from the same company. Not only can you save up to 15 percent on separate car and home insurance costs, your insurance company will be less likely to drop you if you have an accident—it will want to keep the rest of your business.

Hit the delete button. Make sure you're not paying double for the same insurance. Read your policies carefully to determine if you're paying for life insurance (which you already have) as part of your car insurance. Dump any double coverage that you find.

Take a class.

A defensive driving class, that is. You can get a 10 percent discount or more on your car insurance, and you'll learn how to stay away from trouble on the road, which may save you even more money in the long run. Ask your insurance provider, your state DMV, or the AARP for information on these classes.

Make your occupation work for you, even if you're retired. Ask your insurance company if it offers discounts for particular occupations. Some offer dollars off for teachers, engineers, and so on. See if your job, even your former job, has a payoff for you!

Update to keep costs down. Keep your insurance agent up to speed on changes that might affect your rates. Have you given up your extra car? Are you putting far less mileage on your car than when you commuted to work? Only using it for "pleasure" driving, never for business? Even little changes can save you money, so be sure to make that call each year.

Ask for any and all discounts. Your insurance company or agent may not volunteer information about the many discounts available, so ask about discounts specifically: for car security systems, low mileage, a good driving record, safety features on your car, an older car, and more.

Keep quiet. Don't file small claims. If you do, your insurance company is more likely to raise your rates. Absorb the cost of scratches in the paint, dings in the body, or a cracked windscreen (if you don't have specific replacement coverage) to keep your rates from going up, up, up—or your policy being canceled altogether.

Invitations

Don't supersize. Choose regular-size invitations when you're planning a party. Oversized invitations will require additional postage (and will probably cost more, too).

Go high-tech. Send e-mail invitations to your next party. Emily Post may not agree, but you'll save on the cost of postage and the cost of the invitations—and possibly even on the gas used going to the post office!

J Jeans

Flip over your jeans. To make jeans last longer, turn them inside out when you wash them (in cold water on the gentle cycle). If some of the dye escapes from the fabric during the wash, it has a better chance of being reabsorbed into the legs.

Patch 'em up. Are your favorite jeans soft and comfortable and beautifully worn—and in danger of ripping? If so, reinforce the insides of the knees, the corners of pockets, and any other places that look likely to split with iron-on patches. You'll help make your beloved jeans last even longer.

Wash and dry with care. Don't toss your jeans into the wash if you've worn them only once. Wait until they're dirty enough to need cleaning. And don't just throw them in the dryer, either. Use a no-heat setting, or better yet, hang them to dry, out of direct sunlight. You'll save wear and tear on your jeans and on your energy bill, too.

Jewelry

Fix it and forget it. Reset loose stones in your costume jewelry easily and inexpensively with nail polish. Simply use clear nail polish as the glue; it's a quick fix that no one will detect.

Jewelry box

Do double duty. Why spend money on a fancy jewelry box when any number of other organizers will serve the same purpose just as well or even better? Try using an ice-cube tray, a silverware tray, or a craft box designed for beads if you want to separate your jewelry. Hang your necklaces and bracelets from push-pins on a bulletin board. Put post earrings on a mesh pen holder or an upended colander. Your choices are unlimited (and the price is right!).

Jigsaw puzzle

A custom-made puzzle for the price of cardboard. Make a jigsaw puzzle by gluing leftover wallpaper or magazine photos, or even a picture you took yourself, enlarged on the computer, onto cardboard. When it dries, cut it up into the kinds of pieces—small or large, simple or complex—that you want for your puzzle. You'll save $10 to $20 just by using what you have on hand, and your grandkids will be thrilled.

Key

Lock out the locksmith. Make an extra set of house and car keys and give them to a trusted neighbor or friend. Next time you lose your keys or lock them in the house or car, you'll save yourself the expense of a locksmith.

Kitty litter

Make it cheap and easy. There's no need to spend a fortune on kitty litter. Just mix a 75-cent box of baking soda with an inexpensive brand of cat litter for immediate savings and the same odor effectiveness of the more expensive brands.

Keep it in your car.

Strange as it sounds, you should keep kitty litter in your trunk during the winter months. It provides excellent traction if you get stuck and is a lot cheaper than a tow truck.

Knee pad

Dig up your garden, not your pants. Save wear and tear on your pants when you garden by wrapping a plastic bag around each knee. You'll want to spend your money on beautiful flowers, not on a new pair of pants.

A mouse for inside and out. Use old computer mouse pads when you need to kneel in the garden. They'll cushion your knees just as well as cushions you buy at your garden store.

Laundry

A little care goes a long way. Turn dark-colored clothing inside out in the wash to prolong the color. Put lingerie and other fine washables in mesh bags to prevent snagging.

Keep it cold. Do your wash (including the rinse cycle) in cold water. A typical family of four can save $120 per year by not using hot water in the washing machine.

Give it a soak. Stained white tablecloths and napkins aren't destined for the dumpster or pricey store-bought solutions. Instead, soak them in a solution of water and 2 tablespoons of baking soda and launder as usual.

Lawn

Step on it. Don't waste water (and money) on your lawn; an average lawn requires just one hour of watering per week. How can you tell if yours is dry? Step on the grass. If the blades don't jump back up, you need to water. If they spring back, hold off on the sprinklers.

Offer an early drink. Water your plants and your lawn early in the morning. If you water later, the sun will burn off the moisture you so carefully put down before it has a chance to soak in.

Lawn mower

Leave it long. If you cut your grass too short, you'll cut down on saving water (and money). Set your mower blades to the 3-inch setting. Taller grass holds water longer than shorter grass.

Keep it "reel." If you have a small lawn, buy an old-fashioned push lawn mower— also known as a reel mower—rather than a fuel-powered mower. You'll easily save at least $100 on the transaction, you won't have to pay for gas or tune-ups, and you'll get great exercise every time you—or your lucky grandson!—mow the lawn.

Lighting

A bright idea. Install motion detector lights or timers on outdoor lights that may inadvertently get left on during the day. The automatic shut-off will give you peace of mind and a few extra dollars.

Convert to CFLs. Use compact fluorescent light (CFL) bulbs. They last 8 to 10 times longer than incandescent bulbs, put out less heat than incandescents, and, most importantly, use minimal energy. Putting CFLs in just a quarter of your fixtures may cut your lighting bill in half. Put them in all your fixtures and watch the savings skyrocket!

Dim the lights.

Save energy and money by using dimmer switches on your lights. If you dim an incandescent bulb 10 percent, you can save about 5 percent on electricity use. If you dim it 50 percent, you can save 25 percent on electricity. In both cases you'll also extend the life of the bulb.

Three ways to save. If you haven't yet converted to CFLs, use three-way bulbs in your light fixtures. Use the lowest wattage whenever possible, and you'll save on electricity costs.

Stick to the task. Rather than light an entire room when you're working in one corner, use efficient task lighting. It's an easy way to pay for only what you use.

Lotion

Stand your lotion on its head. Turn your almost-empty moisturizer bottle upside down. The lotion will fall into the cap, and you'll squeeze several more uses out of the bottle (you can do the same with shampoo and conditioner and any other cosmetic that will stand upside-down).

Magazine

Get your fix with a friend. Are you hooked on magazines but discovering that you have an expensive habit? Ask a few like-minded friends to each subscribe to one magazine, then swap the magazines so everyone gets to read them all. Depending on the number of magazines (and friends) involved, you could save a bundle.

Makeup

Cap your costs. Don't bother buying concealer if you already use foundation. You can find the perfect cover-up in the cap, where the foundation has settled. It's the right consistency, and you can't find a better color match!

Use it in a different form. If your lipstick is broken, don't give up on it. Instead, push the remainder of the lipstick down into the tube, and then use a lip brush to apply it. You can also put the broken bullet into a small empty makeup container, melt it with a blow-dryer, let it dry, then use it in its new form.

Take it off, take it all off. Try some extra moisturizer in place of your expensive makeup remover. It's a perfect substitute: It removes makeup quickly and easily for a lot less, and you don't have to buy extra products.

Match

Don't eat the match. Why spend money on extra-long matches when you probably have a perfectly good substitute on hand? Use a piece of dried spaghetti next time you need to light a hard-to-reach wick or multiple candles.

Meat

Tough it out. You know that tougher meats are less expensive than tender meats. But did you know that many butchers will run these cheaper cuts through the tenderizer if you ask? Your tough cut will turn into a more tender bite at no cost.

A wise buy for a wise guy (or gal). Boneless meat may cost more per pound, but it usually gives you more for your money than a cut filled with fat and bone.

Slice it thin to keep your wallet fat.

Ask your deli man or woman to slice your meat and cheese thinner than usual. You'll most likely use less in each sandwich you make, which is good for your wallet *and* your waistline.

Microwave

Zap it once to save twice. According to the U.S. Department of Energy and the Environmental Protection Agency, using your microwave oven for small portions can reduce your cooking energy by up to 80 percent. Plus, your air-conditioning costs will be lower in the summer if you use your microwave, since it doesn't generate heat the way your stove or oven does.

Mop

Flip it. After you've used your disposable mop pad, turn it over and use the other side. Then throw it away, knowing you've gotten twice your money's worth.

Movies

The early bird gets the...movie.
Want to see a first-run movie for less than the cost of a child's ticket (often for less than your senior discount price)? Check out A.M. Cinema, run by AMC Theatres, which offers movies for $4, $5, or $6 (depending on the theater and market) before noon on certain Fridays, Saturdays, Sundays, and holidays.

Movie magic for members. Costco members can buy movie tickets at discounted rates for theater chains including AMC, Cinemark, and Regal Entertainment. You buy in bulk (five tickets at a time) and save about $2 per ticket.

Free movies. Choose from hundreds of classic comedies, dramas, horror movies, musicals, Westerns, and more and watch them for free on *Entertainment Magazine*'s Web site, www.emol.org. Some of your favorite classics that are now in the public domain are available here, such as *My Man Godfrey* and *His Girl Friday*, as well as wonderful TV shows from days gone by, such as *The Honeymooners*. It's all easy to download (the site has detailed instructions if you need help) and perfectly legal, and, best of all, completely free.

Mulch

Chips all around. Rather than buying expensive garden mulch, contact your local tree doctor or sawmill, and ask them to deliver wood chips directly to your backyard. Biodegradeable, safe, and natural looking, this terrific mulch also may be free or much less expensive than buying bags of mulch.

Museum

Free art. Most private museums, both large and small, offer free admission on certain days or at certain times. And independent art gallery openings are usually free and open to the public. Plus you may score a free glass of wine, a cube of cheese, and a chance to talk to the artist.

Nails

Fingernails, that is. Stretch out the time between nail appointments: if you normally get your nails done once a week, mark your calendar to get them done once every two weeks instead. At $10 an appointment, you'll save $260 per year, not including tips! Ask the manicurist *not* to put a sealing topcoat on your nails. The thicker the coating, the faster it will peel off.

Very cool nails! Cold nail polish lasts longer and can be applied more smoothly. So take it out of the closet or medicine cabinet (or wherever you store it) and put it in the refrigerator.

Get more from your manicure. Your manicure will last longer if you clean your nails with vinegar. Use a cotton ball to apply the vinegar before you paint your nails, then enjoy the extra time you have before your next manicure.

Napkin

Cut from the right cloth. Sometimes it's hard to remember that cloth napkins still exist. They may require a little care, but they'll add a touch of elegance to your table—and more importantly, save you money over paper napkins in the long run.

National parks

Spend $10 to save hundreds. If you enjoy national parks, you'll enjoy the savings you can get with the America the Beautiful Senior Pass. As long as you're a citizen or permanent resident of the United States and at least 62 years old, you can buy this pass for $10 and get free or reduced admission to any federal recreation site—for the rest of your life! Get the pass from a national park, wildlife refuge, or participating federal recreation site or office.

Newspaper

Let's make a deal. Call your local newspaper and ask if it offers a discount for paying for your subscription a year in advance.

Pick and choose for less. Do you read only a few sections of the mammoth Sunday newspaper? If so, ask friends who always get the Sunday paper to give you the sections you like when they're done with them. You'll avoid waste—and the cost of the Sunday paper.

Save $4 on Sunday. If you're a news fiend, save money by swapping different Sunday newspapers with a friend. You read one in the morning, he reads the other, then you swap around noon. Or if you read only one Sunday newspaper, save several dollars by taking turns buying it. Just be sure to set a time to turn over the newspaper to your friend (and vice versa).

Dispense with the subscription altogether. Nearly all the major national newspapers in the United States can now be read online for free. You may have to register, which is also free, but in exchange you'll get news that's frequently updated, as well as additional photos, interactive graphics (at some sites), and, in many papers, additional articles and details there weren't room for in the printed paper.

Notary

A notary for nothing. Where can you get important documents notarized for free? Try your bank, the library, your employer, or a local government office. Call to make sure this service is offered (and that it's free) before you head out the door.

O

Obedience school

Sit, stay, save! Whether you enroll your dog in obedience school or train him yourself, you'll find savings in his good behavior. Because he'll be less likely to run into the street or eat things he shouldn't, you may save the price of medicine or even a big vet bill.

Odd job

Go the nonprofessional route. You don't always need an expensive professional to help you with jobs around the house. Call the job placement office at your local college to get students to help you with moving furniture, painting, gardening, lawn care, and more.

Orange juice

Cycling for sales. Start paying attention to when your grocery store puts your favorite brand of orange juice on sale. Chances are, you'll discover a pattern, or sales cycle. Soon you'll know when to buy orange juice and when not to. Sales cycles apply to ice cream, pasta, and cereal, too. When it's on sale, buy two or three and store them.

Outdoor furniture

Towel it off. Make your vinyl outdoor furniture last longer by sitting on a towel if you're wearing sunscreen. The sunscreen can eat away at the furniture's protective coating, allowing dirt to lodge permanently in the destroyed coating—making it impossible to clean. So sit on a towel and save yourself the cost of new furniture.

Oven

Keep it closed. Try not to open the oven door to check on the progress of your dish—the oven temperature drops by about 25 degrees every time you do (and you'll have to pay to get the heat back up to the right level). Use a good old-fashioned timer instead.

Turn it off and save.

Don't wait until your dish is completely cooked. Turn off the oven a few minutes before the recipe says you should. The heat left in the oven is sufficient for finishing the meal.

Choose your dish wisely. Use glass or ceramic baking dishes in your oven. Because glass conducts heat differently than metal, you can lower the temperature about 25 degrees (from the temperature the recipe says), and your food will still cook at the same rate.

Double your money. Save on energy bills by cooking two dishes in the oven at once. You can cook two items for the same meal—a chicken for dinner and brownies for dessert—or two items for two different meals, such as a roast for dinner and cinnamon rolls for breakfast the next day.

Over-the-counter medicine

Look past the packaging. Just as you save by buying generic prescription drugs, you can save by buying store brands of over-the-counter medications. Other than the packaging and, most importantly, the price, store brands are often no different from name-brand medications. Read the fine print to find the name and percentage of active ingredients—if they are the same as the active ingredients on the big-name brand, it's the same stuff. Ask the pharmacist, if you have any doubts.

Price your pills. And your gel caps and your capsules. You may find that each form of your medicine carries a different price tag. Choose the right form—and the right price—for you.

Overdraft protection

Guard your checking account. Sign up for overdraft protection at your bank, just in case. It usually costs nothing and saves you the possible expense of returned check fees.

Owner's manual

Save instructions to save money. Keep all owner's manuals, receipts, and warranties. You may be able to easily fix your appliance, tool, or electronic device by consulting the manual, or you may be able to get it fixed for free if you check your warranty. If you've lost the manual, these days you can probably find it online—search for the brand name and the type of product.

Packing material

Ship and save. Don't waste your money on bubble wrap or other shipping materials. Just insert a straw into an almost-closed zip-top bag, and inflate the bag. Remove the straw, zip the bag tightly shut, and use as packing material.

Painting

Roll up the savings. Put a plastic grocery bag completely around your roller pan, roller inside, when you're in the midst of paint jobs around the house. If you tie the bag closed around the pan, the paint will stay fresh for up to several days. When you're done, simply wash the roller and throw away the bag (and the pan, if it's a disposable one). You'll save time on clean-up and money on multiple roller pans.

Pantry

Stay organized. You'll save two ways if you keep your pantry organized: you won't go to the grocery store as often because you'll know what you have (thereby avoiding impulse purchases), and you won't buy the same item that's already sitting on your pantry shelf.

Paper towels

Mop up the savings. Stop using paper towels every time you have a spill. Use your handy dandy sponge and discover savings every time you keep a paper towel on the roll.

Go heavy duty.

Buy heavier weight paper towels, and use them the way you would if they were cloth: rinse them in water, squeeze them out, and drape them over the edge of the sink to live another day.

Pets

Lower the cost of a special diet. Did your vet put your pet on an expensive diet? If so, ask a nearby discount pet store if it can order what your pet needs for less than what the vet charges you. There may also be a generic version—ask at the store for any advice they can offer you to help keep your pet well and your wallet full!

Don't overfeed or overspend. An easy way to save money on pet food is by feeding your pet what is recommended and not overfeeding. Follow the guidelines on the package of food and adjust according to what your pet needs. You should be able to feel your pet's ribs, but his backbone shouldn't stick out.

Trade pet-sitting services. Do you have a friend with a pet? Ask her to swap pet-sitting services with you. She comes to your house to feed and exercise your pet when you're away, and you do the same for her. You both save on boarding costs, and your pets will be happier, too.

Spay and neuter for health and savings. You'll save money not caring for litters and by keeping your pet healthy. Female pets will have lower rates of breast, ovarian, and uterine cancer, and male pets will have lower rates of testicular cancer.

Take a shot at savings. Fido may need to be vaccinated, but he doesn't need the most expensive shot-giver around. Take him to a veterinary college, or even a pet store or mobile vaccination clinic (sponsored by a pet store) for reduced-cost vaccinations.

Place mat

Place a towel, not a mat. Use brightly colored dishtowels for slightly-oversized place mats. They're less expensive than fabric place mats and easier to clean. If you buy the dishtowels in bulk, you can save even more.

Hit the fabric shop. Like to sew? Even if you don't, most fabric shops offer bits and remnants of great material in pieces too small to sell by the yard at ridiculously low costs. Pick up what appeals to you, and sew a straight hem around the edge. Presto! Instant place mats!

Plants

Look forward to an eternal spring. Plant bulbs and perennials, which bloom year after year, rather than annuals that you have to replace every spring.

Save on seeds. Collect seeds in the fall that you can plant in the spring. Put dry seeds from flowers like zinnias and cosmos in a paper bag, and store the bag until you're ready to plant the seeds the following year. You'll have beautiful flowers for free!

Go native. Use local plants and flowers in your garden. Why? They require less fertilizer and water because they've already adapted to your soil.

Spring into action. Keep your eyes peeled for discarded plants during spring clean-up time. Many people rip out their perfectly good plants to make way for a new garden design. Pick up these discards when you see them.

Ask for help. Your local landscapers not only know a tremendous amount about gardening, they know where they're tearing out plants that will go to waste—unless you ask for them. Say that you'll pick up the greenery and cart it away, and you may get some wonderful new plants for free.

Know what's growing before you buy. It's springtime and those nasty weeds in your yard are starting to sprout…only they may not just be useless weeds: they might be purslane, or, if you live in the Southeast, ramps (wild leeks), and they cost a fortune at the grocery store. Caveat: always make sure that what you're planning on cooking is in fact edible. If you're not sure, pull a few and take them to your local horticultural specialist.

Buy this summer for next spring.

Once the spring and early summer perennials have bloomed and faded at the garden store, look out for terrific bargains on plants that have shed all their blossoms. They can often be bought for as much as 75 percent off. You can plant them in late summer, let them get well established, and then you'll have a stunning array of new flowers come next spring.

Prescription medicine

Get a $4 prescription. Target, Wal-Mart, and the pharmacies of many other stores across the United States, such as Hannaford grocery stores, have begun offering a list of more than 400 generic prescription drugs for $4 for a 30-day supply. The price of a 90-day supply is in the neighborhood of $10, depending on the pharmacy. You can get a list of the drugs available at the stores' Web sites or a printed copy at the stores' pharmacies. Ask your doctor if the drug he is prescribing is on the list—or if there's a suitable substitute on the list.

Buy at a wholesaler (even if you're not buying in bulk). Save money by filling your prescriptions at a wholesale club, even if you're not a member. The pharmacy may tack on a small fee, but you have the right under federal law to fill prescriptions at any pharmacy, so tell the person asking for your ID at the front door that you're only visiting the pharmacy. (And don't get carried away—you won't be able to buy anything else without a club membership ID.)

Do the splits. Ask your doctor if your tablets or pills can be split to save you money. You'll probably pay the same amount for the 10-milligram dose and 20-milligram dose, so if you buy the 20-milligram pills and split them in half, you've split your costs in half as well. (Note that you can't do this with time-release or long-acting pills or with capsules.) For best results, buy a pill-cutter at the drugstore, to make sure each pill is evenly divided.

Switch and save. Some pharmacies will reward you with discounts when you transfer your prescription from another drugstore. You may see advertised incentives to switch—like a gift card from your new drugstore.

Be loyal. You can score substantial savings if you're a repeat customer at a particular pharmacy. One major retailer we know offers discounts throughout the store for loyal pharmacy customers, and Kmart is testing a program that offers store-brand pain relief and cold medications for $1 if you purchase or refill a prescription at a Kmart pharmacy.

Ask for samples. Drug company representatives often shower doctors with samples of their medications, and your doctor is probably happy to share these free samples with you. Just ask if your doctor has any samples available. You'll save on a trip to the pharmacy, as well as on the prescription.

Go generic. You'll save big by using the generic version of your prescription drug. If a generic doesn't exist, ask you doctor if there is a similar, older drug that works just as well and is available as a generic.

Think like your insurance company. Request a copy of your insurance plan's formulary, or preferred drug list. You'll find drugs—both generic and brand name—that cost less and require a lower co-pay than drugs not on the list. Share the formulary with your doctor, and ask him to prescribe the drugs you need from the list, if possible.

Printer

Preview your savings. Don't automatically print a page from the Internet—it includes ads and icons you probably don't want. Instead, click on "print preview" or "print version" to see exactly what you're printing, then delete what you don't need. You'll save money on paper and ink as well as wear and tear on your printer.

Think about saving ink. Make your ink cartridge last longer by setting your printer to the lowest quality setting possible.

Double up. To save paper when you use your printer, try printing on both sides. Or print on the blank side of already used paper. Better yet, don't print out at all: store e-mail messages and other potential print-outs on your computer.

Produce

Weigh in on savings. Use the produce scale to weigh the packages of produce you plan to buy. That 5-pound bag of apples may not really weigh 5 pounds; it may weigh less (and if it does you shouldn't buy it) or it may weigh more (and if it does you should march it right over to the cash register). Always make sure you're getting (at least) what you're paying for.

Shake it, baby.

The produce, that is. Many grocery stores spray fruits and vegetables to keep them looking fresh. But the water makes them heavier, and if you're paying for produce by the pound, you may be paying extra for water. Always give a head of lettuce, for example, a vigorous shake before bagging it up, and add up your savings.

Grow your own. There's no better way to save money and eat well than to grow some of your own produce. Instead of spending $10 a week on salad greens and vegetables and shelling out gas money to get to the grocery store, plant a few seeds in a small plot or in pots on your deck. You'll be mightily rewarded with fresh produce from April through November, depending on where you live.

Professional organization

Join the crowd. In addition to AARP, many professional associations offer discounts on health care, car rentals, and more to their members. Look at the type and quality of discount from the organizations for which you qualify to take advantage of these savings.

Quality

Always buy well if you can. It's true what they say: if you have a choice between buying something crafted well versus buying something shoddily produced, always opt for the better quality, if you can. It will last longer, won't have to be replaced, and likely won't have to be repaired as often as its cheaper sibling, thus saving you money in the long run.

Quantity

Two for one isn't always profitable. Before you grab "two for the price of one" in the grocery store, make sure that the individual price hasn't been elevated, too. And if you need only one (of anything), buy only one.

Q

Radiator

Reflect on savings. Save on your heating bill by installing a heat reflector behind your radiator. (Create a reflector from foil-covered cardboard or by wrapping foam board in foil.) Make sure the foil faces away from the wall, and that the reflector is either the same size as the radiator or slightly larger. It will help push the warm air (that you've paid for) back out into your room.

Receipt

The thrill is gone. Shop only at stores that let you return merchandise, and always ask about their return policy. Hold on to receipts and don't cut tags off new purchases for two weeks. By the time two weeks have passed, you'll know if you really want the item you may have bought on impulse. If you're not wild about it, return it and stash the cash.

Refrigerator

Vacuum up the savings. Be sure to vacuum the coils at the bottom or back of your refrigerator twice a year to keep the appliance working efficiently. You'll pay more if your refrigerator needs to work harder because of dust in the coils.

Extra fridge in the basement?

Unless it's Thanksgiving or Christmas and you're entertaining a crowd, don't keep it cold "just in case." Pull the plug if it's empty, and sharply whittle away at your electric bill.

Rental car

Time it right. When renting a car, try to fly in and out of the airport at the same time of day. That way you can avoid paying for an extra day of rental when you've used only a few hours.

Take the shuttle to the car. Renting a car at the airport—particularly in big cities—can be expensive. You can use the free airport shuttle to avoid this cost two ways: first, take the shuttle to your hotel and rent a car there. You can save about 10 percent on taxes and fees alone. Second, take the shuttle to your hotel, and rent a car the next day, thereby saving the cost of a full day's rental.

Check your policy. You may not need liability coverage when you rent a car. Most insurance policies and some credit card companies offer liability coverage, so be sure to check your insurance and credit card policies before forking over money for what you may already have. Check for collision coverage, too.

Resort

You pay to play. That resort on the beach looks so appealing, with unlimited golf, tennis, and swimming. But wait: you don't play golf—so don't choose a resort that features golf. The cost of golf will be built into the cost of your room. Choose a resort that offers the services and activities you'll use.

Go off-season. Get dramatically reduced rates and less crowded beaches and golf courses by visiting resorts in the off-season. Time your visit just before or after the high-rate season, and you can save big.

Restaurant

Order small plates midday. There's no need to order expensive dinner-sized platters for lunch; they'll slow you down for the rest of the day and make you groggy by late afternoon. Instead, order two small plates from the appetizer side of the menu, and share them with a dining partner.

Start your restaurant meal at home. Enjoy an appetizer in your house before you go to a restaurant for dinner. You'll save on the first course and—if you have a substantial enough appetizer—may save even more by ordering a smaller entrée.

Eat for a week. Many communities offer "restaurant weeks," when you can dine at fancy restaurants for a very deep discount. During these promotional events, restaurants entice you with amazingly priced prix fixe meals—the same food you'd pay substan-

tially more for the rest of the year. Search online or watch your local media for details.

Go gourmet at home. Find several foodie friends and start a gourmet club. "Eat out" at a different house each week, rather than eating at a restaurant. You'll save a ton, and get exciting new food experiences as well.

Think before you drink. Order water instead of a soft drink when you go to a restaurant. Assuming you eat out once a week, you can save up to $100 per year.

Skip the dessert (but not really).

Don't pay for an overpriced dessert the next time you join friends for lunch at a restaurant. Pass on it, then pass by a bakery on your way home and enjoy a fabulous indulgence for a lot less.

Happy hour for your wallet. Check out restaurants and bars that offer happy hours. Along with buying inexpensive drinks, you may be able to create your dinner out of free hors d'oeuvres.

A restaurant's gift to you. Does your favorite restaurant give customers a free meal on their birthdays? If so, you can save the cost of a dinner on your special day. If not, find a restaurant that does!

Rewards program

Reward yourself. Join rewards programs whenever and wherever you can, whether offered by your credit card or an individual merchant or service you utilize often, to earn points every time you shop or travel. Then redeem your points for free merchandise, more travel, or services. Just be sure to note if the rewards program requires a membership fee, and determine if that fee is worth the rewards you earn.

Ribbon

Not just for the kitchen any more. Pull plastic wrap tight and twist it to make an unusual and inexpensive ribbon for your gift. It looks particularly festive atop a brightly colored package.

Do it again. High quality fabric ribbons can be used year after year. Just gently iron them, and they'll look brand new.

All that glitters is...ribbon! Shop tag sales for cheap garments with sparkling or colorful fabric and cut them up with pinking shears for beautiful ribbons. You'll spend less on the tag sale item than you will on new ribbon.

Rug

Stay away from chemicals. Whether it's an inherited Persian rug from your great aunt or a fabulous flea market find, steer clear of expensive industrial cleaners. If you find a troublesome stain, hold the rug up away from the floor, and pour warm water mixed with

baking soda through the stain (be prepared to catch the liquid on the underside with a bowl). Rinse with clear water and blot dry with a clean, soft towel.

Salt

Use kosher salt and save. Inexpensive kosher salt is not only tastier than regular table salt, it's more frugal. Why? Each flake or crystal of kosher salt is far bigger than its table salt cousin, meaning that a single pinch will go a very long way, saving you dough in the long run. (One box lasted one of our interviewees over a year.)

Sandwich

One is better than two. Share a sandwich with a friend when you're out and about and grabbing a quick lunch. One big sandwich costs less than two small sandwiches, so split the sandwich as well as the cost, and save!

Bring it from home. C'mon...bet your fridge is filled with assorted leftovers (ours is!). Why spend $5 for a mediocre sandwich from a deli when an inexpensive loaf of bread can be a vehicle for something you truly love?

Shades

Raise and lower to heat and cool. Save money on heating and cooling costs by using your shades and drapes strategically. In the summer, keep your shades and drapes closed on the sunny side of the house during the day and open at night. In the winter, keep them open during the day and closed at night.

Shampoo

Stretch your shampoo. You already know you should stock up on your favorite shampoo when it's on sale. What you may not know: you can alternate using your more expensive brand with a generic brand, and your hair will still look great.

Pump up the savings. Don't use extra shampoo and conditioner simply because the bottle lets you have more than you need. Pour your shampoo and conditioner into large pump bottles—they'll dole out smaller amounts so your hair care products will last longer.

Concentrate and save!

Most shampoos made today are super-concentrated. When you're nearing the bottom of the bottle, fill it halfway with water, tighten the cap, and shake. Depending on the product, you may have a few days to a few more weeks of shampoos ahead of you.

Shipping

Add up the savings. Whether you're shopping by catalog or on the Internet, find a friend who wants merchandise from the same retailer and place a single order, then split the shipping fees. Better yet, find several friends and place a big order so you get free shipping.

Shoes

Join Project SOS: Save Our Shoes. Double or triple the life of your shoes by repairing them, resoling them, and reheeling them when necessary. Why buy a new pair of shoes when you can save your favorite old pair with new soles for $20 to $50? And don't forget that a shoe repair shop can fix luggage, belts, and purses, too.

Keep 'em clean. Watch WD-40 work double duty: it cleans shoe leather *and* lubricates it so your shoes last longer. Ditto purses, briefcases, wallets, belts, riding saddles, bicycle seats, leather car interiors, and leather furniture. You get the point!

Preventive shoe care. Place foam insoles into all your shoes to save their insides. Buy inexpensive store-brand insoles, and replace them when they become dirty or worn. You'll save money on new shoes, and you'll have more comfortable shoes as a perk.

Shower

Go with the (low) flow. Invest in a low-flow showerhead, and save on water and heating costs. By spending $10 to $20 on a new showerhead, you can save about 7,300 gallons of water and $30 to $100 each year on your water and heating bills.

Soap

Dispense some soap and some savings. Don't just refill your soap dispenser with soap. Add one part hand soap and three parts water for a soap that cleans without cleaning out your wallet.

Go the old-fashioned body wash route. Instead of using a separate bar soap for your body and one for your face, buy an old-fashioned liquid body wash, such as pure castile soap—a tried and true multi-purpose favorite that's not only frugal, it's delightfully pure!

Socks

Getting dressed has never been so easy. Buy same-color socks in bulk. If the dryer eats one, you have an automatic match in your dresser drawer—and you won't need to buy a new pair of socks. Besides, you'll pay less buying packs of socks rather than individual pairs.

Soft drinks

Make your own. No, we're not kidding. Instead of buying chemical-packed flavored orange, grapefruit, or cherry soda, combine a splash of fresh juice with inexpensive club soda. Cheaper and healthier, by far.

Spices

Spice up your life for less. Never buy name-brand dried spices in the grocery store: you're paying for the bottles they're packed in. You can often buy spices in bulk at natural foods stores or ethnic groceries or visit online spice suppliers such as www.kalustyans.com or www.penzeys.com. Buy spices you use infrequently in smaller quantities. Store away from light in glass or metal containers.

Dry your own herbs for savings and flavor.

Have a leftover bunch of parsley (or cilantro, rosemary, or basil) in your fridge? Don't throw it away: dry it. Put the leaves on a clean baking sheet and place in a very slow oven (200°F) for 30 minutes. Remove, crumble, and store in an airtight jar, out of direct sunlight.

Sponge

Microwave your sponge. Make sure your sponge contains no metal fibers, and, if it doesn't, put your wet sponge in the microwave for one to two minutes on full power. You'll kill the bacteria that would normally make you toss the sponge. You'll use each sponge longer.

Sporting goods

Make an exchange. Look for school and community organizations that offer sporting goods swaps. You can also find sports stores that sell perfectly good second-hand athletic equipment, such as skis, for great prices.

Stockings

Freeze your hose. Panty hose, that is. Fill a plastic bag with water, drop in your new stockings, zip up the top, and toss the bag in the freezer. Thaw the concoction at room temperature. You'll strengthen the fibers in the stockings, cut down on runs, and save the cost of additional pairs of hose. You can continue protecting your stockings by refreezing them once a month, without water, for one night.

Stocking stuffer

Make Santa work all year. Buy stocking stuffers that aren't overtly seasonal at half off after Christmas, and you can use them as small Valentine's gifts, in Easter baskets, or as party favors throughout the year.

Storage

Store it well and save. Doesn't matter if it's food, sweaters, or garden tools: it pays to keep what you own stored carefully to avoid spoilage, moth damage, or rust. Double- and triple-wrap cold food items before freezing to prevent freezer burn; store sweaters in sealed plastic containers to prevent visitations from winged creatures; wipe down your garden tools with rubbing alcohol, dry them, and hang them until next year.

Stove

Stay small. Use small pots on small burners to save money on gas or electric costs. In fact, if you use a 6-inch pan on an 8-inch burner, you'll waste more than 40 percent of the energy. If you need to use a bigger pot, be sure to use a bigger burner; the pot won't heat evenly if you use it on a smaller one.

Cook on top. Your stove uses less energy than your oven, so try cooking meals on the stove as much as possible. Better yet, use a toaster oven, microwave, slow-cooker, or pressure-cooker.

Sweater

Buy one when you need one. Sweaters generally show up in stores around July, along with other fall clothes. Why do you need a sweater in July? Wait until October or November when you need one, and you can get the sweater for up to 75 percent less. The same idea applies to bathing suits, which go on sale in March and get marked down in July.

No sweat. You know that baby powder can be an effective deodorant, but did you know that it can also protect white shirts from sweat stains? Simply sprinkle it on the underarm areas of the shirt, then briefly iron. The baby powder will stop dirt and oil from staining the shirt. (This works for the collar, too.)

Tasting party

Excite your taste buds and your wallet. Host an international tasting party to learn more about ethnic food and wine. Have guests bring dishes and drinks to sample. You'll expand your culinary horizons, have fun, and avoid the high costs of sampling food and drink at restaurants and bars.

Taxes

Go directly to the source. You probably know that you can get free tax help over the phone from the IRS (1-800-829-1040), but did you know you can get free tax help in person at IRS walk-in sites? You can visit www.irs.gov, click on "Contact IRS," then click on "Contact my Local IRS Office," and find an IRS Taxpayer Assistance Center near you.

Get free tax help, in person.

You can take advantage of tax help at Tax Counseling for the Elderly, with 9,000 sites around the country. Call AARP at 1-888-227-7669 or visit the AARP Web site at www.aarp.org/money/taxaide for more information. You can search by zip code to find your nearest site for help.

Telephone

Go high-tech for (very) high savings. If you have DSL or a cable modem, download and install Skype software for free and call other Skype users all over the world from your computer—for free! You can also call the landlines and cell phones of non-Skype users at bargain rates. Visit www.skype.com for details.

Make saving a feature. How often do you use speed dialing? Has call forwarding come in handy? You probably don't need—or use—the many telephone add-ons that show up on your phone bill. Reevaluate each feature, drop several, and easily save $10 per month. Special offers from the phone company change all the time, so speak to a customer-service representative to evaluate your options—and be sure to ask if there are any senior discounts on phone service!

Television

Simplify and save. Do you really need over 100 television channels? If you trade your current cable package for basic cable, you may save up to $500 a year.

A super deal for the Super Bowl. Wait until the weeks before the Super Bowl for the best deal on a big-screen TV.

Thermostat

Lower the temperature and lower your costs. The Alliance to Save Energy says that you can subtract about 5 percent from your heating bill for every degree you lower your thermostat during the winter.

Get with the program. You've heard that programmable thermostats can save you money—but how much? If you invest $70 in an Energy Star programmable thermostat, you'll save more than twice that in its first year alone.

Don't exaggerate. In the morning, turn the thermostat up to the temperature you desire—not a higher temperature in the hopes that your house will warm up more quickly. It won't, and your furnace will have to work harder to reach a temperature you don't even want (and that will cost you more).

Toilet

Test for leaks. Add a drop of food coloring to the toilet tank. Wait a few minutes, then check to see if the color has shown up in the toilet bowl. If it has, you have a leak—and it may be costing you up to 200 gallons of water a day. Save water and money by fixing the leak.

Take up space to save.

If you have an older toilet, put a plastic bottle filled with water on the floor of the tank. Because the tank will require less water to fill, you'll save money on your water bill every time you flush. (Don't do this if you have a high-efficiency toilet.)

Tools

Priced for Dad, bought for you. Buy the tools you need when they go on sale around Father's Day in June.

Tag it. One of the best places to buy tools is at a tag sale. Keep your eyes peeled for everything from well-priced (but used) table saws and sanders to hammers with a history. Feel free to haggle.

Toothbrush

No cavities—and a free toothbrush. Be sure to ask your dentist for a free toothbrush next time—and every time—you go in for a check-up. Most dentists are happy to give you one, and some will also hand out free toothpaste, mouthwash, and dental floss.

Traveler's check

Use it when you don't travel. In your wallet, replace your emergency cash—that you may have used for impulse purchases—with a traveler's check. You're less likely to spend it than cash, which means you'll keep it for when you really need it (and not for something you really don't need).

Trees

Naturally cool your house...and your costs. Plant trees on the south, east, and west sides of your house, and save up to 25 percent on cooling costs. And here's an easy and inexpensive way to get trees: if you join the Arbor Day Foundation for $10, you'll receive 10 free trees! Just call 1-888-448-7337 or visit www.arborday.org.

Underwear

Stock up during seasonal sales cycles. Just as retailers reliably put seasonal items on sale, they do the same with necessities like underwear. Since you're always going to need underwear, socks, and so on, stock up when you see a sale.

Upholstered furniture

Pull the shades. Protect your upholstered furniture—and your investment in that furniture—by keeping it out of the sun. The sun can weaken the fabric's fibers and colors, so arrange your furniture to limit its exposure to sunlight, or simply shut the shades.

Vacuum the floor...and the couch... and the chair. Keep your upholstered furniture clean to save money. Vacuum it weekly to get rid of dirt and dust, which can act like sandpaper, grating on the fabric whenever anyone uses the furniture.

Utilities

Get audited—and like it! Ask your utility company for a free energy audit. A representative will come to your house and explain what you need to do to make your home more energy efficient. You can save $100 per year by sealing leaks in windows and doors and insulating ducts—all of which your energy audit will highlight. Your water company may provide this service for free, too.

Ask for off-peak rates. Find out if your utility company offers cheaper rates for running appliances at certain hours—usually off-peak—and save.

Stick *very* close to home.

Want to share your family heritage and introduce the grandkids to Italy, for example, without spending a dime on airfare? Throw an authentic Tuscan picnic in the privacy of your own home, complete with authentic food, photos, and history. Visit Netflix.com or Blockbuster.com to sign up and order informational videos about your chosen location. You'll have a ball and spend virtually nothing.

Vacation

Make the switch. Trade your house with someone looking to vacation in your area, and you'll save on lodging, car rental (you can trade cars, too), and restaurant bills (you have an entire kitchen at your disposal!). Even if you pay up to $100 to list your house on a home-exchange Web site such as www.digsville.com, www.homeexchange.com, www.homelink-use.com, or www.intervacusa.com, you still come out far ahead. (And don't forget that you can view listings for free.)

Stick close to home. Vacation in your hometown or a nearby area. Have you seen all the museums near you? Hiked on all the trails in local parks? Visited nearby historical sites that you learned about in school? View your hometown with a tourist's eyes, and you can have a great vacation at a fraction of what you normally spend.

Ask for (free) help. Call or visit the Web site of the visitors' center or Chamber of Commerce in the area where you'll be vacationing. You can get maps, sightseeing brochures, and information about lodging, restaurants, and local attractions—even money-saving offers—for free. Call local information for the phone number or search online for the name of the area plus "visitors' center" or "Chamber of Commerce."

Guide yourself to a great vacation. Bypass sightseeing tours that take you and your wallet for a ride. Instead, look for self-guided walking and driving tours at the visitors' center at your destination. You may find a free or inexpensive guided tour as well.

Vaccination

Flu-free. Call your local health department to ask if it offers seniors free or inexpensive flu immunizations. Since the government recommends that seniors should have a flu shot, you can often find reduced-rate or free flu shots for seniors at community centers and pharmacies.

Vacuum cleaner

Bag it. Prolong the life of your vacuum cleaner by changing the bag when it feels about two-thirds full. Otherwise, the motor will have to work harder, since the air sucked into the vacuum passes through a bag filled with dirt.

Veterinarian

Two for one. Find out if your vet offers a discount for a multiple-pet visit. Bring your two cats in at once, but pay for less than two visits.

Vintage goods

Older is better. Call it what you want: vintage, antique, or simply used, you'll find amazing bargains on clothes, furniture, and other previously owned goods at thrift stores like the Salvation Army or on sites like eBay.com. Not only will you get a great price, you'll also help the environment by buying items that might get tossed—and you won't be buying something that needs to be manufactured and transported. It's an all-around win!

Volunteer work

Work off your taxes. More and more communities are creating programs that allow seniors to volunteer at the library, as a tutor, or in other positions around town to deduct around $500 from their property taxes. Check with your local government to find out if it offers such a program.

Wall hanging

Look great and insulate. Think about energy savings next time you look for art for your walls. Using quilts or decorative rugs as wall hangings will help insulate interior walls and keep energy costs down.

Washing machine

Keep yours cool. Wash your laundry with cold water and save more than $40 per year if you have an electric water heater or $50 or more per year if you have a gas water heater.

Wash more to save more. Don't wash your clothes more often, just wash more clothes at once. You can save more than 3,400 gallons of water each year if you simply make sure your washing machine is full before you start it. If you need to wash a partial load, be sure to reduce the level of water accordingly.

Water

Bye-bye, bottled water. Save your money and the environment by passing by bottles of water in the grocery store. Instead, buy a reusable water bottle. Assuming a store-bought bottle of water costs $1, you'll recoup your costs after only eight or nine uses of the reusable bottle.

Pitch this idea. Keep a pitcher or bottle of water in the refrigerator so you'll always have cold water on hand. No more running the tap to get water that's cold enough to drink—and no more money down the drain!

Turn off the tap. Turn off the water for two minutes while you brush your teeth or shave and save five gallons of water—and shave a few dollars off your water bill, too.

Water heater

Wrap it up. Save more than $30 per year on your water-heating bill by wrapping your pre-2004 water heater in an insulating jacket.

Keep it hot…Don't let the hot water leaving the water heater cool down before it gets to the tap. You've paid to heat the water! Insulate the hot water piping for additional savings.

...and cool it down. Lower the temperature of your water heater to 120 degrees. You'll still get a steamy hot shower, but for a fraction of what you've been paying.

Turn it off. You may be on vacation, but your water heater isn't. Before you go, turn off your electric water heater or turn down your gas water heater. Your heating bills will enjoy the vacation, too.

Weather stripping

Seal it for savings. Don't pay to heat or cool the air outside your house. Put weather stripping around doors and windows and save about $30 per year in heating and cooling costs.

Wedding cake

Think small. If you're helping pay for a daughter's—or granddaughter's—wedding, suggest buying a small, exquisite wedding cake to cut in front of guests at the wedding reception, but serving a large sheet cake to guests. The fancy and elaborate cake for the photos may be small, but the savings will be large.

Weeds

Shoot 'em dead. Make your driveway and sidewalks last longer by zapping weeds in cracks. Save money in the process by using vinegar in a spray bottle rather than expensive weed killers.

Windows

Sparkling clean and saving. Walk right by window cleaning fluid next time you visit the store. Instead, make it yourself: Mix 1/2 cup ammonia or white vinegar with 1 gallon of water. Then use crumpled newspaper with your homemade cleaner to wash and dry your windows.

Wine

Make your case. Save 10 percent on your wine purchases by buying wine by the case. Many stores will give you 15 percent off if you pay cash. And don't think you have to buy 12 bottles of the same wine. At nearly every wine store, you can mix different kinds and still receive the discount.

Make ice, not waste.

Don't throw away the little bit of wine left in the bottle after dinner is over. Instead, pour it into an ice cube tray and transfer the frozen cubes to a zipper-lock bag. You can use the cubes later in recipes that call for wine.

Wineglasses

Split entertaining costs. Do you have a neighbor or friend who likes to entertain but would like to save a few dollars doing so? Ask if she'll buy matching wineglasses with you. You both buy 12, and lend them to each other as the need arises.

Wrapping paper

Wrap up the season with savings. Score big savings on wrapping, gift cards, and ribbons (as well as decorations and holiday cards) the day after Christmas. You can also save big on Easter wrap, Valentine's Day wrap, and so on immediately after those holidays, too. You'll usually save at least 50 percent, possibly more, and you can use everything you buy the following year.

Be plain. Try to buy solid-colored holiday wrapping paper when it's on sale—you'll be able to use it year-round for birthdays, anniversaries, baby showers, and so on. For example, you'll probably be able to buy solid red wrapping paper after Christmas for 50 percent off that you can use for Valentine's Day.

The copy machine is your friend. Save on gift wrap and make a big impression at the same time. Photocopy pictures of the recipient, tape the copies together, and use the sheets of paper as wrapping paper. Your gift wrap may even outshine your gift!

Map out the savings. Wrap gifts in colorful maps. You can use outdated maps you've used for travel in the past, maps sold cheap at tag sales, or maps you can get for free from AAA if you're a member.

Brides for the bride-to-be. Wrap an engagement gift or a wedding gift in the social pages (that feature wedding announcements) from your local newspaper. Save money on wrapping paper and create a conversation piece at the same time!

Double-duty. Wrap a housewarming gift in a brightly colored dishtowel. You'll save money on wrapping paper by making part of your gift the gift wrap.

Let the butcher and florist help. Buy a big roll of white butcher paper and large bolt of colorful ribbon from a florist supply store or craft store and you'll have plenty of wrapping material for the holiday season (and beyond).

X-ray

Examine your X-rays. Do you really need a complete set of X-rays every time (or every other time) you visit the dentist? Ask your dentist if you can skip a set of X-rays and save the cost.

Yard

Be a yardbird and save! Don't pay a pricey "landscape engineer" to do what will spend your calories while it saves your dough. Get out there and pull some weeds, plant some veggies, and care for your flowers. Most landscapers charge upward of $50 an hour; multiplied by an average of two hours and eight seasonal visits, you've just saved yourself $800!

Zipper

Zip up the savings. Don't automatically throw away a garment if the zipper stops working. Try surrounding it with Velcro; you'll avoid the work of ripping out the zipper and the cost of replacing the item.

Zipper pull

Replace it with style. If the zipper on your jacket or your purse is missing the zipper pull, don't toss it. Simply replace the pull with a small key chain (or just the metal ring of the keychain), a metal ring sporting a charm, or easiest of all, a paperclip.

Zoo

Join the animals. Don't let the high price of zoos keep you away from the lions and tigers and bears. Find out if your zoo offers a day of free admission or pay-what-you-wish donation (like Wednesdays at the Bronx Zoo), corporate days (where employees of certain organizations get free admission on designated days), or memberships that offer admission year-round (plus other goodies) for the set price of membership.

Index

A

AAA
- eyewear discounts, 89
- membership card, 14
- travel discounts, 185, 186, 190

AARP
- Auto Insurance Program, 81
- entertainment discounts, 177
- eyewear discounts, 89
- gym membership discounts, 88
- health-care information, 120
- job market information, 261
- membership card, 14
- restaurant discounts, 55, 56, 58
- tax advice, 246, 324
- travel discounts, 185, 186, 187, 188–90, 194

Accident prevention, 69–71

Ace Hardware, 68

Active adult communities, 272–73

Agility training, for dogs, 226

Air conditioning.
See also Heating and cooling costs
- efficiency of, 282
- filters for, 76
- heat reduction and, 75, 309, 326

Airfares
- best fares, 15, 182–84, 282–83
- in Europe, 197–200
- packing for, 183

Air filters, for cars, 83

Air fresheners, 283

All-American Barbecue Dry Rub, 36

Almonds, 109

Alternative medicine, 283

Alumni gifts, 222

American Family Immigration History Center, 126

American Recovery and Reinvestment Act (ARRA) of 2009, 77

Amerispan Study Abroad, 198

Annuities, 237–39

Antacids, 283

Apartments, 68

Appalachian Mountain Club, 143

Appetizers, 52, 63

Applebee's, 55

Appliances, 283

A&P Supermarket, 26, 119

Aquariums, 136–38

Arby's, 53

ARRA, 77

ArtAge's Senior Theater Resource Center, 162

Art Institute of Chicago, 168

Artwork, 284

Asparagus, 112

Asset appreciation, 252

Assisted living, 276

Atlanta Zoo, 136

ATMs, 284

AT&T wireless, 78

Audiences Unlimited, 173

F

G

H

S

X

Y

Z